CW00655955

The City in the City

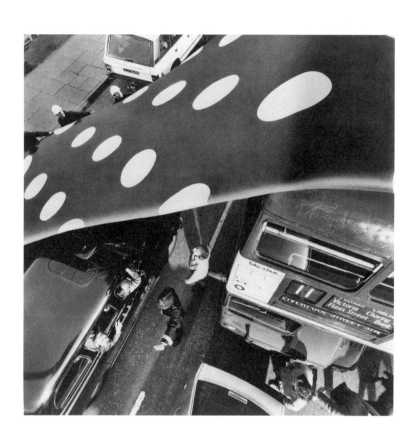

The Big Tie, 1986. Brian Griffin.

The City in the City
Architecture and Change in London's Financial District

Amy Thomas

THE MIT PRESS
Cambridge, Massachusetts · London, England

For Ollie

Prologue

The year is 1945. From a bird's-eye view, London's financial district is indistinguishable from its bomb-scarred metropolitan hinterland. Clusters of financial houses, churchyards, wharves, and warehouses bleed seamlessly into the patchwork of Georgian estates, Victorian thoroughfares, and green spaces beyond. Three centuries of development have eradicated the geographical gap that once demarcated the cities of London and Westminster as the capitals of trade and governance. Yet cartographically, the financial district continues to be represented as an autonomous territory. In an act of political metonymy just two years earlier, a map produced by the progressive London County Council (LCC) for the replanning of London depicted the City as a black hole in the center of the capital. It was the frontispiece to a popular edition of Abercrombie and Forshaw's *County of London Plan*. Demarcated by the graphic ghost of the ancient Roman walls and shaded to remove all topographic detail, this simple diagrammatic trope gestured toward a definition of the financial district as an *other* place. Despite occupying the geographical heart of London, the Square Mile existed beyond the remit of the LCC, and not just in terms of planning.

This is the moment in which this story begins. Examining the postwar history of the City of London, this book documents a spatial and cultural revolution. It covers the period of rebuilding to the explosive climax of financial deregulation in the 1980s and its long aftermath. In this narrative, abstract financial ideas, political ideology, and invisible markets reveal themselves as concrete realities. Despite its physical and political centrality, this period of the City's architectural history occupies an academic lacuna— itself a black hole.[1] Long-standing prejudices about developer-led architecture and the real estate industry have obscured the post-war City's relevance.[2] Added to this are layers of financial verbiage, masking the real, urban consequences of a powerful yet invisible system.[3] But in this period, events took place in the Square Mile that changed irrevocably the course of financial and political life and architectural practice in Britain. This history can only be understood if London's dark center is illuminated: it is a place, not simply a financial space.

THE COUNTY OF

explained by E. J. Carte

Cover of Sir Patrick Abercrombie, Edward J. Carter, and Ernö Goldfinger, *The County of London Plan, explained by E. J. Carter and Ernö Goldfinger* (London: Penguin Books, 1945). Courtesy of Penguin Books.

LONDON PLAN

and Ernö Goldfinger

Politically, the City undoubtedly presents a dark spot. Distinguished by its uppercase *C*, over the centuries the City of London has become the capital's mise en abyme, the City in the city. Existing as a self-governed territory that is juridically, culturally, and spatially distinct from the rest of the capital, the City both represents and contains the power of financial interests. It developed as the center of trade in Britain. Consequently, it became an important source of financing for the monarchy.[4] This provided the economic power necessary to retain its independence from the state, and to resist the invasion of William the Conqueror and thus inclusion in the Domesday Book. Established before the existence of Parliament, its municipality, the City of London Corporation (previously the Corporation of London) still claims to be "the oldest continuous municipal democracy in the world," with "its constitution ... rooted in the ancient right and privileges enjoyed by citizens before the Norman Conquest in 1066."[5] It operates on an ancient nonparty political system of governance. This involves a court of elected common councilmen, aldermen, and sheriffs, all headed by the Lord Mayor (distinct from the mayor of London). Its apolitical character enables it to retain a nonparliamentary representative who attends the Commons Chamber in the Houses of Parliament. This individual, known as the Remembrancer, is a lobbyist for the City charged with protecting its rights and privileges, and sits opposite the speaker. The combination of political influence and geographical isolation ensures that the City of London continues to run like a city-state in the heart of the capital, a status not unnoticed by critics.[6]

But Abercrombie and Forshaw's representation of the City seemed to evoke more than a straightforward municipal exemption. It implied something darker, linking the City's geopolitical independence with urban practices that were anathema to the aspirations of the new welfare state. Drawing on the rhetoric of reformers and observers past, the black hole evoked darkness as a moral metaphor for London: a space created and sustained by wealth at the expense of the less fortunate. Like William Cobbett's Great Wen, the sebaceous cist that drained life and land, or Samuel Johnson's "curst Walls, devote to Vice and Gain," the LCC's map drew the City as a stain or blot on society. It equated market-led development with a state of mind, or culture; "every black'ning Church" was for William Blake a product of London's "charter'd" streets.

This rhetoric was not unjust. Over the centuries, the City's traditionally inscribed rights had become inextricable from the interests of the finance industry and, in turn, the real estate market.[7] Historically, the guilds or *livery companies*, which acted as regulators/educators for their respective trades within the City, were responsible for voting in senior officers such as sheriffs and the Lord Mayor. Today, most members of the Corporation's Common Council also work for companies in the City. Unlike any other political constituency in Britain, businesses form the majority of the electorate.[8] This intertwining of governmental and private sector interests made the City a sympathetic environment for speculative building after World War II—pandering to private and commercial interest rather than planners. However, it was not until the 1980s that growing competition between global financial centers compelled the Corporation to actively use planning to provide "the right business conditions, built environment and infrastructure ... to compete internationally as a global center of business excellence."[9]

Yet while the City was defined by a laissez-fair approach to building and expansion, its building culture was also a product of containment. Since its inception as a Roman port fortified by walls and gates in AD 50, the City's boundaries have been critical to its political power. Reinforced by King Alfred in the ninth century, to which time much of the present street formation dates, today the City's concrete walls are replaced by the Corporation's less obstructive, though equally commanding, griffin-topped posts.[10] Despite dramatic shifts in the nature of the activities carried out within them, the City's outer limits have remained more or less stable since the sixteenth century, covering just over one square mile—hence the famous epithet. Thanks to the relative fixity of its circumference, the commercial center developed in isolation from the rest of London, which steadily expanded to fill the gap between the City and Westminster. Famously, the devastation caused by the Great Fire in 1666 did nothing to disrupt this pattern of containment, as the interests of (predominantly merchant) freeholders of land prevailed over state-sponsored, wholesale replanning by Christopher Wren or any other architect.

The City is a strange place. On the weekend, its streets are empty, shops closed. Yet on the weekday the pavements, squares, shops, and pubs are teeming with office workers. Despite its prime location in the center of London, barely anyone lives there. But this wasn't always so. Initially comprising a much broader range of markets and a large residential population, it was only in the latter half of the nineteenth century that the City began to specialize as a financial center. It became the financial heart of the British Empire.[11] This provided the infrastructure of imperial trade and investment; its grand banking houses and exchanges were unrivaled internationally in scale and reputation. The City also became home to commodity markets, warehouses, and industrial buildings on account of its proximity to the Port of London, which accommodated the flow of over half of Britain's trade in five gargantuan docks downriver.[12] Such diversity and concentration of services rendered the Square Mile highly desirable for businesses of all kinds, driving up rents and wages and forcing out its hitherto residential population. Added to this were revolutions in transportation, with new bridges across the Thames; a comprehensive bus network; the construction of four major railway stations in the City between 1861 and 1874 (Cannon Street, Fenchurch Street, Broad Street, and Liverpool Street); and the advent of the London Underground connecting the City to newly built suburbs in Hertfordshire, Kent, Surrey, and Middlesex, from which wealthy City workers could commute, avoiding the urban smog.[13]

The effect on the demographic composition and use of the City was staggering. Whereas in 1851 the worker and residential populations were approximately even, totaling around 128,000, by 1935 the number of workers had increased to around 500,000 (a figure only recently surpassed), while residents dwindled to around 10,000.[14] By the early twentieth century, the City had become the world's leading commercial and financial center alongside the world's largest entrepôt port.[15]

As a piece of infrastructure, the City's success has always rested on the long-standing power of its business community to shape space. Carved out by the movements of messengers and the influence of money, the morphology of the City was prescribed by the business activities it accommodated. On the eve of World War II, banking houses clustered around the Bank of England in the historic core, radiating out to the shipping and insurance markets in the east, stockbroking in the area to the north of the Stock Exchange, and the legal, newspaper, and publishing district gathering around the Inns of Court in the southwest. Elsewhere were the remnants of a local community of domestic trade, each with strategic geographies linked to the dominant industries in the area, including rope-makers, timber yards, and flour mills on the north bank of the Thames; the fur trade in the south on the former banks of the Walbrook, once used to wash imported furs, close to the wharves where colonial trading in animal skins thrived; the publishing industry around St Paul's, the traditional area for bookbinders, and later for the newspaper industry, which slowly spread west along Fleet Street, and north to the Barbican, where commercial printers settled; export and shipping companies clustered around Cornhill, the location of coffee houses and the Royal Exchange in which seamen and merchants gathered daily to trade commodities; warehousing and textiles located near Commercial Road in the east, on route to the docks; and furniture makers scattered along Cheapside and around St Paul's, the City's high street. In addition to these less formal agglomerations, wholesale markets at Smithfield, Leadenhall, and Billingsgate, each owned by the Corporation, formed anchor points for distribution networks throughout Britain.

Yet as the dust settled after World War II, the City began to be entirely reordered. Incendiary bombing during the Blitz destroyed over 30 percent of the City, creating a shortage of office accommodation, compounded by the enforcement of heavy restrictions on office building during the reconstruction process. Increases in rents and the LCC's decentralization policies made it very difficult for firms displaced during the war to return to business in the City.[16] Warehouses and industrial buildings disappeared, and between the debris of bomb sites and crumbling architectural carcasses, the City rose again as a highly specialized financial center.[17] Despite losing its position as the main international financial center to New York with the dissipation of the empire, Britain's departure from the gold standard in 1931, and a succession of interwar financial crises, the Square Mile continued to preserve its independence and insularity after the war. Developers and businesses, rather than planners, determined its growth.

Real or imagined, the territorial schism with London was undoubtedly a defining narrative for the City after World War II. Planning policies, techniques of representation, and architectural strategies were frequently, though not always intentionally, in opposition to the ideals of London's municipal authorities. Twin narratives of independence and integration persisted throughout the decades, giving way to a very public identity crisis for the financial center. Debates about the built environment were often center stage. This false binary was also the point from which a counternarrative of integration emerged from the 1960s onward, as the political swing toward economic liberalism demanded the convergence of the City and London to bolster Britain's international position on the world stage.

But as with all cartographic traditions, the LCC's partisan act of representation concealed as much as it sought to reveal. A more intricate political-spatial interplay between the financial district, the capital, and the nation belied the dark spot in the middle of the map. As currents of local government reform, nation-building, and globalization swept across Britain, the City became an ideological battle ground for debates between politicians and financial institutions, real estate developers and architects, preservationists and so-called proactive planners throughout the latter half of the century. Its urban development, public spaces, architectural surfaces, and complex interior worlds became a stage set for the other side of public life under the welfare state and its neoliberal successor: the drama of work, not home.

It is in this theater of *haute finance* that the contradictions and conflicts at the heart of the neoliberal economy were performed. The process of dismantling the City's infamous world of conservative clubs and gentlemanly agreements, culminating in Margaret Thatcher's epoch-defining move to deregulate the stock market— the so-called Big Bang—left an archaeology of transformation on the City's desks, in its floorplates, and hiding beneath its high-tech facades. Fraught with tension between the old and new, this narrative saw traditional rituals, novel technology, and new regulatory policies frequently in uneasy coexistence, often colliding in explosive moments of boom and bust, of creation and destruction. Yet viewed through a magnifying glass, the seemingly chaotic spectacle of financial deregulation and societal transformation in the postwar decades revealed itself through sometimes subtle and often mundane material interventions.

In his famous "air-view" over London, John Summerson claimed that "a town, like a plant or an anthill, is a product of collective unconscious will, and only to a very small extent of formulated intention."[18] Historically we know this to be true of the City. Its biography is based on the capriciousness of the market and the logics of property ownership. But this perspective precludes a more intricate understanding of the way that financial and political power produce real urban places and indeed of the effect they have on real people's lives. So what happens if we approach that distant territory or zoom into the map? It is a well-worn story that after World War II, the Square Mile shifted from being a domestic bastion of conservativism to a global financial center, reflected in the modernization of its architecture and culture of public spaces. Yet the complex realities of this transformation cannot only be understood through the macroscopic view; the specific dynamics of this "collective unconscious will" modulate at each scale. As the frame shifts from city to building to office, new actors, relationships, processes, and philosophies emerge, giving texture to the picture, adding depth and intentionality to the ant heap.

1 *City*

Vested Interests

The story begins with a set of underwhelming perspective drawings commissioned for the Corporation of London's 1944 "Preliminary Draft Proposals for Post-War Reconstruction in the City of London." Transmitting an overall feeling of continuity and reminiscence, rather than a bright future, the drawings encapsulated the contradictions inherent in the Corporation's plans for redevelopment. In these projections, well-known perspective artist J. D. M. Harvey sketched out a vague vision for the City of the future, which paradoxically transported the viewer back in time. One drawing showing the proposed ring road from the north depicts the financial center as a village-like cluster of low-rise buildings and church spires emerging in the midst of a pastoral hinterland. More reminiscent of Pugin's *Contrasts* than the Beaux-Arts city of monuments, the image presents the City as a preindustrial paradigm of Englishness: urban lots are transformed into a patchwork of farmland bathed in golden light and framed by Constable-like skies. In another illustration, St Paul's forms the centerpiece of a picturesque scene of barges and sailboats bobbing on the Thames, and an overall aerial view from the south shows a

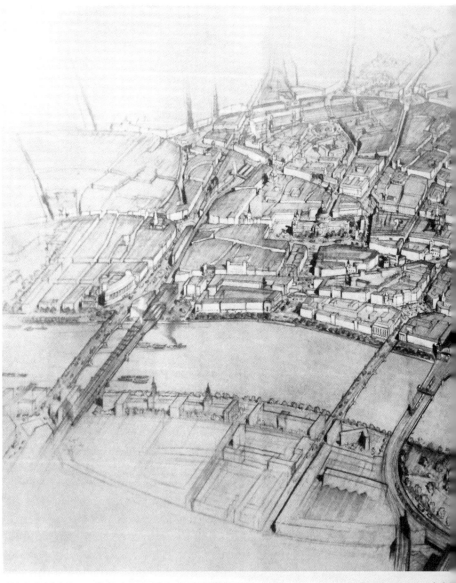

Preliminary proposals for
BIRD'S-EYE GENER

This view indicates the general effect of the main proposals described in the Report and contain
page 32. Outstanding features are the Embankment continuing from Blackfriars to London Br
ring route from the Tower round the north of the City to Holborn, with major junctions where
the open space exposing the London W

Bird's-eye general view from the south. Perspectives for "Preliminary Draft Proposals for Post-War Reconstruction in the City of London," 1944, by J. M. Harvey. Courtesy City of London Corporation and J. D. M. Harvey Estate.

F. J. Forty, City Engineer.

n the City of London.

ROM THE SOUTH.

1—3b. It is taken from a view-point west of the aerial photograph of the City which faces
wide inland street to Tower Hill so that the Upper Pool continues as a part of the Port; the
incipal existing radial roads into the County; the environment of St Paul's Cathedral; and
he Church of St. Giles, Cripplegate.

simplified gray mass of built volumes where all roads lead to the Bank of England, the Old Lady fortress in the beating heart of the Square Mile. These imprecise renderings are somewhat out of character for Harvey. Known for his ability to combine a high level of architectural precision with a more gestural and artistic flare for landscapes, the artist was a prolific architectural draftsman who was commissioned by several influential planners during the war, including Edwin Lutyens and Partick Abercrombie, to communicate their bold proposals for the reconstruction of English cities.[1] In these commissions, Harvey brought life into otherwise dry planning concepts, but also had the technical skill to be able to translate detailed and elaborate architectural elements, as proposed by Lutyens and his contemporaries.

The lack of detail and articulation of a highly romanticized setting in the renderings of the City of London point to fundamental gaps in the Corporation's reconstruction proposals, which became the starting point for decades of debate about the Corporation's legitimacy as a planning agency, and the political status of the financial district in the capital. Compiled by the City Engineer, Francis John Forty, the preliminary draft proposals were full of hollow grandeur: "The future of this ancient City, the Capital of the British Commonwealth of Nations and the centre of the World's commerce ... is dependent upon its reinstatement at the earliest possible moment," explained the Improvements and Town Planning Committee in the introduction. "It is with that desire uppermost in our minds," they went on, "coupled with planning that shall be worthy of the great position our City holds ... that we present this Report."[2] As the City was still considered to be the financial heart of Britain's dwindling empire, and had received the highest concentration of bomb damage in London, with over a third of its floor space obliterated under enemy fire, the gravitas of the language is on one level understandable. Reconstruction was deemed essential to restoring the economic health, and wealth, of the nation. However, the Blitz also presented opportunities for the wholesale replanning of the Square Mile that were unparalleled since the Great Fire of 1666. The Forty plan, as it became known, was not only unambitious in this regard, but deliberately sought to restore the *status quo* as quickly as possible by allowing developers and building owners to rebuild according to the existing planning controls, which centered on cornice height regulations, rather than offer any positive guidelines. Harvey depicts this

The northern arm of the ring route between Holborn Circus and Aldersgate Street. Perspectives for "Preliminary Draft Proposals for Post-War Reconstruction in the City of London," 1944, by J. M. Harvey. Courtesy City of London Corporation and J. D. M. Harvey Estate.

Eye-level view of St. Paul's Cathedral from the proposed embankment on the Southwark side of the river. Perspectives for "Preliminary Draft Proposals for Post-War Reconstruction in the City of London," 1944, by J. M. Harvey. Courtesy City of London Corporation and J. D. M. Harvey Estate.

City

regulation with an almost cynical veracity in the perspective of St Paul's, where a faint cornice is the only concession to architectural detail upon otherwise blank, facade-less blocks in the foreground.

The visual reference to a city of spires, domes, and cultivable land was more than a gesture toward the historic importance of the business district. Forty's proposals conflated nostalgia for the historical autonomy of the City with a laissez-faire approach to redevelopment. "Can it seriously be thought that we, proud to have been promoting its welfare, are unconscious of the romance and history which the very street names breathe?" Forty wrote. "Whatever the surface destruction—the City can in no circumstances be regarded as virgin land, upon a blank plan of which the pencil of a planner, conscious of his responsibilities, can freely or fancifully travel."[3] The plans refused the standard compulsory purchase powers given to local authorities to facilitate rebuilding (the so-called lessor scheme), on the basis that the market would regulate itself, as it always had done.[4] Forty justified this approach by reminding the reader that after the Great Fire, Christopher Wren's plan had been rejected by City landowners. This was not a "lost opportunity," he claimed, because it was "no less in the national than in the Citizens' interest to rebuild as rapidly as possible. The Corporation ... exerted itself to the utmost and, in the face of truly gigantic difficulties, set about rehabilitation in order that the normal course of life and business could be resumed in the shortest time."[5] Historically, the Corporation had indirectly facilitated the business community by allowing the markets to dictate the location, type, and quantity of office spaces. Planning constituted the provision of infrastructure, rather than guiding architectural development, which was limited to the City's civic buildings, such as the Guildhall, Mansion House, and its churches. Reconstruction after World War II was in the national interest, but the Corporation had always resisted external intervention in the name of municipal autonomy and continued to do so in the early conversations about rebuilding.

A three-decade-long battle with London's centralized planning agencies ensued following the publication of these draft proposals. They were almost immediately rejected by the Ministry of Town and Country Planning (MTCP), which sought a universalizing and comprehensive plan for the entire metropolitan region and had already suggested the Corporation bring in external consultants rather than giving the task to the city engineer.[6] Forty was an engineer by training and title, which left him open to attack from senior members of the ministry, attributing the blandness of his designs to the scientific nature of his post. Although seemingly inappropriate for the job, the choice was not surprising in the context of the City of London, where the roles of city engineer, city surveyor, and city architect—which had historically coexisted and at points been interchangeable—were not formally delineated until the early twentieth century.[7] But the most irksome aspect of the Forty plan from the perspective of the ministry was its political conservativism; the Corporation's rhetoric of autonomy, centrality, and growth contravened the progressive social agenda and decentralization policies at the heart of Patrick Abercrombie's County of London Plan, commissioned by the LCC in 1943. Unlike the Corporation's nostalgic breed of market determinism, Abercrombie's plan used sociological data to divide the capital into social and functional areas, using this operative logic to create specific planning regulations for the different communities. Based on the Barlow Commission's recommendations of 1940 to contain the capital's growth, Abercrombie prescribed a dispersal of around one million people from Greater London to the suburbs via the decentralization of offices, housing, and other commercial activities.[8] The Corporation's proposal, on the other hand, aimed to reinforce the City's historic concentration of offices and promote a 50 percent increase in floor space using height restrictions and site boundaries to regulate the quantity of new buildings. Their reticence to adopt compulsory purchase powers in favor of a market-led approach further convinced the ministry that it was "waiting for developers to shape the City instead of planning for them."[9]

Abercrombie had been well aware of the "problems of local government reform" posed by the City of London's independence, and its reliance on private development was viewed as a threat to the efficacy and democratic goals of a London-wide proposal.[10] The County of London Plan actively sought to diminish the power of these "vested interests." The "popular" version of the plan written by the librarian of the Royal Institute of British Architects (RIBA), E. J. Carter, and modernist architect and writer Ernö Goldfinger in 1944 articulated the LCC's antipathy toward developer-led planning: "The Blitz has cleared some sites and we must clear many more—but for what? ... Have we the imagination and power to realise our hopes, or shall we just return to the old unplanned city blocks, to the same old wild activity of private speculation, to recreate the same old jumble of courtyards and streets and competing facades? An inheritance for the future as grim as anything we know to-day. The land speculator's boards are up ... OR can we plan our London?"[11] The ministry branded Forty's attempt as an "amateur effort of the most dangerous kind," which posed a threat to the centralized reconstruction efforts.[12] Yet Forty himself saw the differences as methodological rather than ideological, arguing that "we may appear not to have approached some questions from the same standpoint ... ; divergence of approach, however, does not imply a conflict of ideals."[13]

Their approaches were certainly divergent. Whereas the Corporation kept the plans largely secret in order to quell initial speculation in the real estate market, the LCC embarked on a vigorous public information campaign, including publications, education packs, a film, and a major exhibition in 1943 attended by over fifty thousand people at County Hall which was subsequently moved to the Royal Academy of Arts.[14] Carter and Goldfinger's popular explanation was intended for the masses, representing part of a broader shift of belief within the profession that architectural publications should be accessible to the public in form and content. Carter was among many individuals in the field who saw planning, and in particular planning literature, as a vehicle for promoting the cause of modernist architecture, which had suffered due to its inherent elitism. In 1944, the modernist Modern Architectural Research Group (MARS Group) announced in its newsletter, of which Goldfinger was editor, a shift of focus from the profession to the public in the nature of its work, becoming a consultant to the Ministry of Information and Political and Economic Planning.[15] The war presented an opportunity for largely unemployed architects to use the reconstruction debates as a platform to popularize the central functionalist tenets of modernist discourse. As Carter wrote in an article on the subject, "Now it seems that we can see light through the ruins, and the light is in all this literature of planning."[16]

Forty's plan was disappointing to the LCC and the ministry precisely because it lacked the modernist sensibility, leftist ideals, and mass appeal that these publications espoused. It is perhaps unsurprising then that after a period of further refusals, the ministry compelled the Corporation to work with influential and progressive planner William Holford and his team to reimagine the City's reconstruction proposals. Holford held a long list of impressive posts, including Lever Professor at Liverpool University, a member of the Royal Fine Art Commission (RFAC), chairman of the Committee on Buildings of Special Architectural or Historic Interest, and honorary technical advisor to the MTCP. But as Holford's biographers Gordon Cherry and Leith Penny note, it was as a town planner that he was most renowned as "one of the professionals who was in a position to directly influence the recasting of town and country planning which took place between 1939 and 1948."[17] Holford had already expressed his concerns about the Forty plan's focus on ratepayers and divergence from the wider *County of London* plans in a letter drafted on behalf of the RFAC. Yet he was keenly aware of the various interests his team would have to accommodate in the new plan. The representatives of these interests were certainly not all as forward-thinking as his colleagues at the LCC. It is likely for this reason that the highly distinguished veteran architect Charles Holden was brought in as a second consultant. Holden, who was seventy in 1945, had the status and long experience to appease more conservative parts of the City establishment and had already been a reconstruction consultant for the Dean and Chapter of St. Paul's.[18] His role in the new proposals was to conceive of the architectural context surroundings of the cathedral, while Holford and his team did the bulk of the planning work. During this period, tensions between the Corporation and the ministry were further lowered by the 1947 Town and Country Planning Act, which gave the LCC planning authority over the City's reconstruction proposals, rendering it part of the wider County of London development plan.[19] Working from the Tivoli Corner of Bank Buildings alongside the Corporation's newly appointed planning officer, Henry Anthony Mealand (1947–1961), Holford produced a proposal for reconstruction that would provide the basis for the City's planning activities—however loosely—for the next twenty-five years.[20]

Holden and Holford's plan was approved by the LCC and MTCP because it occupied a middle ground between the ideals of the City and those of the *County of London* plan. It acknowledged the Corporation's desire for market-led development and office floor space, yet also limited the free reign of developers through the inclusion of building regulations and compulsory purchase powers. Plot ratios reduced the traditional emphasis on street facades by placing limits on the total area of a building in relation to its site, rather than the traditional cornice height, thus enabling larger public spaces around buildings, better daylight and ventilation in offices, higher densities, and the introduction of modern tower and podium typology.[21] "The tendency of planning regulations will favour the larger block," explained the authors, prescribing developments with a standard plot ratio of five to one.[22] This calculation was based on an extensive floor space survey conducted in 1939, which concluded that the demand for office space was approximately five times the available building sites.[23]

Its success also largely depended on its accessibility and public communication strategy. Packaged in an attractive book entitled *The City of London: A Record of Destruction and Survival*, published by the Architectural Press, the new plan balanced a respect for the City's rich urban history with modernist planning principles. In an attempt to convince the hearts and minds of the City establishment, the consultants filled the publication with nostalgic photographs of streets filled with top hats, cigars, umbrellas, and glistening pavements, close-ups of cracked heavy stone lintels, intimate corners, and neoclassical ornaments, juxtaposed with the naked reality of large bomb sites. Interspersed throughout the book were large foldout maps and lively projective sketches by well-known draftsman Gordon Cullen, synthesizing historic street patterns and buildings with modernist interventions in the form of pedestrianized "precincts," the vertical segregation of traffic and pedestrians, a ring road, and a series of road widening and construction schemes.

Avoiding a radical tabula rasa approach, as put forward in the unsolicited RFAC and MARS Group proposal that had preceded it, the new plan was an experiment in visual planning, or townscape, a popular and modernist variant of the picturesque tradition initiated by Hubert de Cronin Hastings, Nikolaus Pevsner, and Cullen at the *Architectural Review*.[24] Cullen, who worked as an art editor and illustrator for the Architectural Press's two core publications, the *Architectural Review* and the *Architects' Journal*, at the time of the commission, had a background as a commercial artist, working on all manner of jobs ranging from magazine illustrations to catalog advertising, posters, and exhibition panels. His capacity to create dynamic consumer-conscious graphics rendered him popular in an age where public information programs were essential to the reconstruction effort.[25] Cullen was hired by J. M. Richards at the *Architectural Review*. At this time, the editorial mandate of the magazine was to publicize modern architecture to the masses and to directly influence the profession in modernist thinking. Cullen's

Gordon Cullen's illustrations of Holden and Holford's proposals for reconstruction, 1951. Copyright Gordon Cullen Estate / University of Westminster Archive. Courtesy of City of London.

brightly colored, almost childlike illustrations in the Holden and Holford book emphasized the human aspects of the new plan, putting City workers—the consumers—in the foreground of sunny architectural scenes.

Appealing to the nostalgia of the City establishment was one important element of the plan, but it also had to convince rate-payers and landowners that redevelopment would be quick and straightforward. In order to mitigate between the seemingly conflicting demands for rapid reconstruction to rehouse the business community and adherence to the slow-moving, long-term *County of London Plan*, Holden and Holford divided the proposal into two phases: the short-term, ten-year program, which included street improvements and the acquisition and development of bomb sites; and a thirty-year plan, which would depend on the LCC's progress with larger infrastructure projects like the provision of the London Underground and railways. However, the rising investment potential of City land in the ensuing decades, alongside manifold adjustments to London's building regulations, meant that the longer-term plan was largely unrealized. Whereas the rest of the United Kingdom was focused on the provision of schools, housing, and public amenities, the Corporation's priority was to secure its position as an international financial center by restoring office accommodation, and therefore employment, to just below prewar levels (taking account of changing space standards in office design).[26] During the bombing, some 26.8 million square feet (31 percent) of the 85.8 million square feet of office space had been decimated, leaving little space for business to carry on.[27] Holford calculated for a future daytime population of 427,000, far higher than ever realized in the postwar decades, which according to existing space standards required over 82 million square feet of new floor space.[28] Like many other local authorities during this period, the Corporation therefore enlisted—or in this case enabled—private enterprise to facilitate development.[29] However, whereas housing and schools were publicly debated, office buildings were not subject to the same levels of scrutiny and as such offered a relatively frictionless building opportunity for developers.

The first major property companies emerged during this period, founded by a small group of opportunistic men who amassed great fortunes by capitalizing on vacant bomb sites and deficiencies in the postwar office market.[30] These deficiencies took several forms. First, the dramatic imbalance of supply and demand following the Blitz, as well as heavy building regulations, increased rental values and therefore property prices.[31] Through compulsory purchase, the Corporation sold large tracts of bombed land to developers on long leases in order to assist the provision of office space (the lessor scheme). This would prevent drastic increases in land values and provide developers with the opportunity to build on sites that would previously have been unavailable or costly due to the complex patchwork of land ownership in London. In 1939, livery companies owned around one-fifth of the land in the Square Mile, with smaller private interests taking up the remainder, meaning that even prominent institutions such as the Stock Exchange had taken up to 150 years to accrue sufficient title rights to be able to build bigger premises.[32] However, the unintended outcome of this process was to enable developers to rapidly grow their capital base by subletting the land at substantially higher prices.[33] In contrast to the small infill blocks that characterized development before the war, the availability of these large sites, in combination with the introduction of plot ratios, enabled the construction of much larger buildings.

Second, the initial proliferation of planning regulations paradoxically enabled developers to take advantage of loopholes in the system, exploiting development charge exemptions on war-damaged buildings and so-called dangerous structures.[34] In addition to the availability of building plots and relaxation of building regulations in 1953, the credit squeezes of the 1950s and early 1960s meant banks were keen to lend to developers, despite the risks involved with such young companies, thereby ensuring sufficient short-term finance. In addition, the Bank of England's cheap money policies in the late 1950s caused insurance companies to seek out new repositories for long-term investment, as returns on government stock were low.[35] Commercial property in the City became a secure investment thanks to a surplus of reliable, institutional tenants who were seeking long leases. A thriving office market emerged, bringing a surge in commercial construction. As the Economists Advisory Group (EAG) stated in 1971, "It was estimated in 1935 that ... three-quarters of the buildings in the City were over thirty years old. Of the 77 million sq ft of floor-space available in 1968 ... more than 20 million sq ft had been erected in the previous twenty years."[36]

Around half of the largest schemes constructed during this period were built on bomb sites, largely facilitated by the

Corporation's compulsory purchase powers.[37] The Corporation's land holdings had tripled by the end of the 1960s, with a substantial part directed toward three major precincts recommended in the Holden and Holford plan, which were directly supervised by the LCC: the Barbican area in the north; London Wall, a scheme of five eighteen-story office blocks; and Paternoster Square, a large office and plaza development adjacent to St. Paul's Cathedral.[38] The Barbican was the only noncommercial scheme and also the most contentious, consuming an enormous forty acres at the northern tip of the City. What to do with this prime site, so close to the City center, was a prickly issue, causing the land to remain vacant for over twenty years. Conflicting proposals for the area included a mixed-use development, cultural center, and offices; the symbolism of the site appealed to politicians, arguing for a commemorative public space, while its location, less than a mile from the historic core of the City, appealed to the purses of developers. The winning design by Chamberlin Powell & Bon (1959–1981) was a private housing complex (accompanied by an arts center two decades later) aimed at doubling the residential population of the City, which had dwindled to around five thousand prior to the war. Targeting young, wealthy bachelors, the social function of the Barbican complex was certainly at odds with its physicality; the scheme's three towers with jagged cantilevered balconies, and sculptural low-rise blocks on pilotis spoke the language of the European socialist housing, taking "the expressive potential of concrete to a theatrical extreme."[39] What seemed on the surface to be the most radical architectural program to emerge in the postwar City was in fact one of the largest luxury housing schemes ever to be built in London.

Aside from these developments, by the end of the 1950s much of the optimism surrounding the Holden and Holford plan had dissipated, and the Corporation came under fire again for enabling developers to lead the way. The high demand and low-risk nature of the market enabled property companies to build poor-quality structures at a high profit. New developments were for the most part built to the minimum possible specification, designed by architects working in close partnership with developers to design the maximum amount of lettable floor space at the lowest cost. As tenants were desperate for spaces in central locations, office blocks could command exorbitant rents. Developer Jack Rose subsequently labeled these structures "the essence of attainable

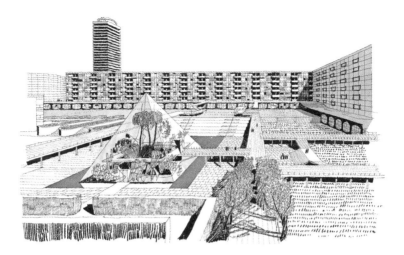

Early drawing of the proposed Barbican redevelopment, 1956. Sketch by Gordon Cullen showing the garden layout, including the conservatory and ornamental water. Courtesy of City of London Corporation.

maximum rent," which "conformed to a sellers market," comprising the minimum floor-to-ceiling heights, no air conditioning, a lack of power outlets, and basic curtain wall construction.[40] The sellers' market continued well into the 1960s, ensuring that prices remained high and quality low, with speculative buildings costing up to 60 percent less to build than occupier-owned properties.[41]

In 1957, Nikolaus Pevsner, a frequent detractor of the modernizing financial district, summed up the architectural establishment's negative feeling towards the City's reconstruction efforts, commenting that "the building necessities in the City for the next few years are enormous. ... What is going up now is mostly not promising. Vast opportunities have already been missed. ... Here the problem exceeds that of better architecture. It becomes one of overall planning."[42] Among the British architectural establishment, the City developed a reputation for generating poor-caliber commercial architecture and facilitating bad practice within the profession. Characters like Pevsner, J. M. Richards, and Ian Nairn drew connections between the Corporation's lack of vision and its paternalistic politics, whereby architectural conservatism was simply another expression of the City's desire to preserve its independence from the rest of London, both juridically and ideologically. But underlying this prejudice was a more generalized disdain for developers and their influence on the intellectual world of architecture. Among the high-profile individuals to speak out on the subject was Lionel Brett (Lord Esher), president of the RIBA between 1965 and 1967. Brett described the developer as the *middleman*, who, he argued, had historically been hated for intervening between "the makers and users, between the respected world of imagination, enterprise, skill and sweat and the great body of consumers."[43] For Brett, the property company hindered good architecture by placing economic restrictions in the way of the design process, bringing architects in too late in the process to have any technical or artistic input.

The reality was somewhat different: the practices working for developers were not progressive firms stifled by pragmatic developers, but were established with commercial motives from the outset. There were ten commercial practices, which received the bulk of the commissions in the City in the two decades after the war: Gollins Melvin & Ward (GMW); T. P. Bennett & Son; C. H. Elsom & Partners; Newman Levinson and Partners; Fitzroy Robinson & Partners; Richard Seifert & Partners; Lewis Solomon Kaye & Partners; Stone, Toms & Partners; Trehearne & Norman, Preston & Partners; and Roland Ward & Partners.[44] According to a great chronicler of the London real estate boom, Oliver Marriott, these architects were successful for the simple reason that they "were in every case directed by one or two men who were businessmen as well as architects."[45] Rather than being brought in at the end of the process, the architect often did initial work for the developer on the basis that they would only be paid if the job went ahead. As Marriott explains, "This was against the rules of the RIBA. The architects were needed at that stage to perform one of their most vital functions as far as the developer was concerned: obtain planning permission."[46] These practices became indispensable to developers as negotiators of an increasingly complex planning system that had emerged with the 1947 Town and Country Planning Act and was further complicated by stringent building regulations connected to decentralization policies in the 1960s. Because the visual character of the building was of so little importance to the developer, they would often strike a deal to hand over some aesthetic control to local authorities in return for efficient treatment of the planning application. Thus, for the most part, imagination was very low on the list of desirable attributes for a developer's architect. In fact, in some of these practices, the founding partners were not always fully qualified architects, having completed only part of their qualification before deviating into business, or holding only the RIBA licentiate status (membership without examination that required ten years practicing or studying the profession, abolished in 1956). In addition, some of the practices had actually begun their lives as developers, within which architecture departments grew to become the main line of work.[47]

Critics like Brett were disdainful of commercial architects because they worked so closely with developers and, in doing so, undermined the nineteenth-century distinction of architecture as an academic pursuit. This distinction was evident in the categorization of "acceptable" commercial work. For example, firms like Easton & Robertson, York Rosenberg Mardall (YRM), and Chamberlin Powell & Bon were classified as practices working within the private sector, and were readily appointed by local authorities in the postwar decades to help build new university campuses and city center retail spaces. Labeled as *design-led practices*, their work was admitted into the canon of British architecture, including large exhibitions at the Royal Academy of Arts and the RIBA, because it was seen to retain intellectual content.[48] Equally, it was perfectly acceptable for architects working for local authorities, like the LCC Architects' Department, to take on a commercial project so long as creative freedom was permitted. *Commercial firms* or *developers' architects*, on the other hand, worked from the cost calculation outward. They relied upon offering competitive rates to be successful, so a good knowledge of accounting, surveying, and planning law was the most important dimension of their practice. In other words, processes associated with business acumen took precedence over artistic invention.

But these categories were a matter of emphasis. There were of course rafts of ordinary salaried architects working for local authorities for whom cost evaluation and efficiency planning were the main activity.[49] Conversely, many commercial practices used the techniques of modular construction and systems building being explored by state-funded projects for schools, hospitals and housing, office buildings and shopping centers.[50] Brett and his colleagues' antipathy toward the developer-architect relationship, an articulation of the long-established feeling among the British intelligentsia that one should stay well away from "trade,"[51] was also underpinned by anti-Semitism and classist attitudes, as a high proportion of developers and commercial architects were Jewish.[52] Underlying the transformation of commercial architects into industry exiles, then, were more profound discrepancies in the classification of architectural labor and social structures in Britain.

Richard Seifert & Partners became the most successful (and most vilified) commercial practice of this period due to Seifert's exceptional aptitude in this area.[53] As the architect would later remark in a speech at the RIBA: "The introduction of the Town and Country Planning Act of 1947 caused architects for the first time to apply their minds to complex and essential rules which penetrated every facet of the profession. Satisfied clients who were seeking to cut through red tape obstructions, new approaches to architectural design ... and the speedy completion of the building contract which has always been the keynote of my practice, led to renewed and growing interest."[54] This knowledge rendered Seifert particularly attractive to the property companies operating in the City of London, where office space was at a premium but land scarce, and his practice expanded rapidly, from twelve employees in 1955 to 240 in 1967.[55] Seifert built his partnership on the basis of close relationships with developers, in particular Harry Hyams (founder of Oldham Estates), with whom he collaborated on a number of speculative London projects including Centre Point (1963–1966), Drapers Gardens (1962–1967), and Royex House (1963). Together they become notorious among planners for their manipulation of plot ratio regulations and for taking advantage of planning loopholes. As one member of the LCC's Town Planning Committee later commented: "The trouble with Seifert was that he knew some of the regulations far better than the LCC itself. Every now and then we had to bring in clauses to stop up the loopholes exposed by Seifert. We called them 'Seifert Clauses.'"[56]

Among the British architectural establishment, the City developed a reputation for generating poor-caliber commercial architecture and facilitating bad practice within the profession. In the first decade after the war, most office blocks were neo-Georgian or stripped classical, condemned by critics like Pevsner, who called it "a style of timidity ... introducing just enough of the twentieth-century to avoid being ridiculous and keeping just enough of ... the ... paraphernalia of Empire to stake the claim of remaining a great nation."[57] Pevsner's critique was double-sided: it was, on the one hand, capitalist (that is, classicism was used unabashedly to articulate the desirable virtues of banking: strength, wealth and prowess); on the other, its timidity expressed the City's impotence in a postimperial age. This image was compounded by the restrictions on business after World War II through Keynesian regulatory policies, coupled with decolonization, meaning that the City lost much of the excitement of the former century. The unadventurous image of City architecture was reinforced as British banks developed a reputation for stability and conservativism based on their ability to endure consecutive financial crises in the first half of the century.[58] The City's image as an economic powerhouse in British life was replaced by that of an old-fashioned, yet safe, bureaucratic entity. For Pevsner, then, the Corporation's embrace of developers and their architects embodied this duality: it was not simply unenlightened, but also submissive, embodying an attitude in which "enterprise and courage stand for nothing."[59]

A Few Houses and a Few Personalities

Despite the financial establishment's anodyne international reputation, it continued to wield great influence over the geographical arrangement and sponsoring of postwar redevelopment. Holden and Holford recognized the power of the City's institutions and markets in their report, articulating that the "subdivision and allocation" of land would be "a matter on which the long experience of [the Corporation's] Committee will have its most direct and most appropriate bearing." Rather than enforce strict zoning, the consultants accepted that "land values, rents, and the natural tendency towards the concentration of like uses will ... afford sufficient protection for the established character of particular zones."[60] This policy was reflected in two color-coded diagrams depicting the sectoral clusters before and after reconstruction. As if to reference Abercrombie's famous egg diagrams, the maps' blob-like and imprecise style point toward a sort of organic functionalism in the Square Mile; business built the City and would continue to determine its form for as long as it remained a designated commercial zone. After three centuries of activity, the banking, financial, shipping, and insurance institutions had cultivated an almost mythical status, with their closed communities and idiosyncratic customs supposedly preserved by the architectural containment afforded by exchanges, clubs, and clandestine courtyards in the deep heart of the City. The maps revealed the spatial corollary of their political authority as guardians of the natural order.

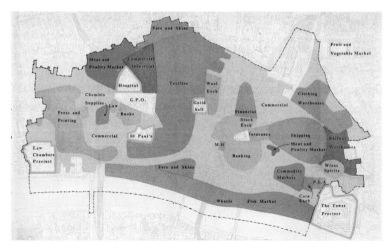

Map showing the distribution of markets and activities in the City, 1951. Courtesy of City of London Corporation.

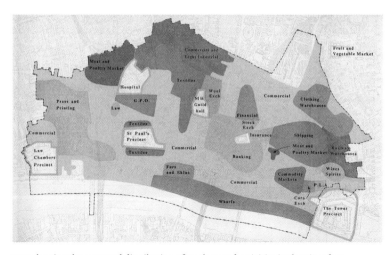

Map showing the proposed distribution of markets and activities in the City after reconstruction. Courtesy of City of London Corporation.

Whereas the planners and municipalities' influence over reconstruction was direct and public, the financial community exerted sway through covert conversations, discreet correspondence, and good contacts. Invariably this was done through the Bank of England, as the node between central government and the financial district. This was the case with the establishment of the City of London Reconstruction Advisory Council, which comprised representatives and senior personnel from every sector in the Square Mile.[61] Amid the rival designs being produced by the LCC and the Corporation, a quiet conversation ensued between the Bank of England and the Treasury on the formation of a council to advise those in charge of rebuilding on the needs of the markets.[62] In a letter to the Bank director via the hand of none other than Maynard Keynes, a high-ranking Treasury official expressed doubt concerning the ability of the Corporation of London to handle the rebuilding of the City, labeling it too "feeble and senile" for the job, claiming that "the ceremony and legal life and dignity of the City owes much to the City Corporation, but in recent years the real life and development of the City owes much more to a few Houses and a few personalities."[63] His proposals called for a plan to be drawn up under the consultation of these "personalities" for submission to the Ministry of Planning, which would highlight certain landmarks, such as the area surrounding St. Paul's, the riverfront, and the Guildhall, "for special treatment."[64] The Bank agreed to the idea, on the grounds that the City's reconstruction was part of a bigger national project that would "attract visitors and thereby increase our invisible exports as well as our prestige," but also because the financial institutions that would constitute the organization would likely be responsible for financing its development.[65]

Although the council never realized its ambition to be the main agent of the City's reconstruction before suspending its operations in 1951, it was an important representative voice in the planning debates.[66] Comprising nearly all major institutions and committees in the City, including the Accepting Houses Committee (representing the merchant banks), Baltic Exchange, British Insurance Association, City Churches Commission, City livery companies, Corporation of Lloyd's, Port of London Authority, and London Stock Exchange, its usefulness was acknowledged in both Forty's and Holden and Holford's reports, with the former deeming it "so representative and informed a body," and the latter praising the advice of such "long-established City interests."[67]

Holden and Holford's diagrammatic blobs expressed the informality of the City's web of influence, which was momentarily formalized in the Reconstruction Advisory Council. Unlike any other London borough, the City's occupants had political leverage due to the historical linkage between business interests and the municipality via the guild system, and because of their strong links with central government. Postwar reconstruction was protracted and difficult in large part because of these entanglements, and of course due to the financial sector's pivotal role in reviving the British economy. Long-term plans were sacrificed for expediency in order to restore accommodation for financial institutions. As the same institutions were financially backing the office market, a lack of planning regulation was perceived to be mutually beneficial for developers and occupiers. They therefore behaved as a crucial but hidden regulatory force in determining the City's geography and morphological structure, on account of centuries of continuous activity and unique rituals. However, in the next decades, the geographical stability of this system was challenged as financial deregulation came into conflict with the long-standing tradition of self-regulation.

Defined by the rubric of informality, which extended to nepotistic recruitment processes, internally monitored business practices, and a system of trust based on verbal guarantees and reputation, the postwar City was a microcosm of the networked society that had ensured the dispersal of privilege in Britain and its empire for centuries. This style of business was the legacy of what historians Cain and Hopkins have called *gentlemanly capitalism*, referring to the increased collaboration and comingling between the financial and political elite that occurred following the financial reforms of the late seventeenth century.[68] The consolidation of the power of landed families and the growth of a merchant oligarchy resulted in the professionalization of private sector occupations, such as banking and later stockbroking. As the government depended increasingly on banks to fund wars and trade across the globe, finance became associated with public duty. Over time, politically powerful families came to occupy key positions in financial institutions, which gave the City autonomy, while the social life of finance became an extension of polite society. Financiers became more influential in government as the financial sector expanded with Britain's empire, further cementing the political power of the City.[69]

This peculiarly British setup was underpinned by an overt philosophy of mutual regulation, characterized by the formalization of apparently informal institutions into a collection of exceptionally powerful club-like establishments, such as the Stock Exchange, Baltic Exchange, and Lloyd's.[70] Such a system was maintained by strict membership policies on the exchanges, through architectural containment, and via spatial regulations and procedures that demanded proximity and visibility. For example, the exchanges insisted that all member firms were located in the immediate vicinity to facilitate the spread of information.[71] Similarly, the town clearing system, a messenger-operated centralized settlement system, required all banks to be located within a half mile radius of the Bankers' Clearing House on Lombard Street.[72]

At the geographical and regulatory heart of this system was the Bank of England, around which the financial district had developed since its establishment in the seventeenth century. Its regulatory method was predicated on close surveillance, which was facilitated by its central location, exercising control through the imposition of spatial rules to which all companies and institutions had to conform, the most important being the insistence on the close proximity of all banks to the Bank of England to facilitate supervision and its own centralized settlement system, which it operated in its capacity as the "banker's bank."[73] Rules such as these positioned the Bank at the core of a precisely orchestrated spatiotemporal system, revolving around the hours of trade, settlement, and clearing times, and the changing bank rate. In their planning proposals, Holden and Holford understood that this symbolic importance translated into a higher demand for office space in the area surrounding the Bank intersection, which allowed for an extension of plot ratios in the half-mile radius of the Bank to 5.5:1.[74] Although automation and advances in telecommunications gradually removed the need for proximity between institutions in the 1950s, rents averaged 20 percent higher in the half-mile radius of the Bank than in developing areas.[75]

Acting simultaneously as the City's and the government's representative in each territory, the Bank's power over the Square Mile was part of what has been termed the *City-Bank-Treasury nexus*, rendering it the crucial point of contact between the market and the British state.[76] After the war, this role calcified due to the government's increasing involvement in British financial services as the City lost its strength on the international stage. By 1945, New York had superseded London as the world's leading financial center, and the dollar replaced sterling as the dominant currency in the global market; the collapse of the gold standard in 1931, World War II, the decline of the empire, and the weakening of the pound triggered a heavy-handed approach from the state. Higher taxation, war-time exchange controls (which were preserved until as late as 1979), and most importantly the nationalization of the Bank

An elevated view of the front of Threadneedle Street from the southwest looking across Bank Junction. Courtesy of the Bank of England Archive, Ref. No. 15A13/1/2/14.

of England in 1946 reinforced the dual nature of the Bank as regulator of, and spokesperson for, the City.

However, as British historian David Kynaston notes, the new status of the Bank was initially not considered by either the government or the City, as there had been "no vision of how a central bank should function in the new era of a more planned economy; no convincing model of the ideal triangular relationship between government, central bank and commercial banks; and no insistence that the Bank shed its highly damaging culture of secrecy and the deliberate cultivation of mystique."[77] This mysteriousness was perpetuated by the entanglement of the Bank's administration with key families in the City; until well into the 1980s, the Bank's governors and senior personnel were drawn from the upper echelons of the merchant banking community. At a time when the City's autonomy and international role was at threatened by nationalist politics and industry-oriented policies, City elites exercised strategic influence over government policy (and vice versa) through a system of fraternal networks.[78]

Secrecy and the "deliberate cultivation of mystique" was at the core of the City's strategy for self-preservation during this period of nationalization and with a growing state. For the Bank, these attributes were also critical to maintaining control over a largely informal code of conduct in the City, where regulation largely happened through unofficial conversations behind closed doors, in the fortress that was the Bank of England. Occupying an enormous island site, the building, which had been almost entirely remodeled by John Soane from the 1790s to the 1820s, was substantially enlarged by Herbert Baker from 1921 to 1942 in an often criticized, neoclassical style.[79] Its giant grandeur not only revealed its status in the City, but also reflected the shifting institutional role of the Bank in the late nineteenth century, from a mediator between public and commercial financial realms to a predominantly bureaucratic establishment. In Baker's design, Soane's exterior ring of grand public banking halls became clerical spaces, enclosing an inner ring of cellular offices for officials and a garden court in the center. The latter acted as the entrance to the private ceremonial spaces, the vaults, and the governor's apartments, which were housed in a towering superstructure emerging from the Bank's core. Baker's alterations served to enforce a hierarchical organization of spaces; the governor and his advisors were now raised up to preside over the City, yet separated from it by Soane's defensive perimeter walls and an army of personnel.

Although seemingly impenetrable, the Bank's outer walls were semipermeable in order to preserve contact with the financial markets. One important portal for this was the Discount Office in the administrative outer ring, the so-called eyes and ears of the Bank; bill brokers from a small number of designated banks, labeled *discount houses*, would visit it each morning and evening.[80] It was just one of the daily and weekly rituals exercised by the Bank that enabled its surveillance of the City via a kinetic network of messengers and brokers that moved between the institutions and markets of the City on its behalf. In addition to this daily intervention in the market, the Discount Office was the mandatory (yet unofficial) first port of call for any new bank setting up in the City. Through this system, the Bank acted as a warning mechanism for other banks, alerting the City to any disreputable establishments and dissuading undesirables from establishing a place of business.[81]

One way of doing this was by restricting the physical presence of new overseas banks via an unofficial—but generally accepted—hierarchy of spatial standards. Under the Exchange Control Act of 1947, foreign banks were strongly encouraged to register first under the temporary legal and architectural status of a representative office before opening a branch. The label restricted the bank's activities to those of a listening post, established solely as an agency to make contacts and send clients back to the head office (in the country of origin) and therefore unable to carry out any transactions on its own account.[82] The form of these offices was proportionate to their legal status: small, unbranded, and invisible to passers-by. As a Bank of England memo put it, "A Representative Office … can be staffed at a minimum by one person with a telephone, and can simply involve renting one room in an office block."[83] By absorbing these banks' representative offices deep within existing blocks and therefore limiting their conspicuous visibility, the central bank was able to segregate them from the market as well as the City's self-regulatory networks; for the Bank, to have a visible establishment was to be established.[84]

The Bank of England's spatial mediation enabled the continuation and reproduction of a distinct set of class-based, gendered social structures, which protected the autonomy of the British financial sector and the invented traditions of Englishness. This further helped to preserve the City's independence.[85] Yet this largely unofficial system was predicated upon the survival of a close-knit, imperially oriented regime, founded on the strength of sterling and strict controls on the participation of foreign firms in British markets. Although this arrangement of surveillance was still in place until the late 1970s, the breakdown of exchange controls and regulatory barriers throughout the 1960s and the influx of international business gradually eroded the Bank's ability to regulate in this way.[86] Specifically, the birth of the Eurodollar market substantially undermined the Bank's supervisory position and in turn transformed the shape, rhythm, and structure of the City, as well as the City's planning approaches.

After World War II, politicians and financial institutions believed that by securing the strength of sterling, the City's role as an international financial center would be restored and reinforced—a wisdom that was later questioned as the pound grew increasingly volatile with the growth of wartime debts.[87] As such, a series of measures, including the 1947 Exchange Control Act, were enacted by the government to secure Britain's currency reserves and prevent capital outflow from the sterling area—Britain's empire-based currency zone. This had the effect of dividing British banking into the regulated domestic (sterling) market, and a largely unregulated—and effectively offshore—international market.[88] Such a distinction produced a regulatory blind spot, which subsequently enabled a collection of overseas and new merchant banks in the late 1950s to legally solicit the trade in dollars between nonresidents. As this market avoided sterling altogether, the Bank considered it to exist "elsewhere" and excluded it from Britain's accounts, which rendered it invisible and beyond the taxable boundaries of the British state. The informal nature of the Bank of England's supervisory role in the City meant that there was no legislation permitting the Bank's interference or obstruction in the development of a Eurodollar market. Consequently, the surveillance system that the Bank had previously established was entirely undermined by the legal invisibility of the new market, triggering a slow yet substantial spatial transformation of the City in the subsequent decades as more foreign businesses arrived to take advantage of the new markets.[89]

The Eurodollar market emerged as one response to the decreasing value of the pound on the world stage as the sterling area dissipated with decolonization and postwar exchange controls. Britain had initially attempted to revive the declining value of sterling by investing in the colonies, via the Colonial Development and Welfare Act, which aimed to boost colonial industries to supply Europe with raw materials and to balance Britain's accounts.[90] Maintaining the value of the pound in this way proved to be bad for British industry and exports as it increased prices. Britain accrued horrendous debts with sterling area countries as it had to sell assets at terrible prices while simultaneously dealing with a dwindling export capacity. Simultaneously, independence movements gathered pace from the 1950s, with India in 1947, Sudan in 1956, Malaya, the Gold Coast in 1957, the West Indies forming a federation in the same year, Nigeria and Cyprus in 1960, Jamaica in 1962, Kenya in 1963, and Malta in 1964. As the empire disintegrated, Britain turned to Europe and America as its main trading partners. Whereas in the late 1940s, around 50 percent of foreign trade was conducted with the Commonwealth and other sterling area members, and only around 25 percent with Western Europe, by the 1970s the opposite was true.[91] Advocates of the Eurodollar market saw it as a way of reestablishing the City as a leading international financial center, breaking free of its imperial shackles. Spreading through a small group of clearing banks and a progressive set of merchant banks, including S. G. Warburg and Kleinwort Benson, the market was approved by the Bank in

1963.[92] Steadily expanding over the next decade, the Eurodollar market soon became the largest source of capital in the world, reaching around $46 billion by 1970.[93] Its impact on the City, and indeed the global economy, is difficult to overestimate. It marked the beginning of the City as an offshore financial center and the decentralization of regulatory control from the Bank. In conceptual terms, the market divided the Square Mile into two layers: the highly visible realm of financial exchange, limited by the Bank of England's spatial and economic boundaries; and a legally invisible, permissive space that not only escaped the Bank's surveillance, but also quietly manipulated the geographical limits of exchange.[94]

Between 1960 and 1970, the number of foreign banks in the Square Mile doubled in response to the Eurodollar market and subsequent emergence of a highly lucrative international capital market known as the Eurobond market (referred to collectively as the Euromarkets).[95] Faced with stringent postwar currency restrictions in their home countries, these banks took advantage of the light touch regulation in London, a process known as *regulatory arbitrage*.[96] American banks were the biggest participants in this activity, arriving in droves following the imposition of new controls on foreign exchange on the US economy in 1963.[97] In the 1960s, twenty-three American operations opened sizable offices, including companies such as Bankers Trust, Chase Manhattan, and Citibank, the latter employing almost seven hundred people. These companies established branches in cheaper parts of the City where they could occupy larger office buildings more akin to those in American cities, and thereby dispersed the field of banking activity just beyond the traditional remit of the historic core. Moorgate was particularly popular, soon earning the title of the Avenue of the Americas, while others such as Continental Illinois National Bank, which moved into 160–162 Queen Victoria Street (formerly home to *The Times* newspaper) in 1964, opened offices further to the west.[98] Kynaston notes that less than a decade earlier "a stockbroker who sought premises in New London Wall, past Moorgate and towards Aldersgate, was deemed to be committing commercial suicide."[99] Yet while this early move may have demonstrated the Americans' cultural indifference toward the sociospatial traditions of the City, the geographical shift can also be attributed to the lack of space in the historic core and the abundance of new office buildings in the London Wall area. Bomb damage was heaviest in this part of the city, and it was thus the most comprehensively redeveloped, with modern, American-inspired mid- and high-rise buildings. It was also an area formerly dominated by commerce and light industry—hence its status as an unprecedented location for financial firms.[100]

Nonetheless, the emerging cosmopolitanism and geographical enlargement of the financial district began to disrupt the traditional social codes that had historically preserved its autonomy. This trend increased throughout the 1960s and into the 1970s, as the creation of the Euromarkets, in tandem with Britain joining the European Economic Community (EEC) in 1973, initiated the diversification of financial activities, changes in business practices, the creation of new markets, such as the interbank market, and the emergence of new financial instruments. More aggressive attitudes to business practice accompanied a progressive relaxation of economic controls, instigating corporate expansion and the formation of international banking consortiums. In tandem with the implementation of the Companies Act of 1967, which allowed the boards of firms to expand beyond twenty partners, these developments led to the dramatic growth of firms, forcing many to seek accommodation beyond the City's boundaries in the West End and at times on "the wrong side of the river."[101]

These changes marked the beginning of the end for the City's self-regulatory practices, as well as the unquestioned authority of the Bank.[102] As the British government's ideological stance became more market-driven, it took a greater interest in opening up the City to foreign capital and removing barriers to trade. Yet just as the City-Bank-Treasury nexus facilitated new financial activities to ensure the financial district's survival in the new international economy, so too did the physical City make space for the new market within and beyond historic core, in essence dislocating the existing social and spatial systems of the old City to make way for the new.

The Corporation's Two Faces

If the Nation continues to think it worth while to maintain the symbol of self-government which the City has represented for over a thousand years, the machine should be kept in working order, no matter what changes in the administrative picture there may be.
Holden and Holford, *City of London*, 1951[103]

The City of London Pavilion at the Brussels Expo, 1958. Courtesy of British Bankers'
Association.

Reestablishing the City as a leading international financial center was a slow process, fraught with conflicts between the financial institutions, government policy and ideology, and the London planning authorities about what exactly the role of the financial center should be in British public life and how it should operate. From one view, modernity was everywhere. Thanks to innovations in financial markets and telecommunications, by the end of 1965, there were ninety-eight foreign banks in the Square Mile—compared to sixty-three in New York, forty-eight in Paris, and seventeen in Zurich.[104] Britain's first international airport at Heathrow facilitated the arrival of a new, cosmopolitan executive class and the importation of American corporate culture, which revealed itself in the steel-and-glass office blocks that began to emerge in the City's postwar property boom.[105] And yet international financial activity was severely stifled by government restrictions, which aimed at stabilizing the British economy by imposing exchange controls, protecting sterling, and boosting British exports. Economic policy emphasized national industries rather than international finance, and the City's role was limited to facilitating investment in British manufacturing, gaining a reputation as a staid, conservative community.[106]

Amid all this, the City's role in public life became a source of debate and the Corporation, a target. For those that sought to internationalize the City, the municipality was lambasted for its emphasis on traditionalism and failure to provide the right infrastructure to accommodate foreign markets. In an age of welfare-state led reforms, the Labour Party left viewed the Corporation as anachronistic and undemocratic, epitomized by the medieval trappings of the Guildhall and the Mansion House. Right at the core of the problem was the fact that the City's two personalities—the modern financial City and the civic City—were no longer synonymous.

Nowhere was this tension more explicit than in the Corporation's first major public exhibition, the City of London rooms in the British Industry Pavilion at the 1958 Brussels Expo. Viewed by the Corporation as "a model for the blend of tradition and modernity which characterises the City today," the exhibition was an extravaganza of obvious architectural symbolism, in which a curved entrance, framed by the heraldry of the guilds, led the visitor through to a small circular scale model of the City's latest modernist buildings in the center of the room, with the backdrop of the Corporation of London's coat of arms on a wall comprising a map of the world and symbols of trade and industry.[107] This central space, described as the *beating heart*, was crowned by a scaled-down model of the dome of Wren's St. Stephen Walbrook, weighing down on the modern developments below. Another overblown replica in the form of the coffered ceiling of the Egyptian Hall in the Mansion House covered the rest of the pavilion, in which interactive trade exhibits, organized in partnership with the major City institutions, were positioned alongside instructive placards about the Corporation's history and mannequin models of guildsmen.[108] Modern buildings and exhibits perched submissively under the weight of the City's neoclassical heritage, which exuded luxury, power, and prestige.

Commissioned by the Federation of British Industries (FBI), and designed by its exhibition company in collaboration with the City Corporation, the 1958 exhibit won universal acclaim and was awarded a silver star by the international jury, despite its lack of cohesion. It was the first of a number of public-facing interventions made by the Corporation to unite the civic and financial City, using visual strategies such as film, publications, exhibitions, and touring installations to advertise the activities of the municipality. At the core of this initiative was the promotion of the Square Mile's architecture and infrastructural projects, which it viewed as an opportunity for public engagement, yet ultimately became a proxy for political conversations about traditionalism versus modernization and domesticity versus internationalism in the City.

Public relations first became a topic for discussion within the Corporation in the immediate aftermath of World War II, in response to the Ministry of Health's call for all local authorities to establish a public information center for residents.[109] By 1947, this advice had extended to promoting publicity for government, in order to cultivate more "day-to-day, all-the-year-round, democratic interest in local government, and to attract the best men and women to its service as members and as officers."[110] Recommending the use of "exhibitions, films, posters, leaflets, etc." for propaganda purposes, the ministry advised municipalities to establish "public relations committees and officers" to carry out such duties.[111] In the City, an Information Office was established in 1951 as an independent, temporary building to represent the City of London during the Festival of Britain. Located to the southwest of St Paul's Cathedral, the center was designed by Albert Richardson as a small yet conspicuous information hub in the tourist heart of the City, partly funded by the festival authorities.[112] It was here that an officer was first appointed to deal with the press and publicize the exhibitions and events organized by the Corporation throughout the festival. However, it wasn't until 1958 that the Special Committee of the City Corporation recommended that a public relations officer be formally appointed "and that the public relations section of the Town Clerk's Office be developed to deal with an increased degree of public relations for the Corporation."[113]

Publicity intensified during this period due to the large-scale program of rebuilding being implemented by the Corporation, attracting attention from the press and the public. The initial building boom was also in full force, with fifty-two new developments completed just between 1958 and 1959, totaling over 3.8 million square feet of new floor space.[114] In 1956, the Town Planning and Improvements Committee had requested "the engagement of professional assistance for the interpretation to the public of the planning activities of the Corporation,"[115] but the request was withdrawn until two years later, when a number of large schemes were moving toward completion, such as Route 11 (opened 1959), alongside securing planning permission for Holford's Paternoster scheme and the Barbican towers.

In the same way that the pavilion in Brussels had emphasized tradition above all else, the initial output of the Corporation's PR office promoted the "Old City," symbolized by the pageantry of common council and guilds and the celebration of its ancient buildings, rather than looking toward the national and financial concerns of the Square Mile. In 1950, the information officer had been instructed to produce "brightly written and illustrated booklets of popular character" on the ceremonial functions of the City, which largely went on to inform the printed output of the Corporation for the next decade.[116] Titles such as *What Is the Corporation of London?* (1963) were produced alongside a series of architectural and tourist guidebooks focusing on St. Paul's, Christopher Wren's churches, the Mansion House, Monument, and the Guildhall as the key highlights for the City.[117]

During this period, the two functions of the City were for the most part treated as separate entities, with the Corporation representing democracy and the financial and commercial City representing trade. Where publications were produced for the business community, such as the Burrow's Guides, these took the form of directories or manuals containing trade advertisements and contained little reference to the Corporation or its architectural achievements.[118] Their relationship was positioned as one of mutual respect that had been cemented by centuries of (somewhat disinterested) coexistence.

A series of films commissioned by the Corporation in the 1950s encapsulated this dynamic, including *City of London* (1951), *Our British Heritage: The City of London* (1955), and *My Lord Mayor* (1960). Produced for circulation to theaters and schools throughout Britain, the films were considered to be educational tools, rather than promotional material. *City of London* had the widest distribution of the three, commissioned for the South Bank's Telekinema at the Festival of Britain, with subsequent screenings at international film festivals, including those in Venice, Helsinki, and Edinburgh, where it won several awards. Directed by British Pathé, the documentary intended to reinforce the historical significance of the Corporation and reveal "the Spirit of the City," using "pictures and words that ... get over to the general public something of the intangible quality of the City's life—the spirit which springs from the mutual trust and fairness in trading which directly derives from the traditions of the past."[119]

Almost entirely focused on reiterating the history of the City as an institution, rather than its future as a financial center, the film begins with a hazy Turner-esque landscape over the Thames at daybreak, described by the narrator as being "as young as each new morning yet endowed with a wisdom that only comes of age." Here, visual focus is on the empty streets, but, as the director subsequently argued in editorial notes, "the sound track brings back the bustling life and the street cries of London's past ... throughout, although we are always seeing the present, the past will, some way or another, be always with us—hinted at in sound or picture."[120] Throughout the film, scenes of men doing business in the port, wholesale markets, and trading floors are juxtaposed with craftsmen of the various guilds hard at work, or the Court of Common Council in session, showing that "the corporate feeling is ... the result of generations of men with a respect for, and something deeper than financial interest in, their particular trade or business."[121] The business City is cast as the child of the guilds, and therefore intimately wedded to the Corporation's activities.

In all three films, the modern financial center was mostly avoided in favor of establishing the historic lineage of the

Stills from *City of London*. Black and white, documentary film, 1951. Courtesy of London Metropolitan Archives.

Corporation as a municipal body. In the 1960 documentary *My Lord Mayor*, tradition, in the form of the Mansion House and the lavish interior of the Guildhall, was juxtaposed with progress in the form of the Corporation's achievements as a local authority, including the Barbican residential development, Epping Forest, the City police station, and the City's schools, but the film reveals little evidence of the booming property market then beginning to dominate.

Placing emphasis on the Corporation's role as a local authority and ancient municipal body at this moment was perhaps not entirely surprising.[122] The timing of *My Lord Mayor* was almost certainly strategic, as in the year of its release a royal commission was in the process of reevaluating the whole structure of local government in London, in an enquiry that resulted in the formation of the Greater London Council (GLC) in 1963. Despite coming under threat of attack during this period, the report of the royal commission favorably concluded that "[the City] is an anomaly but we recommend that this anomaly should continue," arguing that "its wealth, its antiquity, the enormous part it has played in the history of the nation, its dignity, its traditions and its historical ceremonial" rendered the City "an institution of national importance."[123] Such a sentiment validated the Corporation for the expressions of pageantry which it would be later be publicly condemned for.

In the coming decade, this narrative began to change. In 1964, the Corporation employed outside PR consultants to deal with increased press attention. The Bank of England's official announcement of support for the Euromarkets put demands on the City to modernize. In addition, the royal commission's inquiry had put the City in the spotlight. The firm Mather Public Relations Limited—which would later become the advertising giant Ogilvy & Mather—was an established agency already working with other national governments abroad, such as in Canada.[124] Their initial report agreed that the Corporation was at "a critical stage of its history" and that there was "an urgent need to create a new, more up-to-date and more widely acceptable image." It declared: "A new image must be projected, and this will require an enlightened outlook by the Corporation. The emphasis must be not so much on historical associations as on the role the Corporation plays in the development of business, on its progressive attitude towards cultural and economic relations, local government and the arts. The aim must be to promote the Corporation and the

City of London as an active, forward-looking local (but central) authority which is the hub of National and City affairs."[125] Mather's report marked a dramatic change of direction and demonstrated a shift in the Corporation's attitude toward self-representation. By hiring an external consultant, the organization agreed to expose its internal workings to external criticism for the first time in history. Mather's call for a need to be seen to support business and present an improved attitude toward "economic relations" implied a shift in identity, from an institution that was symbolic of the link between trade and government to one that actively enforced, and promoted, that link through infrastructure provision, publicity, and forward planning.

Architectural and urban planning projects were used by the consultancy as the main mode of public engagement, partly due to their visibility and clarity of message, and partly because this was an area in which the Corporation had historically been highly criticized. Publications no longer drew attention to historic monuments, but instead highlighted modern buildings. In *Walk a Modern City: A Look at the Square Mile* (1967), visitors were guided through slick high-color photographs of the Square Mile's newest schemes, including Owen Williams & Partners "mammoth Daily Mirror Newspaper building, 196 feet high and completed in 1960 ... the largest newspaper in Britain"; London Wall's developer-led glass towers, where "the atmosphere of a new City makes itself quickly felt"; and Holford's Paternoster Square, hailing this "new £9,000,000 development" as "an example of Modern architecture at its best."[126]

The consultants made the City an architectural destination. In 1969, the Corporation appointed its first official "lady guide," to show guests of the mayor around the new architectural developments of the City, such as foreign officials, press, and the monarchy.[127] Throughout the decade, the municipality staged sponsored architectural exhibitions in the disused Royal Exchange building and a new exhibition hall at the Guildhall, including *Modern City* (1969), comprising photographs of the City's newest buildings. The venues were also used for exhibitions and events on proposed developments to enable public consultation, such as the North Bank, Paternoster Square, London Wall, the Central Criminal Court Extension, Barbican towers, various car parks and road safety programs, and numerous private developments like the National Provincial headquarters and the Mansion House scheme.[128]

While promoting modern architecture was a way of fulfilling the consultants' demand for a new "progressive attitude towards cultural and economic relations," it also provided a smokescreen for the sluggish development of the Corporation's building program. In 1964 the government implemented stringent building restrictions and office development permits (ODPs) to encourage decentralization out of London stifled the property boom, deterring new developments and halting existing projects mid-construction.[129] Receiving negative attention in the press, the Corporation used publicity material to highlight the achievements of postwar reconstruction rather than the failures.

One of the more overt examples of this was a film entitled *The Living City* (commissioned 1967, released 1970), made to promote "one of the most complex redevelopment projects in history," celebrating modernist projects like London Wall, with its raised walkways filled with throngs of young workers socializing to a groovy soundtrack. Less desirable facets of the City's infrastructure, such as the heavily criticized road development scheme, are couched in terms of efficiency in the film, while the unfinished office buildings are "compared to individual pieces in a vast and highly complex jigsaw puzzle, which when finished will eventually make up the complete picture." Modern office buildings are celebrated to establish the Corporation's role as a provider for the day-to-day activities of the business community and as an enlightened local authority. Against the scenes of modern office interiors, commuters on London Bridge, and traffic at the Bank of England intersection, the concluding narration explains that the municipality's architects and planners were mindful of two prevailing factors: first, of "the importance of creating a suitable environment in which the highly complex machinery of modern business can function most efficiently"; and second, "of providing all the social and cultural amenities essential not only for the hundreds and thousands of commuters, but for those who live within the City boundaries."

Around the time *The Living City* was commissioned, the Corporation had begun to work more closely with the business community. In 1966, for the first time, the Lord Mayor's annual procession included representatives from various business sectors, subsuming trade into the Corporation's ritual, while two years later, one hundred "leading American businessmen" were invited to spend four days in the City, "visiting the Corporation and the large

Stills from *The Living City*, 1970. Courtesy of London Metropolitan Archives.

institutions."[130] This increased cooperation came at a time when the financial institutions were embarking on their own PR drive to promote the City as an international financial center, in response to political hostility. Harold Wilson's recently elected Labour government accused the City of causing the UK's ongoing balance of payments crisis through privileging the sterling area—and in turn deflecting investment away from the domestic economy— and for generally "destroying the government's grand plans for economic modernisation and social equity" with its opaque and uncompetitive systems.[131] All this was exacerbated by the devaluation of sterling in 1967, which established a period of great financial instability in the City. The government carried out reviews of the City's banking system, and threats of further nationalization abounded.[132] The critique was associated with the City's inability and unwillingness to focus on investment in British industry, at a time when this was being promoted vociferously by both political parties.[133] Following economic devastation of World War II, the government enacted policies that focused on reviving the nation's industrial base in order to boost British exports, rather than on foreign financial markets. The withdrawal of US loans, and the overall drop in exports and earnings to one-third of their level before the war, meant that Britain was struggling to pay for its imports. British industry became the focus of Labour and Conservative governments alike, as a way to improve the balance of payments problem and restore employment levels.[134]

Despite becoming the most industrialized country in the world in the 1950s, with "its highest ever, to that time, proportion of the workforce … in industrial operations," by the 1960s UK exports were plummeting and economic growth was slow in comparison with other European countries.[135] In the spirit of stemming economic decline, the Wilson government, building on the rhetoric of previous administrations, adopted a planning approach that focused on scientific, technological, and industrial advancement to boost the economy and rectify the balance of payments crisis. It sought to achieve this through economic incentives and the establishment of new government agencies, such as the Department of Economic Affairs, the Ministry of Technology, and the British National Export Council (BNEC).[136] Established to encourage the expansion of British trade, the BNEC formed the Committee on Invisible Exports (COIE), comprising senior personnel from major financial institutions, the Bank of England, and the Treasury, to investigate the "invisible earnings" dimension of the UK balance of payments—in other words, services (rather than products) provided to clients outside the UK. As commercial and financial services formed the basis of the UK's invisible earnings, and the City was the main generator of this income, the committee became a vehicle for promoting the City's expertise in international trade as an essential facet of the British economy.[137] Its research proved that invisibles were a long-standing and significant part of Britain's economic output and of equal importance to manufacturing, and that this success was largely dependent on the City of London. This "political and public relations campaign" was integral to the reestablishment of the City as a "post-sterling international financial centre," as it provided a platform for further campaigns on regulatory liberalization and created a new basis for promotion of the financial sector.[138]

Following the formalization of the COIE in 1967, the Corporation's PR activities took up the rhetoric on invisibles as a key part of its strategy. In 1966, Lord Mayor Robert Bellinger commissioned an important planning document dubbed *An Economic Study of the City of London*, which aimed "to report on the whole complicated and esoteric subject of financial activities carried out in the City" and to see "what we, the Corporation, could do so as best to nurture this vital work, particularly in our role of local planning authority."[139] The authors of the report, a new consultancy firm called the Economists Advisory Group (EAG), were also the main researchers for the COIE, which suggests they were selected by the Corporation on the basis of their expertise in this area. Bellinger, who was an active promoter of the City's role in the UK's invisible earnings and who also commissioned a film called *The Hidden Strength* dedicated to this purpose,[140] was emblematic of the Corporation's shifting priorities and of the redirection of its traditions to facilitate the business community.

One notable episode in these early collaborations was the creation of the City of London Transportable Pavilion: a mobile structure comprising exhibits on the City Corporation and every major business sector in the City, to be shown at international trade fairs. The idea was conceived in 1964 in response to an invitation to provide a mobile display unit for so-called British weeks. Taking place in major cities all over the world, British weeks were devised by the Board of Trade with the aim of increasing exports—both visible and invisible—through the promotion of British products and services abroad. With the decline of British exports follow-ing the loss of the Commonwealth markets to competitor indus-trial nations such as America, Japan, and the USSR, the British government had carried out a number of pathfinder missions in 1961 in Western Europe to assess the appetite for "consumer and consumer durable goods."[141] "What they found almost without exception, were rich, fast-developing markets that reflected rap-idly rising standards of living," something hitherto ignored by British manufacturers.[142] British weeks aimed to promote British exports internationally through theater, exhibitions, concerts, and sporting events in the host city. At the exhibitions, pavilions promoted British industries and services, and British shops were encouraged to put together window displays to be given as gifts to foreign tradespeople to be sold in their own shops.[143]

Spurred on by the "enthusiasm which the project ... aroused among influential City interests," the Corporation's decision to commission a pavilion for British weeks was also influenced by the success of the City of London Pavilion in the British Industrial sec-tion of the 1958 Brussels Expo. Yet whereas the latter emphasized

Photograph of the first City of London Mobile Pavilion, 1966. Ronald Dickens and Associates Ltd., printed in A. Abel Smith, "British Weeks," *Stock Exchange Journal*, September 1965, 8–10. Courtesy of the *Stock Exchange Journal*.

heritage and tradition, the 1965 City of London Transportable Pavilion focused on the Corporation's role as a provider of international business services and progressive local authority. Designed by Ronald Dickens, Fellow of the Royal Society of Industrial Artists, who previously produced stands in the Festival of Britain, the pavilion eschewed neoclassical forms in favor of a modernist, circular form, "based on a spiral which admits the viewing public to an inner chamber first, then to the outer gallery from which [the] final exit is made."[144] The sequence of exhibits inside the structure was telling of the Corporation's priorities: the inner chamber—its *beating heart*—contained the section on the Corporation, including information panels and "a 10' diameter model of the City as it is today," which would begin in daylight and "as the lighting dims, the glow of lights from the commercial buildings [showing them] as they would appear at night." As visitors moved away from this they were met with four "slowly rotating cylinders" containing color transparencies of the Corporation's key activities such as "Housing, Police, City Health, ... Schools, Open Spaces, Barbican scheme etc." These were set into a wall decorated with "a painted mural illustrating The Lord Mayor, his coach, Liverymen, Bank Messengers, City Workers etc." A series of diorama models of London trade from Roman days to the present adorned its outer gallery, followed by the various trade exhibits in the form of loop films, drawings, models, maps, and charts, contributed by various financial institutions, showing the significance of the City's trade to the rest of the world. Finally, the exit sequence was designed to filter out the crowd via vertical screens comprising "impressive facts" relating to the trade relationship between Britain and the host country. Upon leaving the pavilion, the visitor would be channeled outside to see the exterior, composed of angled facets, each covered with cropped, blown-up photographs "which when viewed askew, build up into a panoramic view of the City."[145]

Viewing the exhibit as a successful exercise in "soft power," the pavilion was subsequently exhibited in Amsterdam, Milan, Oslo, Lyons, Brussels, Stockholm, Tokyo, and San Francisco.[146] However, press coverage in April 1966 was not so positive, following an arson attack on the transportable pavilion during its display at the Oslo British week. The perpetrator was a fifty-seven-year-old Norwegian businessman who claimed he acted on "an irresistible impulse" and was "protesting against the British 10 per cent import surcharge and subsidies to British shipping," and hence more broadly at the Labour government's commercial policies.[147] Ronald Dickens was called in to build a temporary structure and eventually redesign the exhibit. The second transportable pavilion was larger, spread over two stories, on account of the huge number of visitors its predecessor had received, but with a more transportable, prefabricated plywood and timber structure.[148] The pavilion continued to tour, alongside various other mobile display units devised by the Corporation to share the demand of international trade shows, for another five years. On the surface, the point of these touring exhibitions was to promote Britain's financial and commercial activities abroad, but the deeper significance was undoubtedly for the Corporation to sell an image to the British people at home of a municipal body that was in touch with the business activities going on within its boundaries. However, while "the City's New Image," as one newspaper put it, was being recognized in the press, the Corporation struggled to escape criticism. As the PR consultants commented in 1968: "While there may be an improvement in the Corporation's image, many people still think of the Corporation as an extension of the Dick Whittington myth. That this is nonsense is obvious: in Public Relations terms, however, it is difficult to put such a legend 'on ice.'"[149]

Despite the Corporation's efforts to work with the business community, changes in the regulatory structure of the finance industry and the political turmoil of the 1970s provoked deeper divisions between the City's two personalities. The Organisation of the Petroleum Countries (OPEC) oil price hikes and concomitant flow of petrodollars through the City (expanding the offshore currency markets) continued to render it an attractive place for foreign banks to establish headquarters, with over ninety foreign banks locating in the City between 1971 and 1976, while a change in legislation enabled foreign securities houses to set up in London.[150] Despite the raising of most of the US restrictions in 1974, American banks continued to operate in the City, with nine relocating to the Square Mile in the same year.[151]

However, the City's international ambitions required wholesale changes of its regulatory and social system. Bretton Woods collapsed in 1971, then the secondary banking crisis took grip in 1973, followed by the sterling crisis of 1976, collectively providing the impetus for the implementation of monetarist economic policies in Britain. Public opinion grew increasingly hostile to the City's paternalist traditions and the closed self-regulatory system, which were perceived as barriers to a free market system. This critique threatened to erode the Corporation's legitimacy and undermine the public services image that it had spent the previous five years cultivating. Britain's anticipated entry into the EEC (and thus the Common Market) was felt acutely in the City, with an initial surge of business and foreign companies well beyond the capacity of its existing office stock. Economic think tanks put pressure on the City of London to lower rents, while critics began to question the competitive future of the Square Mile as an international financial center in the broader context of European regulation.[152]

In essence, the City's informality—both financially and architecturally speaking—was perceived to be a problem: some commentators worried that if the EEC were to impose blanket regulations on financial activities for all participating countries, the necessary removal of the City's flexible approach and club-like arrangement of regulation might take away its competitive edge. Similarly, the same critics were concerned that the City's medieval form and concomitant dearth of standardized building plots near the center would render it uninhabitable for European banks wishing to set up headquarters in the capital, on account of scarce and substandard accommodation.[153]

A major problem for the Corporation was that a second property boom was well under way, yet the combination of a lack of available building sites, the government's tight restrictions on new development, and high demand for space was driving up land values in the Square Mile. This reflected badly on the municipality. "At present, some of the very institutions and businesses which make the City great are in danger of being forced, by high rents, out of that 'close physical proximity to one another' which (in [Governor of the Bank of England] Leslie O'Brien's words) 'is a major factor in promoting the City's efficiency,'" wrote Ogilvy & Mather in its 1970 report.[154] In theory, the Corporation had attempted to preempt this problem by commissioning the Economists Advisory Study in 1966, which incorporated a comprehensive overview of the City's current and future planning requirements in view of projected economic and political fluctuations.[155] However, this study was carried out under the assumption that, aside from the effects of technological innovation, the business City's traditional way of operating would continue unchanged, without the imposition of centralized regulation. Furthermore, the persistence of government controls on development and influx of foreign firms meant that prime rents had increased substantially, rising from £5 per square foot in 1968 to £20 per square foot in 1973.[156] As a result, key members of the business community as well as figures from national organizations such as the Trades Union Congress began questioning the value of the Corporation as the provider of an effective business environment.[157]

Two responses were put forward by the Common Council: the first was to openly challenge the GLC's blanket approach to building in the capital in its *Greater London Development Plan* (1967) and to criticize the government's system of building controls. Other experts in office development had been critical of the GLC on this matter. In 1969, planners Peter Cowan and Daniel Fine wrote a report for the Joint Unit for Planning Research (a collaboration between University College London and the London School of Economics), in which they claimed decentralization was counter to the strategies for economic growth being put forward by the government. They explained: "The Central London office function is one of the keys to economic growth in Britain; its financial and banking sectors provide the bulk of our 'invisible exports,' while the prestige commercial offices of the West End are the headquarters of the marketing, advertising and after-sales services which are so vital in competing for industrial and service orders both at home and abroad. If Britain joins the Common Market these functions will have to expand many times. Yet growth in this sector is being stunted, surely without adequate knowledge of the effects."[158] In line with this critique, the Planning and Communications Committee of the Corporation stressed to the GLC the need to maintain the City of London's position as "a national and international centre for finance and trade" via "increased workforce, derestriction of office building," and "encouragement of small businesses."[159]

Its second response was to refocus the activities of the PR office toward presenting an image of the Corporation as sympathetic to the needs of the financial community, focusing less on its role as a local authority, particularly where the built environment was concerned. Until now, Ogilvy & Mather had spent most of its time answering enquiries and dealing with planning issues concerning a number of new and contentious developments, such as Mies van der Rohe's unrealized Mansion House scheme, the Bishopsgate redevelopment, and the decision on whether to go forward with the Barbican Arts Centre. Time had been devoted less to strategic office policy and more to iconic buildings. In 1971, when the Barbican Arts Centre was finally confirmed, the PR office expressed relief: "it leaves the Corporation free to stress its civic task of helping to improve the environment in which the Business City can function and flourish."[160] An exhibition the following year entitled Europe and the World was constructed to commemorate Britain's forthcoming entry into the EEC, while the Lord Mayor's theme for the year was ambitiously entitled The World Is Our Market, aimed to "stress the toughness of the task ahead."[161]

In addition to new publications, the Corporation commissioned yet another film, entitled *Capital City* (1973) and depicting the City of London as the center of Britain's invisible exports, with a focus on workers filling its streets, trading floors, and offices.[162] It aimed to highlight the City's international connections, with shots of foreign banks housed in modern high-rise office buildings, lit up at night. Presented as a businessman and ambassador, rather than a ceremonial figurehead, the Lord Mayor was depicted wearing a suit rather than livery, and sitting either at his desk conversing with the export group manager or in meetings with City executives, discussing a business project. Scenes of the common council were kept to a minimum, and the Guildhall itself was promoted as a mere tourist attraction. Furthermore, redevelopment and public services were presented as facilitating the business community, with the Barbican representing a key resource for maintaining the City's labor force, while high figures were quoted for infrastructure expenditure, such as the £11 million road improvement project. As the narrator put it, "The City Corporation's a big spender." The aim was to reinforce the idea that "the business City depends for its environment and efficient running on the public City, which means the Corporation of London."

Despite these efforts, as the financial City began to deregulate with the support of the government, the Corporation, became a symbol of stasis. In 1973, a prominent report jointly commissioned by Lord Rothschild and a government think tank argued that the Corporation of London could not "represent ... the financial services industry," calling for government intervention.[163] In the following year, the London Labour Party demanded the Corporation's abolition, decrying the municipality for its arcane and undemocratic processes. This plea won a majority support from the GLC and was eventually put forward in Parliament.[164] While ultimately unsuccessful, the campaign lasted for over a decade and brought the Corporation under extensive public scrutiny, with over three thousand articles and broadcasts about its affairs appearing in the media in 1973.[165] More than ever, the ongoing conflict between the Corporation's two identities was damaging its public profile. "The 'image' of the Corporation of London and the 'image' of the City have long been confused in the public mind," wrote the PR consultants. "But the one cannot speak on behalf of the other, and the result is often that an attack on either tends to reflect on both."[166]

Once again, this crisis of representation manifested through the built environment. In the 1970s, the Corporation's planning approach became increasingly conservation oriented with the continued agitation by heritage interest groups.[167] As the oldest part of London, it contained some of the capital's most significant historic sites, many of which were destroyed through its often-careless postwar rebuilding program. In response to vehement criticism from conservationists for its cavalier attitude to demolition during the boom periods of the 1960s and early 1970s, the Corporation redrafted its planning policy to be predominantly conservationist. Jane M. Jacobs has articulated how the Corporation's emphasis on heritage preservation toward the end of the 1970s and into the next decade was ideological, and a way of reaffirming the City's image as the "heart of the empire" during its resurgence as an international financial center.[168] Yet there were also pragmatic reasons for adopting such strong conservationist policies, which were, on the face of it, more economically than politically motivated. Reusing existing buildings became a necessity with the instability of property markets; the 1970s began and ended with periods of serious demand, yet the lack of available land and regulations on development put pressure on the Corporation.[169] A heritage approach was not only economical and, in theory, marketable, but also satisfied the Corporation's policy to provide accommodation for small businesses and countered fears that the City may become too expensive, weakening its ability to compete.[170]

The City was changing. Growing internationalism and murmurs of impending financial deregulation created a growing demand for office space. But despite this, in 1984 it released a new draft local plan (DLP), which designated over 70 percent of the City's core a conservation area and effectively prohibited any new developments. The response was devastating for the Corporation. Critics claimed that the DLP wildly misjudged the economic climate, failing to anticipate the new floor space demands, sending a message that businesses should look to alternative locations, including the new rival, Canary Wharf.[171]

An influential report by a right-wing think tank, the Centre for Policy Studies (CPS)—led by Sir Keith Joseph, a minister and personal friend of Margaret Thatcher—outlined the dominant criticisms of the DLP, which claimed that the Corporation was not only seriously misguided in its recommendations, but also that the impact of the DLP on financial services would be harmful for the British economy.[172] Arguing that the Corporation had "little understanding of the economy of the City," the scathing report revealed that the DLP used data that was in some cases over ten years out of date and had no clear comprehension of the impact that computer and communications technology would have on needs of occupiers. It also criticized the DLP for too heavily emphasizing the nonfinancial aspects of the City, "such as industry, wholesaling and housing," with too many "nanny policies" and conservation regulations based on the "negative planning" approach in the 1976 *Greater London Development Plan* (produced by the Labour-dominated GLC). In short, the authors argued, "it does not indicate that the Corporation wishes to promote the financial economy of the City."[173]

Such sentiments reflected the Conservative government's antipathy towards the City's old boys' network and restrictive practices, which crystallized with Thatcher's early financial reforms at the end of the 1970s. In 1979, the City's major regulatory institutions were overhauled: the London Stock Exchange was listed on the Office of Fair Trading (OFT) Restrictive Practices Register, and the Banking Act and the removal of exchange controls reduced the Bank of England's informal regulatory authority, for the first time enshrining it in law.[174] In this political climate, which emphasized free market principles and competition, the City Corporation's conservation policy represented the visible face of the old reactionary system, whereby the emphasis on heritage stifled innovation.[175] As the CPS report wrote, "the past is firmly enshrined in the plan; the present is not understood; the future may be merely considered," a philosophy that "illustrates the national malaise of looking to the past not to the future, which is at the root of Britain's economic decline."[176] To a certain extent, these accusations were extensions of the negative critique leveled at the City since the early postwar years from the business community, which had become more pronounced as the rhetoric of internationalism grew more prominent. But the pervasiveness of Thatcher's reforms across economic, political, and planning policy, in tandem with more global changes in international finance, meant that for the first time the various forces attacking the Corporation were unified in their analysis. The municipality would have to more closely represent the interests of the financial City, or risk extinction.

Proactive Planners

On October 27, 1986, the *Financial Times* published a captivating double-page photograph: a construction worker stood stoically looking out across a large building site, his back turned to the camera, his overalls and hard hat bathed in a luminescent glow cast by spotlights beaming from the rubble and a large firework exploding overhead. At a glance, the photograph venerated the worker; the mysterious central figure echoed the many anonymous heroes depicted in Soviet propaganda posters, while the striking geometries of light and building infrastructure had constructivist overtones. Yet the real scene couldn't have been further from communist Russia. Commissioned by the marketing agency Peter Davenport Associates for the developer Rosehaugh Stanhope Developments (RSD), taken by the iconic British photographer Brian Griffin, the image was in fact an advertisement for the Broadgate development, the largest office complex ever built in the City of London. For those in the know, the visual metaphor was blatant: this was the day of the Big Bang, one of the most transformative financial revolutions in history, which would irrevocably change the way the UK banking and securities sector operated and in turn herald a new dawn in British commercial real estate. Broadgate represented a new kind of workplace, developed by a new kind of developer, for a new kind of financial district.

On the face of it, Griffin was not the obvious choice for a real estate advertising campaign, as an artist who had become known for subversive photographic critique of Thatcherite Britain, an approach he dubbed *capitalist realism*. Born in Birmingham, Griffin started out at age sixteen as an engineer before rebelling and joining Manchester Polytechnic to study photography at twenty-one. He made his name working for the industry magazine *Management Today* under the Swiss-German art director Roland Schenk. His pseudo-surrealist portraits of executives for the magazine brought a dark humor and sense of unease into these business images, as if to question the power dynamics at play in Britain's ever-growing corporations. He continued these themes in two acclaimed books, *Power: British Management in Focus* (1981) and *Work* (1988), which included collections of portraits of politicians, executives, trade unionists, educators, and manufacturers.

Quite ironically, Griffin became immensely popular among corporate clients during the 1980s, subsequently receiving commissions from Lloyds TSB, British Airways, Coutts Bank, and BT. Perhaps it was the overt and unabashed depiction of wealth and power, and the hint of bad taste, that attracted these clients. Or perhaps it was the ease with which Griffin spoke the client's language. Either way, for Stuart Lipton and Godfrey Bradman of Rosehaugh Stanhope, the attraction was undoubtedly about creating a new kind of image for the corporate real estate world. At the time of construction, Broadgate was the largest, most advanced, and most technologically sophisticated speculative office building in Britain. It was the first of the new American-style "groundscrapers" to emerge with the financial transformations of the 1980s, curated as a dense hub whereby the corporate workplace was reconfigured to include large art-filled public spaces, retail outlets, and leisure facilities. Rosehaugh Stanhope was not simply introducing a new set of buildings; it was introducing a new idea of corporate life in the heady boom period of the 1980s. Griffin's work drew attention to these cultural shifts. Hired by Peter Davenport to produce a series of brochures to publicize Broadgate and show development progress, two other photographic series emerged from the commission. One entitled *The Big Tie* was part of a brochure advertising the upcoming ice rink in the heart of the Broadgate circus. It told the story of a giant polka dot tie—an emblem of eighties corporate excess—being dragged from an executive, who was leaning over a model of Broadgate, into the real Broadgate project by construction workers. In each photograph, the giant tie swooped down on the City, where it was ultimately carried overhead like a royal bier, ending in the prestigious Broadgate circus, where the executive "walks up the red carpet that is his tie and skates on the new ice rink."[177] The other was a compilation of eight portraits of skilled workers from the Broadgate site, each depicted lying as a tomb effigy of a recumbent knight, with a tool of the trade pressed like a sword to their lips. Griffin's work, which was not only published in book form and in print media but also exhibited at the National Portrait Gallery, bestowed the Broadgate project with an

Big Bang, Broadgate, City of London, 1986. Courtesy of Bridgeman Images. Copyright
Brian Griffin.

air of cultural awareness and unapologetic confidence, but it also indicated a drastic shift in the cultural position of corporate architecture in the City that would emerge post-Big Bang.

Broadgate was arguably *the* architectural icon of the Thatcher era, symbolizing and embodying the pinnacle of the economic, regulatory, and political changes brought in by her government. Big Bang was an epoch-changing agreement forged between the Thatcher government and the Stock Exchange, resulting in the opening up of the UK stock market to international members and the erosion of the jobber-broker distinction, which had hitherto restricted participants' activities in the market to the buy or sell side. This meant that institutions could now take part in all areas of the market, ultimately enabling the formation of new multifaceted financial conglomerates.

Regulatory change transformed the organizational and technological character of financial firms and their accommodation requirements. First, the scale of these companies increased dramatically. Unlike Wall Street, which already had a number of large investment banks due to brokerage deregulation in 1975 and partial repeal of the Glass-Steagall Act in 1980 (hitherto separating investment/retail banks), in the early 1980s the City still comprised smaller, market-specific firms, which were unsuitable for the size and diversity of the new securities market. To compete, they needed to consolidate and grow, triggering a spate of unparalleled expansions, amalgamations, and acquisitions between firms, with the aim of offering "the widest possible range of services to the widest possible range of clients in the widest possible range of countries."[178] The mergers incorporated clearing, merchant, and foreign banks, jobbers and brokers, securing their future in the marketplace by expanding their in-house capabilities.[179] In the first three months after the Big Bang, daily turnover nearly doubled.[180] The banks also grew in size. For example, Morgan Grenfell expanded from two hundred to two thousand employees between 1975 and 1986, increasing in value from £160 million to £4 billion.[181]

Second, the Big Bang created unprecedented technological demands. The introduction of a new electronic trading system at the Stock Exchange, modeled on its NYSE rival NASDAQ (National Association of Securities Dealers Automated Quotation System), instigated the abandonment of traditional face-to-face, or *open outcry*, trading in the City after 1986. The latter had dramatic spatial implications, rendering the centralized Stock Exchange trading floor completely redundant by enabling its members to trade from their own in-house dealing floors across the financial center.[182] The new dealing floors had specific and costly infrastructural and architectural requirements, including large slab-to-slab heights to house the cabling for computers and air conditioning above suspended ceilings and beneath raised floors, and deep floor plans.[183]

The firm to revolutionize office design in response to these organizational shifts, and to introduce the concept of space planning in the UK, was DEGW. By foregrounding change as the core design problem, the firm became one of the most prolific and successful commercial practices operating in the City from the 1980s onward. Cofounded in 1973 by Duffy and John Worthington, DEGW pioneered user-oriented design with a particular focus on workplaces. Duffy, who has also published widely and occupied the position of RIBA president (1993–1995), drew on his postgraduate education at the College of Environmental Design at UC Berkley and at Princeton. Here Duffy was exposed to a school of thought derived from the multidisciplinary environment-behavior studies (EBS) movement in the US, which analyzed individuals as part of their sociophysical environment.[184] Building on this methodology, DEGW approached the office building as a complex, multilayered organism that changed with the needs of the tenant, rather than a rigid, unchanging form. In short, the firm's philosophy reconfigured the office from a prescriptive environment to a responsive one.

The biggest innovations in the City emerged from their highly influential ORBIT (Office Research: Buildings and Information Technology) study in 1983, a two-year research project that aimed to assess "the impact of information technology upon office work and office workers" and its consequences for the design of office buildings.[185] As the first of DEGW's many multiclient studies, the project was sponsored by industry giants from the supply, rather than the demand, side of the commercial property world (i.e., the producers of buildings, rather than the users/clients), including the British Telecom and Department of Industry regulatory bodies; suppliers of office space, including Greycoat Estates in association with developer and investor Norwich Union; surveyors Jones Lang Wootton and Fletcher King; the development corporations of three Scottish New Towns; and firms in office construction, including building services engineer Matthew Hall, fee-management contractor Bovis, and Steelcase, which was the largest office furniture manufacturer in the world at the time. With subjects ranging from ergonomics and organizational change to surveys of technical equipment and economic analyses of the office market, the variety of research fields addressed in the report reflected the diversity of the patrons. As almost all the sponsors were prominent institutions in the City, the report became hugely influential regarding the future organization of work, and workspace, in the financial district.

The report sought to understand the scale and nature of imminent technological change in Britain, its impact on organizations, and the effect of this on building specification, construction, and the real estate market. IBM's launch of the personal computer in 1981 heralded a new era in IT, which brought about new possibilities and challenges with regard to office buildings. Where previously the bulk, heat, and noise of mainframe computers had forced them to be located in separate rooms, floors, or, in many cases, buildings located outside city centers, the microcomputer could sit comfortably on any office desk. The impact of this in organizational terms was potentially enormous as it would improve communication speeds (thereby affecting locational requirements in real estate terms), increase investment per head, and transform space needs. In addition to the technological unknowns, the future of organizations was made all the more uncertain by the state of British politics at the start of the 1980s: the new Thatcher government's free market policies promoted deindustrialization and the growing dominance of the service economy, the deregulation of financial markets, and the globalization of production.[186] Furthermore, the shifting demographics of the workplace, such as the slow ascendancy of women to positions of power, and the rise of HR-based management policies called into question the existing cultural and spatial requirements of firms.[187]

ORBIT's main conclusion was that as IT became essential in the operation of firms, the building would become increasingly important to the user. As buildings and technological infrastructure became more mutually dependent, occupiers would demand higher specification buildings and a greater level of shared expertise among suppliers.[188] The implication was that the built environment professions would need to coordinate and collaborate in ways that they had not before. Regulators would need to work with developers and surveyors to produce adequate policies for office production, in an economy that privileged information and services. Developers and surveyors would need to work more closely with architects, engineers, and building contractors to ensure that the economic potential of office buildings would be renewable over time. Architects, interior designers, and furniture suppliers would need to liaise directly with building managers and IT specialists. And ultimately, all parties, at least in theory, would need to work with occupiers in a management climate in which employee preference was of critical concern regarding the design and let-ability of office buildings.

All these developments cast the City Corporation and its DLP in a very bad light. News of deregulation unleashed a slew of criticism. In 1985, the Corporation held public consultations and received comments on the plan, which it published in a report, containing statements from most major financial institutions in the City, real estate analysts, heritage groups and the GLC. All except the latter two were against the plans and criticized some 1,500 points.[189] Although firms were uncertain what the future would hold under the new regulations, the comments noted that the lack of flexibility in the existing plans would hamper the City's ability to remain competitive as an international financial center.[190]

In particular, there were concerns within the Corporation that firms were already leaving the City as more institutions moved beyond the traditional banking district to the north of the City, south of the river and to the West End/Mayfair.[191] As the ORBIT study had shown, the technological and regulatory changes in financial services made face-to-face communication less urgent and demanded buildings that were too big for the small building plots in the City core. In addition to the personal computer, new digital banking and trading networks changed physical activity patterns in the City; for example, the Clearing House Automated Payments System (CHAPS) and the Stock Exchange Automated Quotation (SEAQ) removed the necessity for proximity to the Bankers' Clearing House and the Stock Exchange, respectively. As a result, the Bank of England relaxed its unofficial restrictions on the location of banks within the City. In 1984, it acquiesced, saying that with "improvements in communications and other technological developments, the need for physical proximity to the Bank of England has lessened. The extended village concept should be retained."[192] Yet in a speech later that year at the Lord Mayor's dinner, the governor of the Bank conceded that this might even mean moving beyond the boundaries of the City.[193]

As the political instrumentalization of technology became more pervasive, the UK became the first European country to denationalize its telecommunications industry, which had previously been monopolized by the state-owned British Telecom (part of the Post Office). In 1981, the British Telecommunications Act gave the secretary of state for industry the ability to license to other operators for the first time. This was part of the ideologically motivated selling off of nationalized assets that took place in the name of free market efficiency; the government and the finance industry believed that competition was necessary to handle the increasing complexity of digital services.[194] By 1984, BT was completely privatized.[195] Britain became the first country in the world to entirely break the public telecommunications monopoly by licensing Mercury Communications, a competitor, to operate in the City of London in a "duopoly" with BT, and by 1990 over forty licenses were given to competitors to operate across Britain, representing the complete deregulation of the sector.[196] In addition to destabilizing a powerful public-sector union, the government was responding to the financial services lobby at the core of the telematic coalition, which argued that more efficient telecommunications were necessary to bolster London as a "premier centre of international finance."[197]

These changes made it more convenient for firms to locate on the edge of the City and even outside it. New purpose-built office complexes were built at London Bridge City, Butler's Wharf, Surrey Docks, and most notably Canary Wharf, to service the growing financial services industry.[198] Built in a so-called urban enterprise zone (UEZ), the latter was a product of the government's business-oriented policies to incentivize development. These (largely formerly industrial) sites were intended for commercial redevelopment, offering businesses who located there huge incentives, such as "100 per cent capital allowances for industrial or commercial buildings, exemption from the Development Land Tax, a streamlining of the planning process, exemption from industrial training boards and minimal requests from the government for statistical information for a 10-year period."[199] The Department of Industry (DOI) oversaw the development of fourteen UEZs between 1981 and 1982, distributed across the UK, with just one in the southeast—the well-known London Docklands redevelopment.[200] Emerging from the radical Non-Plan antiplanning movement, conceived by Peter Hall, Cedric Price, Reyner Banham, and Paul Barker in *New*

Society magazine in the 1960s, this once-anarchic concept became an emblematic campaign for the conservatives. It was touted by Keith Joseph—the then secretary of industry—in 1979 as providing demonstration areas for Thatcherite, supply-side economics, "where conditions more encouraging to enterprise might be established—to show what would then result."[201]

As plans for Canary Wharf were unveiled in 1985, promising just under one million square meters of floor space, the need to reform the DLP became all the more urgent. In Manhattan, the new spatial and technological demands caused by deregulation were accommodated relatively easily thanks to large gridiron building plots, which enabled the construction of big buildings with deep window-to-core distances. Canary Wharf offered large standardized floor plates and all the amenities required for the new investment banks, while catering to existing American expectations. Not only did the City have insufficient capacity to accommodate the new demands within its existing footprint, but the DLP guidelines on conservation made new developments impossible.

Following the devastating public consultation, the Corporation came to recognize that there was a direct link between its future success as a financial center and its ability to provide an adequate provision of office space to accompany the imminent deregulation of financial markets. In 1986, the Corporation made a radical revision of the policy to promote new developments, giving consent for the demolition of listed buildings. Whereas plot ratios had been zoned previously, in the new plan a blanket ratio of five to one throughout the City was allowed for new developments, and basement areas were entirely excluded from plot ratio restrictions to allow extra enlargement below ground.[202] This achieved the potential for approximately 20 percent more space without radical replanning, although the ratios were still lower than those of New York, at fourteen to one, and San Francisco, at twenty to one.[203] "Air rights" were also included in the new plan to allow developers to build over railway termini and to use the land of abandoned stations and routes such as Broad Street station and Holborn Viaduct, as well as to build over London Wall, which became the site for seven proposed megastructures.[204] In 1986, the same year that the Eurobond market raised an unprecedented 200 billion dollars of capital, the Corporation published the new local plan, which enabled the expansion of total City floor space by 25 percent.[205]

Deregulation had dramatic and instant effects on the City. In the three months following the Big Bang, the average daily turnover in London almost doubled to £1,161 million.[206] Although employment as a whole declined in the City during this period, the proportion of workers operating in finance, banking, and insurance increased by nearly 20 percent.[207] Planning statistics show commensurate, and in fact staggering, growth. Between 1985 and 1993, approximately 50 percent of the total office volume of the City was rebuilt.[208] Planning applications tripled between 1985 and 1986, doubling again from 1986 to 1987, and approximately only 4 percent of applications were refused in the entire decade.[209]

With uncharacteristic speed and conviction, the Corporation transformed itself from a local authority to a proponent of the financial City within the space of a year. Notably, the planning department was reorganized and restaffed, beginning with recruiting a new head of planning, Peter Rees, in 1985. This newly established post was created as it was felt that the then city architect and planning officer, Stuart Murphy, held too wide a responsibility. However, when Murphy retired in 1987, Rees was made city planning officer, a title he retained until 2014.[210] Trained as an architect at the Bartlett School of Architecture, University College London, and formerly apprenticed to Gordon Cullen, Rees previously worked as assistant chief planner in the Borough of Lambeth for six years, where he had been responsible for conservation and regeneration work—a combination of activities that appealed to the department following the heritage debacles of the last decade. He was brought into the planning department during the consultation for the revised DLP. As Rees notes:

> My first task was to sit down with the team that were producing the planning policies and revise all the planning policies to suit what was going to be a totally different City. The first step in doing that was to go out and talk to the top people in all the banks and the insurance companies and find out what they thought they'd need—and of course they had no idea because they didn't know what was going to hit them. But we did our best to consult on it and, in talking to them and to other various experts ... we looked forward into a world that was going to change with the incoming American and Far Eastern banks, and tried to imagine a different sort of City.[211]

Such a level of collaboration demonstrated a shift of policy that was more in line with the government's approach to economic policy, which promoted a reorientation toward enterprise and an emphasis on market-led approaches to planning.

Under Rees, the Corporation adopted a model that it later referred to as *proactive planning*. This involved an active relationship with developers and architects, who would discuss and cultivate plans for new construction with Rees before putting them before the Corporation's nonpartisan Planning Committee.[212] As Rees commented:

> Even though we have a reactive planning system I see it as my role within the City of London to be proactive in encouraging development. Other planning authorities' members take a much more hands-on approach to policy and development control and will have a much more executive approach to the work they are doing but that makes it very difficult on major developments because when a developer and an architect comes to see me, I can give them a very clear idea of what I think I can get planning permission for. What I can persuade the members for. Because the members are used to listening to my professional advice and in 99% of the cases they will accept what I say.[213]

Whereas in the postwar years the Corporation's unique political organization and autonomy were perceived by outsiders as a hinderance to progressive planning, these were the very attributes that made proactive planning possible. Unlike all other constituencies in Britain, the City's planning committee comprised mostly business representatives rather than publicly elected councilors and was almost double the size of other London borough planning committees, which meant it relied more heavily on the advice of the planning officer and advocated any developments that would service the business community.[214] Furthermore, the Corporation's nonpartisan character meant that it was not directly subject to the influence of national or local politics, which made it easier to implement and follow through with long-term strategic planning.[215] In other words, it was comparable to a single-party system. As Rees commented in 2013, "we see our role as protecting the business environment, above anything else. ... At least you know that in the City you can have a consistency of policy. Most of the policies that we put in place back in 1985/86 are still in place."[216] The Corporation's administrative infrastructure had been structured historically to protect commercial interests, yet it was only within the new political climate—which privileged competition above all else—that this unique system was exploited in planning terms.

Under the new strategy, the Corporation reduced the friction of the planning process for real estate companies, while ensuring a more stringent vetting process in the construction of buildings. From the mid-1980s onward, the Corporation was thus more directly involved in the development of commercial architecture— and indeed, the wholesale development of the Square Mile—than ever before, representing an unprecedented entanglement of regulatory forces in finance, politics, and planning. This approach was aligned with the new Conservative government's emphasis on private enterprise as a catalyst for economic development in Britain in the 1980s. Under Thatcher, the state reconfigured its relationship with the construction, design, and real estate industries to facilitate its vision for deindustrialization, outsourcing, and growth of the service sector. Building on the public-private partnership initiatives established in the 1970s, during its first term the Tory government developed a number of planning instruments such as urban development corporations and enterprise zones, designed to directly engage developers, rather than planners, as the main drivers of new construction initiatives and to reduce the role played by local authorities.[217] The goal of such bodies was to create attractive conditions for the real estate industry to encourage development, and in turn create a spin-off effect, using property development to encourage more property development.[218] In other words, they were intended to stimulate enterprise rather than behave as tools for comprehensive planning.[219]

Within this regulatory overhaul, the marketization of planning, implemented through legislation (such as the 1980 Local Government, Planning and Land Act), circulars, and policy, caused local authorities to lose much of their power.[220] In line with this approach, the GLC was abolished in 1986. In planning terms, this meant the removal of the *Greater London Development Plan*, and the transference of planning powers solely to the Corporation, which avoided abolition due to its special status. In the future, all boroughs were to receive individual "strategic guidance" from the secretary of state for the environment. However, in practice, this did not prove fruitful, and consequently the London Planning Advisory Committee (LPAC) was formed as an independent organization comprising the heads of planning from every borough, acting in place of the former planning department.[221] These political transformations also rendered developers, surveyors, and large-scale building contractors more powerful in the building industry. Government policies that weakened local authorities simultaneously strengthened developers by shifting the planning process in the developer's favor—such as the imposition of time restrictions for processing planning applications and financial penalties on local councils for making "unreasonable" refusals—thereby facilitating the rush of successful applications for commercial development in the 1980s.[222]

These opportunities, in tandem with the ready availability of credit, gave rise to a new breed of financially innovative and ambitious developer. The strength of these firms was that they were able to become very profitable, very quickly, by restricting their activities to "property trading and development for sale" and by embracing new financing mechanisms that enabled them to build up huge debts while keeping them off the balance sheet. This made it easier to finance much bigger and more complex projects at relatively low risk.[223] In tandem, developers, surveyors, and large-scale building contractors were able to grow by becoming "hollow corporations," relying on just-in-time construction techniques, subcontracting, and temporary, self-employed staff, thanks to the weakened position of the unions.[224] Under proactive planning, these companies became an essential part of the City's long-term planning strategy, which, in tandem with the removal of planning barriers, facilitated the rapid redevelopment of the City after 1985.

As a result of their increased status, developers also became more involved in the architectural process, shifting toward a model of developer-as-patron. Stuart Lipton of Greycoat (who later founded Stanhope), was an example of the new "enlightened" developer; he became known for his close working relationships with high-profile architects, as well as his role in British public and cultural life.[225] A member of the Royal Fine Art Commission, Lipton later became the chairman of the Chartered Association of Building Engineers (CABE), and was made an honorary fellow of the RIBA—the latter a rare honor for a developer, whose profession was condemned twenty years earlier by then RIBA president Lionel Brett for being nothing more than opportunist intermediaries, interfering between "makers and users."[226] Yet ironically, it was precisely through such intervention that developers like Lipton became so successful.

As DEGW had argued in its introduction to the ORBIT study report, increased reliance on IT and organizational change had "the effect of making sophisticated organizations increasingly dependent on buildings."[227] The growing dependency between user and building reciprocally heightened the dependency between market and user, forcing developers and architects to produce appealing, functional, and adaptable buildings in order to obtain the competitive advantage.[228] As Duffy noted elsewhere, "Poorly designed, ill-conceived, unusable offices will stick: well-thought-out, skillfully designed and highly usable ones will be let."[229] Developers shifted away from a purely spatial concept of value (minimizing gross to net ratios) to a qualitative definition of value, whereby impressive architect-led developments were more likely to attract publicity and tenants.[230]

As such, it became an essential part of the successful developer's business model to partner with well-known architects to obtain prestige project status. Lipton, for example, became known for his early collaboration with Richard Rogers on the ambitious Coin Street Development (1978–1984), on the South Bank of the Thames; although never realized due to local backlash and activism, it solidified his reputation among architects and government agencies.[231] Such partnerships extended beyond the architect, as Lipton surrounded himself with specialists to advise on projects. As real estate chronicler Alistair Goobey noted, for the development of the City's first high-tech American-style office building, 1 Finsbury Avenue, designed by the well-regarded Arup Associates, the developer curated "a team of ad hoc advisors on whom he relies and with whom informal discussions on all aspects of design, building and legal matters are often held. Among this group are Francis Duffy, the architect head of DEGW, Gary Hart of lawyers Herbert Smith, and executives from the Economist Intelligence Unit and Schal."[232] Finsbury Avenue, like Broadgate and Heathrow's Stockley Park to follow, was considered to be a risky investment due to its position outside the traditional heart of the financial center, in addition to the aforementioned uncertainties surrounding users and the office market. But Lipton understood that in such circumstances, good research was essential to producing a development that was financially viable and "future proof."[233]

Just as the nature of corporate real estate development transformed in the new economic environment, so the scale and quality of real estate in the City was entirely overhauled. Between 1986 and 1993, around three million square meters of floor space was constructed in the Square Mile, and 19 percent of planning applications were for structures upward of 25,000 m².[234] Many of these were built at the City's periphery, due to the lack of space in the historic core. Major developments beyond the Bank intersection were planned for Paternoster Square, Cutlers Gardens, Finsbury Avenue, London Wall, Upper Thames Street, Spitalfields, and Liverpool Street. The latter was the site of the Broadgate complex, which was the most celebrated of these new developments. Built on the northeastern border of the City, the development took advantage of the new air rights in the local land and built around 400,000 m² of office floor space, spanning the tracks of Liverpool Street station and the former Broad Street station.[235] Broadgate was the first major City project by Lipton's firm Stanhope, which, with Godfrey Bradman of Rosehaugh, established a new development company—Rosehaugh Stanhope Developments (RSD)—to execute the scheme. Designed by Arup Associates (phases 1–4) and Skidmore, Owings & Merrill's (SOM's) (phases 4–8), with a range of consulting space planners, engineers, and construction firms, the complex was the first of the American-style groundscrapers that would fill the City. It was an attractive proposition to investors and occupants as it took advantage of the existing infrastructure and nearby services. The planning department saw it as an attempt at developing a new attitude toward planning through placemaking, incorporating an ice rink, public square, shops, cafes, and public art.[236] For a complex that was considered to be far away from the Bank intersection, the latter was particularly important. As P. W. Daniels and J. M. Bobe remarked, "With the provision of high-quality office space configured to meet the most exacting contemporary requirements and the probability of lower rents than those prevailing for 'traditional' City locations, it was anticipated that new occupiers would relinquish their reticence about non-traditional locations."[237]

This increase in peripheral developments indicated an acceleration of the social transformations that had begun in the 1960s with the arrival of foreign firms in the City, whereby the importance of proximity to the Bank of England and other important institutions slowly diminished.[238] After the Big Bang, the demographic of banking and finance in the City became younger, more international, and extended beyond the traditional class structures. In other words, the traditions of proximity were not engrained in this new group. As Maria Kaika notes, "The City's traditional British-based banking élites who had remained loyal to the traditions of the Corporation for many generations were replaced by a new generation of élites ... who revel in the amenities and kudos that a City location may offer, but do not necessarily express place-loyalty."[239]

In addition to the change in architectural demands under deregulation, the loss of centrality was caused by government policy to dismantle the City's self-regulatory system by making its primary regulatory institutions less powerful. The Banking Act put the Bank of England under more stringent supervision, while the operational changes of the Big Bang quickly rendered the physical presence of the Stock Exchange redundant, as the new investment banks created their own dealing floors. Little more than a month after the act was instituted, the Stock Exchange floor was almost entirely abandoned as the new investment banks set up dealing rooms in their own premises.[240] New, impartial regulatory bodies, such as the Securities and Investments Board, were formed by the government with the intention of replacing the informal system it had removed. As such, the supervisory regime that previously demanded proximity was gradually dislocated.

After the Big Bang, the attitude toward real estate in the City shifted from a territorial conception based on traditions and proximity to one based on maximizing the operational value of a building. In other words, from location to use value and marketability.[241] By the 1980s, the location of companies was to a large extent being regulated by the market, rather than by work processes.[242] As Daniels and Bobe posit, "In this context the "market" could be defined as locations where maximum returns on capital are anticipated (locations considered desirable to potential tenants) and which are therefore attractive to development capital."[243] Real estate became a more prominent investment, and the City's spatial layout became increasingly dependent on the interconnectedness of developer/occupier markets. By the early 1990s, the social and spatial organization of the City was transformed on the basis of future fluctuations in land values, which were inherently linked to the financial markets it sought to accommodate.

A City, Aligned

From the aerial perspective, a dramatic transformation had taken place in the City. Deep floorplates, unseen subterranean infrastructure, and new public spaces had reconfigured the financial district. But this was underpinned by fundamental structural transformations in the way finance was done. Neoliberal practices of governance in Britain brought about a regulatory convergence within politics, planning, architecture, finance, and real estate markets in the City. This is not to say that these sectors became "compatible," which would imply a historic incompatibility, but rather to say that their methods and practices became more intelligible to one another as economic competition became the guiding principal of urban development. During the postwar decades, the presence of different supervisory regimes among the central government, Greater London, the City Corporation, and its financial institutions prohibited consensus on how the financial district should be planned. Ideological oppositions among the City, the LCC, and the central government rebuilding agencies, combined with the changing status of Britain in the global economy, gave rise to conflicting opinions about the role of the City in British public life, which filtered through into planning debates. The government's emphasis on industry, rather than invisible exports, drew attention away from the City. Building regulations and decentralization policies stifled development, while economic policies aimed at domestic production stifled financial innovation. It was only through the gradual engineering of a new political-economic paradigm, which united the interests of these groups in the desire to promote the City as an international financial center, that such conflicts were erased.

This smooth narrative was punctuated by inconsistencies and perforations. Heavy regulations in both the built environment context and the financial sphere gave rise to explosions of unregulated activity. From this perspective, legal objects like development permits, investment vehicles like compulsory purchase powers, and planning regulations like plot ratios emerged not simply as instruments of restriction and control but as catalysts for new forms of economic and professional relationships among architects, developers, local authorities, and financiers. The Eurodollar market and the building booms occurred simultaneously,

Aerial photograph of the City of London, 1946. Copyright Dave Wood.

Aerial photograph of the City of London. Copyright Mike Hughes / Alamy.

in turn undermining the stable foundations underpinning the postwar City. As foreign currency markets reduced the effectiveness of self-regulation in the Square Mile, so unfettered building production resulted in extreme levels of destruction to the City's built heritage. The backlash against the Corporation resulted in the adoption of punitive heritage-focused planning policies in the 1970s, which ironically became the trigger for the fastest and most dramatic period of developer-led construction in the following decade. The ebbs and flows of building production and planning ideology were linked to the dynamic macroeconomic and governmental context but were not always synchronous. Parallel cycles of construction, use, and debate in the built environment do not always fit comfortably with political temporality, leaving a detritus of stalled construction, abandoned proposals, and empty buildings.

2 *Street*

I venture to call this Essay "Lombard Street," and not the
"Money Market," or any such phrase, because I wish to deal ...
with concrete realities.
Walter Bagehot, *Lombard Street:*
A Description of the Money Market, 1873

The Architecture of the Short View

In the opening lines of his famous nineteenth-century examination of London's financial sector, the fabled editor of the *Economist*, Walter Bagehot, reminded the reader that the operation of the City's markets was inextricable from their urban character. "A notion prevails that the Money Market is something so impalpable that it can only be spoken of in very abstract words," explained Bagehot, "but I maintain that the Money Market is as concrete and real as anything else."[1] Writing at the high point of Britain's global political and financial prowess, Bagehot witnessed the City in the throes of a dramatic physical functional transformation as it shed its residential population and grew to become the predominant international and national financial center. It was a moment when informal relationships and systems of exchange were formalized in the Victorian grandeur of wide boulevards, historicist buildings, and palatial institutions. "The Roman Corso, The Neapolitan Toledo or even the glories of the Rue de Rivoli ...

will be overtopped and out-vied by the continuous line of merchant palaces in Cornhill, and Lombard-street, and Bishopsgate-street, and Cheapside," wrote an observer in the *Builder* in 1866, remarking upon a deluge of new developments that had appeared within the space of just three decades.[2]

In Bagehot's City, these streets also represented the crystallization of specific markets, each becoming a destination for a particular kind of trade. At the core was the Bank of England, constructed on Threadneedle Street in 1732, which by the 1850s had become the point from which land values radiated on account of its centrality in banking operations, causing the surrounding area to become the most valuable in Britain, and arguably in the world.[3] Spreading southward, Lombard Street, which had been the main thoroughfare of banking life since the fourteenth century, continued to be known as the street of the banks; its famous hanging signs and modified town houses with their ground-floor banking "shops" were gradually replaced with larger buildings containing impressive banking halls. Insurance firms gathered westward on the larger King William Street, and on Cornhill to the south, while Fenchurch Street, the curved continuation of Lombard Street toward the southeast, became known for shipping. Mincing Lane and Great Tower Street were the destinations for the colonial trade, and Mark Lane became the center of the corn trade, while the legal profession occupied its traditional warrens around Fleet Street and the Inns of Court along the western axis.

Over three-quarters of a century later, Holden and Holford shared the view that the synchronization of form and function had been an essential characteristic of the City "for over a thousand years," resulting in a place that was "more single-minded than any other square mile of London." Yet for the postwar planners, the large streets that had been adorned, widened, and straightened by the Victorians were less the key to its identity than the density and proximity of its thoroughfares. "All these activities are concentrated into a small area," wrote the planners. "The City man can walk from his transport point to his office, from there to his broker, his bank, his insurance house, his professional chambers, his exchange and his eating-house. If one were to move an important market out of the City, one would have to move quite a number of others, together with their contributory enterprises."[4] Walkability

Facing: Lombard Street, City of London, 1957. Edwin Smith / RIBA Collections.

was deemed essential to the City's functionality, a characteristic that was petrified in the nexus of smaller passages, alleyways, and intimate courtyards that perforated the main blocks and streets. Holden and Holford called these pedestrian ways the *main substance* of the financial center, dedicating two sections of their report to them.[5]

From a practical perspective, pedestrian movement offered an alternative to vehicular transport, which was causing intense traffic in the main intersections of the City, a problem that was a core concern during this replanning process. Holden and Holford saw the pedestrian ways as an effective preexisting network that could be used in combination with modern interventions, such as raised walkways, to improve the flow of people through the City. "There is, of course, a functional pattern even in the ant-heap," wrote the authors. "The planner's problem is to make this pattern more efficient."[6] But their interest in these spaces cannot simply be explained by a concern for expediency. The "Pedestrian Ways" chapter of their report, for example, dedicates pages to explaining the traditions and atmospheres associated with the alleys and courts running around the Bank intersection, with lengthy enumerations of their importance in the social life of the City. They claim that "in the pedestrian ways people become individuals ... the short lengths and turns ... sort them out in twos and sixes and pose them against a multitude of backgrounds which are seen close to and in detail."[7] Such descriptions imply close connections among an intimacy of scale, the visual presence of history, and human relationships in the functioning of City life.

While not unique as a typology, the dense web of alleys, shortcuts, and courtyards had a specific historical link with the operation of the business community in the City, which dated back to its emergence as a financial center. The spatial relationship between streets was a product in part of the medieval morphological development and the dense patchwork of private land ownership in the original square mile of London. Buildings were often buttressed against each other, requiring passages running through and between them to allow access for those working deep within each block. In the seventeenth century, these channels became important places for trade—particularly those running between the Bank of England, the Royal Exchange, and Lombard Street—as they became populated with coffee houses, which acted as specialist markets and information-gathering sites outside the opening

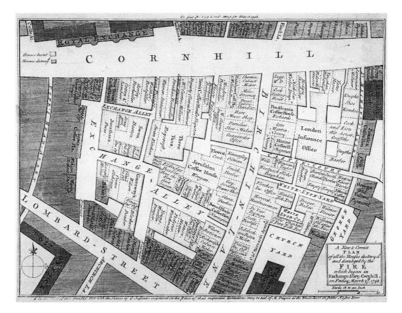

"A new & Correct Plan of all the Houses destroyed and damaged by the Fire which began in Exchange-Alley, Cornhill, on Friday, March 25, 1748." London Metropolitan Archives (City of London). London Picture Archive, ref 1814.

hours of the official exchanges. Alleys permitted face-to-face interactions and rapid communication for brokers and messengers running between markets, forming a collection of shortcuts woven together for efficient transmission of market intelligence. In the eighteenth century, the network provided by alleys and coffee houses also became the informal infrastructure for an early form of international postal service and financial press, as merchants left letters with the coffeehouse proprietors for ship owners to collect on their daily rounds, and jobbers posted price-lists on notice boards at relevant markets.[8]

Gradually the alleys were inscribed into the public imagination, either as places of nefarious activities associated with financial crises, as depicted in Hogarth's satirical etchings of the South Sea Bubble in Change Alley, or as a microcosm for Britain's ever-expanding international activities. Daniel Defoe described "the kingdom of Exchange Alley and its adjacencies" as an empire to be navigated: "Enter Cornhill, visit two or three petty provinces there in your way west; and thus, having boxed your compass and sailed round the whole stock-jobbing globe, you turn into Jonathan's again."[9] By the nineteenth century, these small streets had taken on almost mythical status, described by financial journalist D. Morier Evans as "those indescribable localities that ... excite curiosity in the mind of the stranger from the sort of maze its thoroughfares shadow forth."[10]

The enduring legacy of pedestrian ways in the City is intriguing, not because it tells a truth about the way the financial system functioned, but rather because it highlights the way in which public spaces became part of an essential narrative surrounding how the City was organized and how it operated. Most of these smaller streets survived the interwar period, when large office buildings interrupted the medieval plot patterns, thanks to fire-prevention and daylight regulations that ensured that many of the original alleyways were retained; new blocks were required to contain large light wells in their center, and thus used the network of walkways to connect to the main streets. Developments such as Curtis Green's Scottish Widows complex on Cornhill (1934–1935) actually reinstated the network of alleys roughly on their medieval alignments for ease of access. Yet many were stripped of their original character, with Change Alley described by Pevsner as "little more than white-glazed canyons."[11] Experiencing the social fantasy of alleyways and courtyards thus relied on the telling of their histories, either through photographs and imagery, as in Holden and Holford's publication, or through oral histories passed down through the generations of City workers. For example, when digitalization slowly removed the need for messengers' daily clearing walks in the 1990s, the City's shortcuts were mythologized through anecdote as spaces that had previously provided messengers occasions for opportunist espionage, enabling them to peer into offices, overhear private conversations, and meet competitor messengers.[12]

One important reason for the continued use of the alleys in the twentieth century was the spatial organization of banking and trading in the City, which demanded specific patterns of movement between institutions. Prior to the so-called dematerialization of money markets in the 1980s, which came about with the widespread use of microcomputers, the City's streets were important components in the transactional process. Unlike the digital bank-clearing systems today, up until the late twentieth century, the settlement of accounts between two parties was a physical act, carried out via messengers, choreographed according to a precise timetable. The process was separated into three independent

Photographs of the City's small urban spaces in Charles Holden and William Holford, *City of London* (London: Architectural Press for the Corporation of London, 1951). (top left; bottom right) R. H. de Burgh Galwey / RIBA Collections and City of London Corporation. (top right; bottom left) Dell & Wainwright / RIBA Collections and City of London Corporation.

systems: general clearing, 9:15–10:30 a.m.; town clearing, 2:30–3:45 p.m.; and check clearing, a system initially dealing with payment of salaries. All three operated via the Bankers' Clearing House, the central institution in the clearing system, to which all checks were sent for payment. Situated in the midst of the banking area on Lombard Street, the Clearing House remained empty for large periods of the day, standing in the form of a small interwar building by Whinney, Son & Austen Hall (1937) seemingly incommensurate with the two to three million payments that would be processed there daily—the result of its time-specific functionality.[13]

This system required the strict coordination of bodies in space. Town clearing was the most important for City institutions as it was the only way of processing high-value, same-day payments, thus involving nearly every City establishment. It required all members to reside in the *town clearing area*—that is, the half-mile radius of the Bankers' Clearing House—for expediency.[14] Operated by messengers who would bring all checks accrued by their bank at the end of the day to the Clearing House, the system dealt with high-value transactions with a quick turnover time: a check between two town branches received at 3:00 p.m. would be cleared the same day; consequently, the speed and efficiency of the system was of vital importance to the money market.[15] The result was a highly mechanized procedure orchestrated by a computing army of female clerical staff processing a minimum of two thousand payments per hour, served by hundreds of messengers moving rapidly through the streets at specific times of the day.[16]

The City continued to operate in this way not simply because it offered an efficient and reliable way of moving paper between businesses, but also because it maintained the core values of face-to-face contact and self-regulation expressed by the Stock Exchange motto *Dictum meum pactum*, "My word is my bond." Self-regulation, with the Bank of England at the helm as the arbiter of good practice, ensured continued independence of the City and its class-bound social structure even after the growth of the state after World War II and throughout the encroachment of technologies and financial systems that would theoretically put an end to it. Invented spatial traditions like the clearing system, and the geographical impositions by the Bank of England, were used to protect these structures and give the illusion of historical permanence, forming what historian Eric Hobsbawm referred to as "a set of practices … which seek to inculcate certain values or norms

Stills from Roy Battersby, dir., "A Question of Confidence," *Men and Money*, BBC 2, 1964, showing a messenger on his rounds from the Midland Bank to the Bankers' Clearing House. Courtesy of BBC Archive.

of behavior by repetition, which automatically implies continuity with the past."[17]

The apparent informality and regularity of encounter was held up as being a specifically English way of doing things, to which the great strength of the English banking sector was attributed. As one prominent City businessman claimed, "I think the last thing we have as Englishmen is *Dictum Meum Pactum*. ... It's a very thick, strong ethos to have. And it is counted as such."[18] One example of the various daily spectacles that maintained this idea was the operation of the City's "classical" money markets, the structure of which was understood internationally to be specifically English, in its history, its rituals, and its unique combination of banking institutions.[19] Postwar money markets were based on the prevailing Keynesian approach to monetary policy whereby the nationalized Bank of England controlled interest rates and therefore the supply of money. One way the Bank did this was through the discounting of commercial bills. This process was performed through a ballet of messengers and intermediaries, the most important of which were the discount houses. If the Bank wanted to inject money into the market, it bought commercial bills from the houses; if it wanted to drain money, it sold bills.[20]

Discount house brokers needed to be extremely knowledgeable about the state of the market and, as such, spent the first part of the morning making rounds on foot to banks and City institutions, which on a good day could total over one hundred individual visits.[21] Paul Ferris, a well-known commentator of the City, reveled in the exaggerated performance of the discount banks, known as *top-hatters* for their adoption of a conservative top hat and tails uniform (which they continued to wear well into the 1970s): "Top-hatters ... can be seen queuing at a bank, four or five in a row on a hard bench, striped trousers tugged up to show uniformly dark socks, polished pointed shoes neatly side by side on the cold tiled floor," Ferris remarked. "There is an absence of documents, a bland assurance that events are being coped with."[22] Personal contacts served as a mode of advertising; as all discount houses essentially sold the same product, daily meetings with individuals enabled some differentiation between firms. Personal contact also supposedly enabled bankers to assess the integrity of the particular individual; as most transactions were not finalized on paper until the end of the day, the verbal contract was key.[23] One discount broker explained, "over the phone, you may never know if the man you are talking to is good at his job. He may be a liar or a fool and not give it away on the telephone, but when you see him you get the truth."[24]

Following this, the manager of each discount house would visit the Discount Office at the Bank of England to give the general feel of the market so that it knew how much money to pump into the system (via the minimum lending rate for Treasury bills).[25] If by the end of the day a discount house failed to balance its books, a representative needed to return to the Bank of England to be "interviewed" by the principal of the Discount Office and borrow at the bank rate (termed the *punitive rate*) for at least seven days—an expensive loan.[26] Ferris describes this journey as a psychologically stressful experience, "leaving a man ten minutes in which to take his top hat off the peg, cross a couple of streets, and hurry past the pink-coated attendants into the lofty precincts of the oldest, slyest, stuffiest central bank in the world. ... Through tall windows the mulberry trees can be seen flourishing in the inner courtyard, and above them, on the first floor, a long row of chandeliers illuminates the courtroom. Below the courtroom are the parlours, where the Governor works, and near it on the ground floor is the discount office. ... The market ... has had to go like a naughty boy and ask Grandma to help."[27]

Public spaces in the City were not only essential to financial operations, but part of the rhetorical infrastructure for these narratives. Holden and Holford's report articulated how the expression of informality and tradition in the City's pedestrian ways and hidden courtyards were essential to reproducing the social fantasy of British financial life. In a "partly real and partly imaginary" walk through the City, the authors reinforced the connection between the character of the small passages and a certain gentlemanly sensibility, or Englishness, that belonged to the financial district. "The architecture of the pedestrian ways is one of detail and the short view," the authors wrote in their description of Bengal Court and St Michael's Alley, "built in the days of 2lb steaks and pints of claret" where "ten thousand cornices, doorways and string courses have a full-bloodedness that bears witness to it." They viewed the backstreets with a character embodying that of the City gent. Neoclassical dressings were the sartorial parallel to the top hat; alleys and taverns were where men of integrity operated amid dignified architecture, designed without "short measure" or "milk-soppery," enabling one to "recreate in imagination mid-Victorian City life."[28]

Bengal Court: the architecture of the short view, in Charles Holden and William Holford, *City of London* (London: Architectural Press for the Corporation of London, 1951). R. H. de Burgh Galwey / RIBA Collections and Courtesy of City of London Corporation.

The entry to the churchyard of St Michael, Cornhill.

where the tower of St Michael, Cornhill, rises behind the church of St Edmund the King—these are the elements, in a hundred compounds, of street scenes in the secondary thoroughfares. Bengal Court (p. 238) tapers down to 3 feet wide; its gratings have not yielded to pavement lights and its restaurant has a sanded floor, a Chop Room below and a Joint Room above. In it and St Michael's Alley which runs from it one realises how much the architecture of the pedestrian ways is one of detail and the short view. Often the detail is coarse, but it is nearly always full of vitality. Most of the architecture of the pedestrian ways was built in the days of 2-lb. steaks and pints of claret, and tea thousand cornices, doorways and string courses have a full-bloodedness that bears witness to it. Their designers had a lively horror of short measure and milk-soppery. Bengal Court although not in a damaged area, will probably not survive for very much longer. Few of its windows receive much daylight and it is in an area where there was much rebuilding between the wars. Yet there are few better places in which to recreate in imagination mid-Victorian City life—the times when the main line railway stations were still new and Soames Forsyte was still serving his articles.

Fifty and a hundred yards from Bengal Court are two more of the small open spaces that are strung like beads on the thin lines of the pedestrian ways. Both are a little

240

Another suggested improvement for an existing open space, the churchyard of St Peter, Cornhill.

bigger than the average. The churchyard of St Michael, Cornhill, has been newly furnished and paved in a manner which does not perhaps do justice to the exciting detail overhead and around. St Peter's churchyard is paved over above the graves at a level 3 or 4 feet higher than the surrounding ground and furnished with urns at the corners. In a forecast of what it might be (above), a wider connection is suggested with Gracechurch Street and the higher level has been reduced in area to form a terrace against the church wall.

In Gracechurch Street, just opposite the pedestrian way from St Peter's, is an entrance to Leadenhall Market—an entrance so carefree in style that it can only be called Victorian Rococo. Shopping habits have changed since 1880—through taste or necessity—but the market is very fully used. A great deal of shopping (including rationed foodstuffs)

241

Juxtaposing Gordon Cullen's illustrations of future proposals with photographs of the old City in Charles Holden and William Holford, *City of London* (London: Architectural Press for the Corporation of London, 1951), 240–241. Copyright Gordon Cullen Estate/University of Westminster Archive and R. H. de Burgh Galwey / RIBA Collections.

Here, Holden and Holford seemed to draw parallels between the physical and social character of the financial district: the intimacy of scale gave emphasis to the individual—the basis of competition—while the complex layering of historical details mirrored the organic development of the markets. Such a notion was expressed most emphatically by the juxtaposition of moody black-and-white photographs revealing close-up, intimate perspectives of the alleys and courtyards against Gordon Cullen's almost cinematic projective illustrations of these spaces integrated within the precincts of the "rebuilt" City. Evoking the townscape principles with which Holford and Cullen were associated, this section of the report exposed the messy confusion of the metaphorical ant heap as a kind of natural order to be drawn out by the planners.

Initiated by the *Architectural Review* in the 1940s under the editorial direction of Hubert de Cronin Hastings and Nikolaus Pevsner, the *townscape movement* was propagated by Ian Nairn, Cullen, and other *Architectural Review* authors in reaction to the destructive, alienating tendencies of car-based, modernist planning.[29] Advocating for traditional urban forms that showed the passage of time and traces of use, townscape privileged human interaction and pedestrian mobility in the urban realm, encouraging variety and diversity over geometric monotony. At its core was an

The tower of All Hallows, Staining, from the east. It would form the focal point of the small sunken garden proposed by the consultants.

The ruins of St Olave, Hart Street.

is done in the City—especially at lunch-time. Between noon and 3 p.m. nearly as many people use the pedestrian ways to go shopping, or to shop-gaze, as to go to lunch.

Beyond the Market, east of the long grey hull of Lloyd's, there is a large cleared area between Lime Street and Billiter Street. Here the pedestrian ways are just paths between the cellars of bombed buildings and can be changed at will when rebuilding takes place. Their new form will need to be carefully thought about if, as seems probable, new buildings are designed to have more floor space well back on their sites and less on main street frontage. At present public houses and restaurants often open off the pedestrian ways and there is no reason why a coffee house of 1955 should not be entered from a new-style Billiter Square.

South of Billiter Square, across Fenchurch Street, there is another blitzed area between

Mincing and Mark Lanes, with the stumpy tower of All Hallows, Staining, almost in the middle of it. The drawing opposite proposes that changes of level, a common feature of City open spaces, might here be used to the full to include lower and crypt in a combined pedestrian way and sunk garden, with walls and pavings of varied materials. It has been suggested that at one or two points in the City a church which has been destroyed or ruined by bombing should become an open space of a new kind, in which the surviving walls and memorials should be retained. This proposal was realized, temporarily, at All Hallows, Barking (p. 244), and the ruins of several other churches—for example, St Olave, Hart Street (above)—would lend themselves to execution of the proposal on a smaller scale.

In the last century the City has rather turned its back upon the river, which is no longer the main traffic route for both goods and passengers. A major part of the City's

Juxtaposing Gordon Cullen's illustrations of future proposals with photographs of the old City in Charles Holden and William Holford, *City of London* (London: Architectural Press for the Corporation of London, 1951), 242–243. Copyright Gordon Cullen Estate/University of Westminster Archive and Dell & Wainwright / RIBA Collections.

interest in specific characteristics of place, historic context and older architectural forms, and an emphasis on visual methods in urban design.[30]

In the context of the City, townscape offered a framework for marrying preconceptions about public space and public life in the rebuilding process through a central notion: Englishness. In their theoretical explications of townscape in the *Architectural Review*, Hastings and Pevsner identified the movement as a revival of English picturesque principles, drawing on the ideas of eighteenth-century landscape gardeners Uvedale Price, Capability Brown, and Humphry Repton, who offered ways to "improve" landscapes and provided a theoretical basis for reconciling the conflict between historical and modern situations, which was an inevitable focus in the postwar reconstruction period. But, as Anthony Raynsford writes, the authors also viewed the picturesque movement as a political philosophy characterizing English ideals, borne out of anti-Jacobite resistance to the revolutionary rationalism emerging in France; it drew on a Burkean vision of a cumulative political constitution and was centered on an empirical approach to developing the landscape, finding beauty in the imperfections that existed by virtue of time, rather than creating it on principles based on reason. As Pevsner wrote of picturesque landscapes, "The free growth of the tree is obviously taken to symbolize the free growth of the individual, the serpentine path and rivulet the Englishman's freedom of thought, creed and action and the adherence of nature in the grounds, the adherence to nature in ethics and politics."[31] This "natural" order meant the happy coexistence of seemingly contradictory elements, which had emerged over time. Hastings in particular saw this as the basis for a paternalistic townscape movement, which would return Britain to a nation of "sovereign individuals" through a mode of planning that privileged a naturalized, organic formation of society. Such sentiments echoed the rising waves of neo-Toryism after World War II, which sought to preserve the English values of difference and individualism against an ever-expanding welfare state.[32]

It is clear that Holden and Holford's plans for the City were highly influenced by the townscape ideals and specifically by the *Architectural Review*'s "A Programme for the City of London," an unsolicited plan for the rebuilding of the financial center, published in 1945. It doesn't require close scrutiny of the two plans to recognize the similarities: key policies of the Holden and Holford report, such as the plot ratios and traffic systems, were set out in the *Architectural Review*'s program, as was the emphasis on pedestrian circulation, precincts, and the preservation of historic monuments. Yet more telling was the common connection drawn between culture and environment in the financial district. For Hastings and the other *Architectural Review* contributors, the City embodied the picturesque visual tradition more than any other urban space in Britain, where the "temperamental English bias has nearly always defeated the conscious intention," with a form derived by use and activity rather than classical planning.[33] More than any other part of London, they claimed, the City had resisted heavy planning and as such represented the purest synthesis of form and function, which, like picturesque landscapes, manifested in a delightful chaos of style, scale, and circulation.

Like Holden and Holford after them, the *Architectural Review* editors claimed that these principles were revealed most acutely in the City's pedestrian ways and small-scale public spaces, which, although "unspectacular and often dingy," were, they argued, "fragments of the vigorous idiom which has evolved through the ages as a suitable expression of City life; as such they must be respected."[34] They showcase these in two "peep-shows," the first showing detailed photographs of "the less publicised intimate corners" of the City, and the second with lively projective drawings by the LCC architect Hugh Casson revealing the "pattern of ... courts, walks, paved paths, grass verges" comprising the reimagined precinct of St Paul's. Very likely the basis for Cullen's "partly real and partly imagined" walks in the Holden and Holford report, Casson's drawings revel in the informal encounters and polyphonic richness of its historic environment, contrasting with the modern interventions, while the photographs bring an almost mystical quality to the space.

"A Programme for the City of London" made explicit the intimate connection between the specifically English nature of public life and public space in the City, whereby individuals were "differentiated in the shelter of its many intimate corners" formed as a result of its ongoing "unconventional activities" as a commercial center, such as "transacting business on the street." Hastings further attributes the absence of uniformity in the City's architecture (which in itself is a sign of "overpoliteness," "un-english," and "ill-bred") to a "polite discord ... beneath a suave convention of good manners," as if to evoke the social etiquette in City trading. What was peculiarly English about this existence was the visibility of compromise, conflict, and coexistence in its public spaces, which Hastings attributed to the semipublic way by which City business took place, with an "insatiable appetite for gregarious living" and "overspilling exuberance" for which the City "provided an elastic receptacle." To illustrate the point, the program opened with six pages showing a "pictorial anthology of city life," comprising historic images of celebration, work, and social life in the City's streets, ranging from the exotic parades of the nineteenth-century Lord Mayor Shows to George Cruikshank's brawling pub scenes to gentlemanly agreements on the exchanges to grueling dock work. In every image, the scene is not simply framed by public space; rather, the streets, facades, and pavements are active protagonists in the events, their irregular character only adding to the vitality of every scene.

Although the debauchery of Cruikshank's illustrations was a far cry from the postwar City, semipublic business continued to go hand in hand with semipublic spaces as the pub or chophouse remained a mainstay of City life. Working days often ended mid-afternoon after long, inebriating lunches. Despite the introduction of canteens into some offices in the 1950s, for the most part workers opted to dine out at a range of well-known haunts, most famously

The
ARCHITECTURAL REVIEW
Volume ninety-seven
June 1945

1. S. Magnes 2. Gray Church S. Dunston in the East J. Alhallows barking

THE BRIDGE

A PROGRAMME FOR THE CITY OF LONDON

A VIEW OF LONDON BRIDGE FROM BANKSIDE, BEING A SECTION OF WENCESLAS HOLLAR'S VIEW OF LONDON, PUBLISHED IN 1647

A PICTORIAL ANTHOLOGY OF CITY LIFE

In the functionally grown City of London the visual scene mirrors the life that goes on in its quarters more truthfully than in the cities laid out by classical planners. Because the way the people went about their business, celebrated, met each other, was allowed to mould the face of the City, it became what it still unmistakably is to-day. The atmosphere of the City has undergone many changes through the ages ; in fact an infinite capacity for taking change has been one of its remarkable characteristics. What remained the same was the City's insatiable appetite for gregarious living ; living at close quarters, turbulent in the streets, and differentiated in the shelter of its many intimate corners. From Chaucer's town stocked with merchandise from abroad, the chop houses and coffee houses of Addison and Goldsmith, the Law Courts and merchant firms of Dickens's and Lamb's, or in our day, this life has always been overspilling with exuberance, and the City provided an elastic receptacle for it.

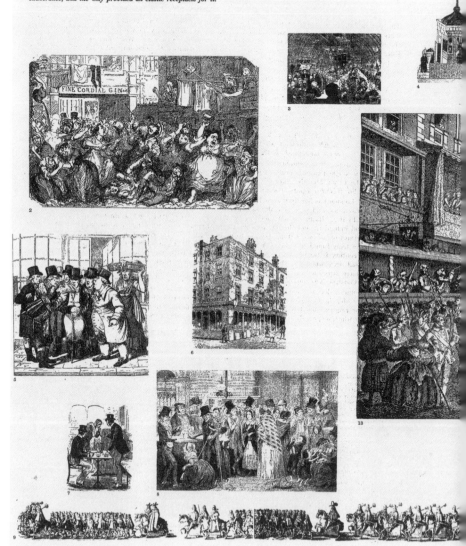

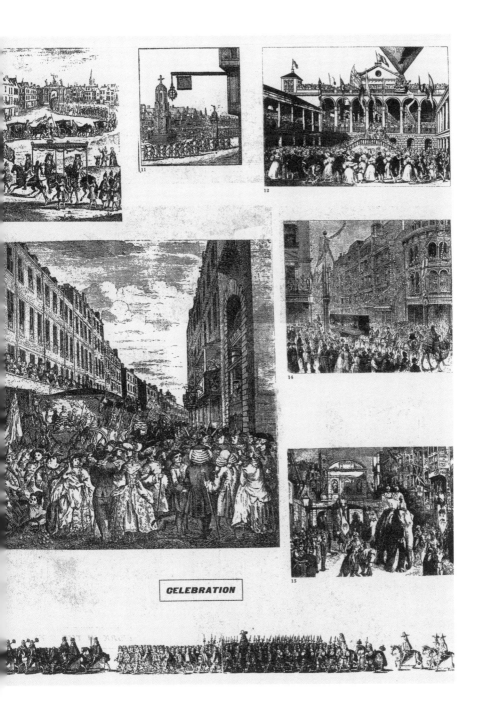

CELEBRATION

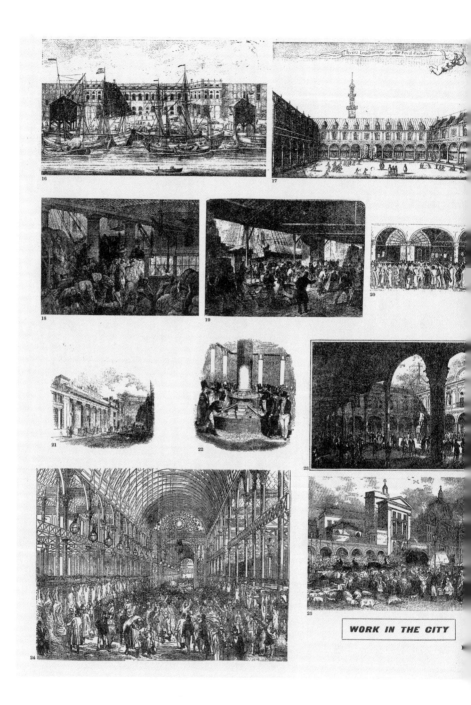

WORK IN THE CITY

LIFE IN THE STREETS

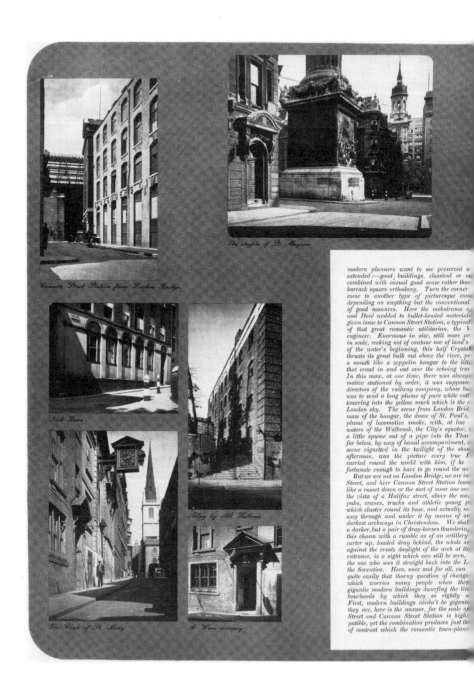

The steeple of St. Magnus

Cannon Street Station from London Bridge

 Feck Lane

Alley by All Hallows

The Clock of St. Mary

A Wren doorway

modern planners want to see preserved a
extended :—good buildings, classical or oe
combined with casual good sense rather than
barrack square orthodoxy. Turn the corner
come to another type of picturesque com
depending on anything but the conventional
of good manners. Here the melodrama o
and Doré wedded to bullet-headed material
given issue to Cannon Street Station, a typical
of that great romantic utilitarian, the V
engineer. Enormous in size, still more pr
in scale, recking not of contour nor of land's
of the water's beginning, this half Crystal
thrusts its great bulk out above the river, p
a month like a zeppelin hangar to the litt
that crawl in and out over the echoing iron
In this maw, at one time, there was always
motive stationed by order, it was suppose
directors of the railway company, whose bu
was to send a long plume of pure white cott
towering into the yellow murk which is the c
London sky.   The scene from London Brid
maw of the hangar, the dome of St. Paul's
plume of locomotive smoke, with, at low
waters of the Walbrook, the City's equator, i
a little spume out of a pipe into the Than
far below, by way of banal accompaniment, i
scene vignetted in the twilight of the sho
afternoon, was the picture every true L
carried round the world with him, if he
fortunate enough to have to go round the wo
     But we are not on London Bridge, we are in
Street, and here Cannon Street Station loom
like a russet down or the sort of moor one see
the vista of a Halifax street, above the wa
pubs, cranes, trucks and athletic young p
which cluster round its base, and actually m
way through and under it by means of on
darkest archways in Christendom.   We shal
a darker, but a pair of dray-horses thunderin
this chasm with a rumble as of an artillery
carter up, loaded dray behind, the whole se
against the ersatz daylight of the arch at th
entrance, is a sight which can still be seen,
the one who sees it straight back into the L
the Seventies.   Here, once and for all, can
quite easily that thorny question of change
which worries many people when they
gigantic modern buildings dwarfing the litt
bourhoods by which they so rightly s
First, modern buildings needn't be gigant
they are, here is the answer, for the scale o
Street and Cannon Street Station is high
patible, yet the combination produces just the
of contrast which the romantic town-plan

Chapter 2

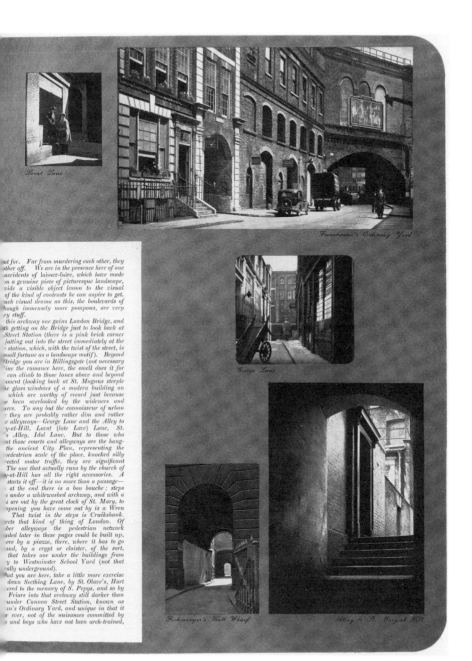

Lovat Lane

Frenchman's Ordinary Yard

George Lane

Fishmonger's Hall Wharf

Alley to St. Mary-at-Hill

...ut for. Far from murdering each other, they ...ther off. We are in the presence here of one ...accidents of laisser-faire, which have made ...m a genuine piece of picturesque landscape, ...vide a visible object lesson to the visual ...of the kind of contrasts he can aspire to get. ...uch visual drama as this, the boulevards of ...hough immensely more pompous, are very ...ry stuff.

...this archway one gains London Bridge, and ...h getting on the Bridge just to look back at ...Street Station (there is a pink brick corner ...jutting out into the street immediately at the ...station, which, with the twist of the street, is ...mall fortune as a landscape motif). Beyond ...Bridge you are in Billingsgate (not necessary ...'ine the romance here, the smell does it for ...can climb to those lanes above and beyond ...ment (looking back at St. Magnus steeple ...e glass windows of a modern building on ...which are worthy of record just because ...e been overlooked by the wideners and ...ers. To any but the connoisseur of urban ...they are probably rather dim and rather ...e alleyways—George Lane and the Alley to ...y-at-Hill, Lovat (late Love) Lane, St. ...'s Alley, Idol Lane. But to those who ...at those courts and alleyways are the hang- ...the ancient City Plan, representing the ...edestrian scale of the place, knocked silly ...rected motor traffic, they are significant ...The one that actually runs by the church of ...y-at-Hill has all the right accessories. A ...starts it off—it is no more than a passage— ...at the end there is a bon bouche; steps ...under a whitewashed archway, and with a ...are out by the great clock of St. Mary, to ...opening you have come out by is a Wren ...That twist in the steps is Cruikshank. ...cts that kind of thing of London. Of ...her alleyways the pedestrian network ...ded later in these pages could be built up, ...ere by a piazza, there, where it has to go ...and, by a crypt or cloister, of the sort, ...that takes one under the buildings from ...y to Westminster School Yard (not that ...ally underground).

...hat you are here, take a little more exercise ...down Seething Lane, by St. Olave's, Hart ...ered to the memory of S. Pepys, and so by ...Friars into that archway still darker than ...under Cannon Street Station, known as ...an's Ordinary Yard, and unique in that it ...ever, not of the nuisances committed by ...and boys who have not been arch-trained,

5

6

Ludgate Hill we are now in Amen Court, **5**, with its
nclosure a good place for quiet rest. Past the west
stop at the bookstalls within the shadow of the north
the cathedral, **6**. Here St. Paul's rises like a great, grey
erpowering with height and weight. On the first floor of the
al Restaurant above, **7**, we get an unprecedented proscenium box
the west front towers, framed in the great plate-glass window and
ceful steel frame of the restaurant facade. Descending and venturing
east we have a last view of the north flank of St. Paul's. Across
et stands the Chapter House, **8**. The new office blocks, the cathedral
old buildings, all seem to have found a way of living with each other.

Street

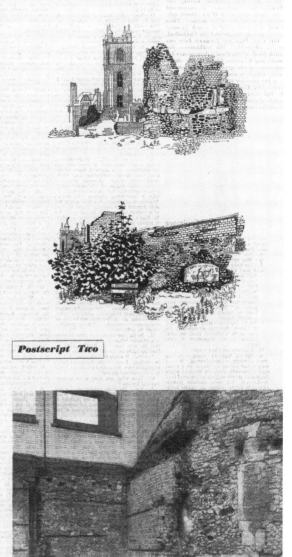

London Wall

Of the problems connected with historical buildings and their share in the City picture, St. Paul's constitutes perhaps the outstanding one; but there are many minor instances of a similar nature which demand careful attention by the visual planner. The City wall, for instance, is such a case. It is the oldest monument in the City, built in Roman days, and added to in medieval times. New sections of it have been exposed during the recent air raids. The wall can be seen in the London Wall (the street) between Wood Street and Aldermanbury; in the churchyard of St. Giles, Cripplegate; at the General Post Office, Newgate Street; in the offices of the Oxford University Press, Warwick Square; at the foot of Jewry Street, Aldgate; in America Square, off the Minories; in Trinity Square, at the Tower, etc. Its position can be traced from the east starting by the river, and following a line slightly westward off the Minories to Aldgate; then curving to the north-west, between Bevis Marks and Houndsditch to Bishopsgate, then along what is still known as London Wall to Cripplegate. From there south to Aldersgate and behind St. Botolph's Church to Newgate; thence to Ludgate and along Pilgrim Street to the Fleet river (which once flowed in the valley now known as Farringdon Street) down to the junction with the Thames. There also was a river wall, of which little is left. The old Roman Wall remained the nucleus of the City's defences throughout the Middle Ages. Its date of origin is put by some at the first decade of the third century, by others at the middle of the second. About 25 bastions were added later, probably in the fourth century. The wall which had a bank and a ditch is built of Kentish ragstone and Roman bricks. Its thickness above the plinth varies from 7-9 ft. The highest recorded piece stands 14 ft. above the plinth. The Wall as it exists to-day, possesses apart from its literary and associative significance—which is considerable—great sculptural potentialities. It is for the visual planner to bring out these qualities and incorporate them in the City picture. If related to the footpath system and leisure spaces, that are to link the City sights, the Wall will take its rightful place in the City scene.

Postscript Two

Cover and pages from Hubert de Cronin Hastings, "A Programme for the City of London," *Architectural Review* 97 (June 1945). Courtesy of *Architectural Review*.

in those clustered around the Stock Exchange and on Throgmorton Street, such as the Gresham; Birch, Birch & Co.; Slaters; and the much-renowned "Long Room of The Throg."[35] Throgmorton Street was used as an example of this culture in both the *Architectural Review*'s and Holden and Holford's reports, with moody photographs showing the street's blackened facades containing a sea of jobbers and brokers. As smoking was restricted to after trading hours in many of the major institutions, like the Stock Exchange, during the day smokers lined Throgmorton Street, providing a ready audience for brawls, or spectacles, encouraged by the City's public school ethos. As one worker recalled, "One day ... I looked up the road ... and I saw all these people standing outside this apothecary ... and they all had their top-hats on ... and they were queuing up. ... As it was, they were all having Alka Selzers for the last night's hangover. ... People used to drink like fishes then. The excess of life was, well, just wonderful really."[36]

Since the days of the coffee houses, pubs were considered a legitimate part of the City's modus operandi, as informal and unofficial extensions to trading floors and offices. Their reinstatement

Photograph of Throgmorton Street in Charles Holden and William Holford, *City of London* (London: Architectural Press for the Corporation of London, 1951). Courtesy of City of London Corporation.

after World War II was considered particularly important, and as such, the City was granted an allowance of one "licensed house" for every 1,600 members of daytime population (rather than the standard calculation of residential population), meaning around 260 licensed premises for approximately 470,000 workers.[37] It was agreed that "100 yards was a reasonable maximum distance for a worker to walk to a public house."[38]

Despite the romanticized rhetoric of both planning programs, both relied on the continued informality and in-person nature of proceedings in the City, which would slowly diminish in the coming decades with shifts in regulation and technology. Holden and Holford's plan embraced the City's "private circulation," proposing a network of pedestrian precincts connected by existing alleyways and courtyards.[39] Efficiency meant greater provision for pedestrians, including: "increased open space, generally in small patches"; the linking up of such areas with "shopping centres, historic buildings, and open viewpoints by means of wider pavements ... or tree planted streets ... or in some cases subways under traffic crossings"; the closure of certain streets to all but service vehicles; and the widening of pavements to facilitate movement.[40] They claimed the implementation of plot ratios would assist the process of picturesque landscaping. By reducing internal courtyards and setting buildings back from the street, it was hoped that this would offer "some open space beside the streets, if only the cleared setting of an historic building, or a view of the River or some distant prospect, for refreshment of the spirit as well as the eyes and lungs."[41] Holden and Holford agreed that "almost every City worker who has any sense whatever of his environment becomes, at least for part of the day, a sightseer."[42]

However, plot ratios were one of the many processes of rationalization that dampened the City's famously intimate street life. Previously, maximum building heights were set at twenty-five meters so as not to detract from St. Paul's, with tiered set-back frontages and terraces on upper floors for fire safety.[43] "The mistake made in developing certain sections of New York was that the skyscrapers were allowed to cover the whole of the sites," the Holden and Holford report claimed, arguing that its new plot ratio system would supersede the austerity of interwar blocks, seen as smothering the traditional street scene. Yet plot ratios enabled tall buildings to be constructed with large public plazas in front, such as the Commercial Union and P&O complex, Richard Seifert &

Partners' Drapers Gardens, and the Stock Exchange in the coming decades, a distinctly "un-English" typology. Furthermore, a new "daylighting code" sought to improve on the dark light wells and courtyards through buildings "which have the bulk of their accommodation towards the centre of the site and then step down in stages to street level." Holden and Holford noted, "The buildings would be turned inside-out, so to speak" and would "draw back from the street frontages and build up toward the middle."[44] But the policy meant that a number of the City's informal spaces of communication were removed through reconstruction during the next decade, notably in areas surrounding Drapers Gardens, Moorgate and east of the Guildhall precinct, and the Stock Exchange. One former messenger observed: "Most of the old passage buildings were torn down and replaced with tower blocks. Firms became bigger and tended to have complete floors. Gradually firms became conscious that financial espionage was something that people were prepared to embark on ... it became harder to casually walk through buildings and, in the end, downright impossible."[45]

In the coming decades, the informality that had come to define both the physical and operational character of the City's public life was superseded by a process of rationalization in both urban planning and financial operations. Holden and Holford were designing for a City based on a Bagehot-like concrete money market, in which trading and exchange were tangible, visible, and personal, even if the financial concepts were abstract. In the coming decades, as financial practices moved slowly into the less visible virtual realm, the abstract and physical worlds of finance grew increasingly at odds with each other, fundamentally changing the meaning of urban planning in the City and the nature of public space. Yet as with all developments in the postwar Square Mile, this process was neither quick nor friction free. The transition to a deregulated financial center was fraught with tensions between its invented spatial traditions and the necessity for modernization.

Knowledge in a Hurry

Not long after the rebuilding process had begun, the synergy between the City's informal geography and its informal mode of transaction was slowly broken down with a gradual restructuring of business operations and the deregulation of British finance. First, a formalization of financial mechanisms took shape throughout the 1960s, including the introduction of analysts who used statistics to assess the market, as opposed to biographical information or company reputation, as well as the enforcement of exams for new brokers on the Stock Exchange for the first time ever. Second, broader shifts in international finance challenged the City's spatial operations. Emerging markets such as the Euro-currency markets, local authority loans markets, and interbank lending triggered companies to move beyond the town clearing area, with the space shortage caused by the influx of international (specifically, American) banks.[46] In addition, the mode of exchange itself changed as interbank markets for the first time permitted banks to lend *unsecured* (i.e., without the liquidity to back up the deal), a concept that was anathema to the City's *Dictum meum pactum* ethos. These new financial instruments ensured that the quantity of transactions was often much higher than the quantity of final payments made, creating a distortion between the spatial act and the transactional process because of the incompatibility of their relative speeds.[47]

A huge strain was put on the City's carefully choreographed pedestrian network of messengers and settlement procedures as a result of these changes, despite the introduction of telephone trading, which still necessitated proximity between institutions for the final settlement of accounts. Paper became a problem in the City, and in financial centers across the world, during this period due to the imbalance caused by the huge increase in transactions and the perseverance of a manual clearing system. Knowing the precise location of any bank certificate in the system and the overall status of accounts at any given moment became a particular issue for concern. One commissioner of the New York Securities Exchange Commission observed in 1970 that in the case of stock certificates on Wall Street, each piece of paper went through fourteen different processes and more than four "street carries" in the space of a few days. He explained: "Involved in this paper pushing process at the securities firm are the branch office, the receiving department, the transfer analyst, the transfer department and the delivery department."[48] Then the certificate was packaged and sent to the transfer agent (where it would be handled by four different people: the window clerk, transfer analyst, examiner, and cage clerk), before going through the typing, proofing, balancing, and sorting departments, after which it was sent to the registrar to sign the certificate by hand. After this, it would be sent back to the transfer agent and back to the original brokerage house to be logged once more, and sent to the receiving party (broker, bank, or individual) if necessary.[49] While the City of London had its own idiosyncrasies, the journey of the stock certificate (or other bill) there was similar to that found in New York, and with the number of items cleared annually at the Bankers' Clearing House rising from 397 million in 1958 to 854 million in 1968, the system became increasingly clogged and subject to error.[50]

Technological solutions, such as punch-card systems and magnetic ink, and the use of CCTV for document transmission, were introduced to limit the amount of paper moving around the City.[51] In 1960, the Stock Exchange settlement department was mechanized, with eighteen machines to carry out activities previously done by 150 workers, while the Bankers' Clearing House acquired check-sorting machines to manage the paper flooding in with the new markets.[52] Britain looked to America as inspiration for improvements in automation, with the US having been at the forefront since producing the first digital computer in 1940.[53] By the late 1960s, many financial institutions had invested in computers to counteract the shortages of clerical labor while also avoiding wage increases and easing space limitations.[54]

Pedestrian trading prevailed in the City until full digitalization in the 1980s, despite these technical advantages, causing the City's planning department to look closely at the relationship between its public spaces and human movement. In 1967 and 1969, two surveys were conducted by the Corporation to calculate the foot traffic of office workers throughout the Square Mile. The first was a "business contacts survey" designed to scrutinize the number of meetings between and within institutions per day, the distance traveled on foot to get there, and the duration of meetings, as well as business telephone conversations and notes delivered by messengers and by the postal system.[55] Forming part of the Corporation's larger 1966 *Economic Study of the City of London* carried out by the Economists Advisory Group to explore the manner in which the City's "innumerable facets ... interlock and overlap," the survey confirmed common perceptions about the spatial character of City life.[56] It reaffirmed that "internal contacts between members of the same firm are very important," that "the City has a high proportion of meetings in relation to other methods of communications," and that "by far the most common way of travelling to a meeting or carrying a message is on foot."[57] Drawing on a similar study of New York, the report concluded that the dominant reason for proximity was the need for "knowledge in a hurry."[58] "There is more than psychological comfort ... in the intimacy that permits brokers and dealers to expose their views to the accumulated wisdom of their compatriots through frequent and personal meetings," the American report had argued; "the participants in the money market are clustered together because the 'costs' of buying and selling can be minimized by maintaining direct and continual contact with the market."[59]

In light of these discoveries, planning discussion of the City's public spaces was overtaken by a rhetoric of "scientific" analysis and complexity. One rather incomprehensible diagram from the study showing the relationship between financial institutions and organized markets reiterated this viewpoint, representing the City as a collection of overlapping and bewildering points of connection, as if to highlight the imperative to rationalize them formally. A second pedestrian movement survey carried out two years later by the Corporation's planning department further attempted to reiterate this point by mapping out the findings of the economic study in order to untangle the complex physical patterns of worker activities and business connections. Using questionnaires, interviews, pedestrian counts, and shopping and commuting statistics, the data was recorded onto punch cards and processed by the Corporation's computer. Pedestrian activity was yet another dimension of the financial district that should be calculated, anticipated, and automated.[60]

Despite the obvious undercurrent of computation permeating the Square Mile during the 1960s, the economic study confirmed to the planning department the ongoing importance of the material markets and reiterated the need to maintain and improve the City's street network and constrained geography. The subtext to these findings was that the decentralization strategy then being pushed by the GLC was unfavorable to the City, or, as the Common Council argued, it was a proposal that "should be approached very cautiously, if at all."[61] In response to the GLC's *Greater London Development Plan* in 1967, the Common Council argued that the City's economic practices did not lend themselves to decentralization, and that instead the GLC should consider "pursuing policies of discouraging through-traffic in the City with a view to creating relatively traffic-free precincts and making provision for improved public road transport for essential business use."[62] They argued that by "ringing" the City and leaving interior roads free for financial business, the policy "would greatly strengthen the Common Council in providing environmental areas suitable to the business activity carried on within the City."[63]

Whereas in the immediate postwar years Holden and Holford had viewed pedestrianization as a necessary counterpart to townscape, which took the picturesque bomb-scarred City as the point of departure, the Corporation of the 1960s positioned pedestrian circulation as part of a more pragmatic (and cost-driven) tabula rasa attitude toward replanning the financial center, which positioned traffic management at the core. Nowhere was this more emphatically expressed than in the so-called pedway project, which aimed to implement a thirty-mile network of raised pedestrian walkways across the Square Mile. If completed, the pedway would have been one of the largest infrastructural interventions ever to be completed in central London, on par with Victorian transformations to the capital. Yet its underpinnings were more practically motivated than ideological, pointing to a general mood in urban planning that viewed car traffic as the enemy to civilized town centers. Rapid growth in British car ownership throughout the 1950s and 1960s induced anxiety surrounding congestion and accidents, giving rise to a planning rhetoric that favored the segregation of pedestrians and cars. At the regional level, this favored the construction of satellite towns like Croydon to stem the buildup of traffic in cities like London. At the local scale, it meant the Corbusian separation of people and cars, with planners such as Colin Buchanan propagating the division of the city into raised pedestrian walkways with motorways below.[64]

Pedways offered the Corporation a way of rationally planning pedestrian activity at a moment when the financial system was placing a huge burden on the face-to-face system of trading in the City. However, the concept of vertical transport segregation emerged over a decade earlier than the pedestrian surveys and was first put forward by the LCC Architects' Department during the reconstruction of Paternoster Square and the Barbican area. While most of the City's planning decisions had been transferred back to the Corporation by 1955—after a spell in LCC hands in the immediate postwar period—the scale of bomb sites in these two areas necessitated a collaborative approach to redevelopment between the two municipalities. Both projects presented

Drawing of Milton Court (top) and London Wall (bottom) pedways in City of London
Department of Architecture and Planning, *City of London Development Plan: Background Study
Summary: Walkways & Pedestrians* (London: Corporation of London, 1978). Courtesy of City
of London Corporation.

Illustration showing vertical segregation in Colin Buchanan and Geoffrey Crowther, *Traffic in Towns: A Study of the Long Term Problems of Traffic in Urban Areas: Reports of the Steering Group and Working Group Appointed by the Minister of Transport* (London: HMSO, 1963). Courtesy of Williams Lea Group Limited.

themselves to the LCC as opportunities for experimentation with "three-dimensional planning" via raised walkways, which initially contravened the Corporation's parsimonious approach, including street widening and the developer-led reconstruction of existing parcels of land. However, by 1959 the LCC had convinced the Corporation to enshrine the separation of pedestrians and vehicular traffic in policy, and the construction of high-level walkways became a priority in the City planning strategy.[65]

Raised walkways satisfied the Corporation's practical and financial goals, for they brought together the dual imperatives of improving traffic circulation and avoiding compulsory purchase of exorbitantly expensive land in the center.[66] Route 11 along London Wall was the first major site to incorporate pedways, or *city walkways*, as they would become known. Situated at the Barbican's southern end, the LCC's planning consent had required the Corporation to connect the Barbican's raised walkways with the six office blocks planned for the area. Podiums, ramps, and bridges connected the modernist blocks as they sprang up, resulting in a parallel streetscape along London Wall with a high-speed road for car traffic beneath. This model later became the prototype for the larger network, spreading duly to Tower Place on Tower Hill,

Stills from *The Living City* showing the pedways in use, 1970. Courtesy of London Metropolitan Archive.

Upper and Lower Thames Street, and Paternoster Square in the coming years.

City walkways were not simply a way of reducing the frictions of human circulation around the City, but also reduced the friction of the planning process for the Corporation. As the full extent of the pedway plan was kept secret until the mid-1960s and not released publicly until 1976, due to being part of an unfinished highways strategy, it was pursued as a piecemeal incentive-based scheme from the outset. Developers were offered enticements for the inclusion of pedway connections into their scheme, usually in the form of plot ratio concessions, and were also permitted to use the connection points for temporary office space while the pedways were under construction, producing additional revenue. Consequently, throughout the 1960s and 1970s, openings for the pedway network were incorporated within most commercial developments.[67] Doubts about the Corporation's ability to enforce these planning conditions led to the passing of the 1967 City of London Various Powers Act, which effectively stated that pedway provisions were compulsory for schemes falling within the areas of the network, but that future maintenance would be provided by the Corporation.[68] This legal move reinforced the Corporation's power as a local planning authority since it was now able to impose a public right-of-way on any completed stretch of the walkways, and in fact became a model for planning authorities across the world looking for planning powers to include raised pedestrian systems in their urban schemes.[69]

Despite their pioneering modernist provenance, the raised walkways were regarded by the Corporation as infrastructure justified by reasons of efficiency and economy, devised and overseen by the office of the city engineer rather than that of the city architect. "Business activities carried out within the City [are] known to be based on a long tradition of personal contact," claimed the walkways study, which sought to legitimize the scheme through analyses of "pedestrian and vehicular movement patterns, land use and activities, and physical development."[70] Pedways were the urban technology for the new, fast-moving City. In a speech to the Guildhall Historical Association, one common councilman explained that because the scale of transactions had become so big in recent years, "time is literally money; hence 450,000 messages go by private messenger per day"; he consequently proclaimed that there was "a certain hard logic behind the miles of walkways planned for the City."[71] In this interpretation of the motivation behind the walkways, the price of time, or profit, depended on the speed of the messenger communicating the bank rate or the broker delivering bills of exchange or the check-delivery vans flooding into the City every hour. Frictionless channels for human movement would facilitate circulation and production, without which the City, and thus the national economy, would not function so well. Literal architecture became financial architecture, and the abstract and concrete were in perfect harmony.

In reality, the pedways were probably intended as simply another facet of the Corporation's traffic management program rather than radical innovations in financial infrastructure. Schemes like the London urban motorway program—and indeed, the City's own plans for Route 11—sought the most efficient manner of dealing with the heavy flow of traffic; pedestrian safety was a necessary afterthought.[72] Viewed as an efficient alternative to what City Architect Edwin Chandler described as "utterly impracticable" alleyways, the raised walkways were intended to be constructed in parallel with the new traffic routes.[73] These included road-widening at Great Tower Street, Fetter Lane, Mark Lane, Mincing Lane, Old Jewry, Bucklersbury, Gresham Street, Cheapside, Cannon Street, Wood Street, and Bishopsgate, and the construction of new roads along Upper and Lower Thames Street and for the Blackfriars underpass, all of which destroyed much of the City's medieval street pattern and architecture along the way. In aesthetic terms, the impact of these planning policies was a steady erosion of the irrational arrangement and intimate scale of its streets, as concrete replaced brick and stone, crooked lines were usurped by straight ones, and elevated modern pubs took the place of embedded taverns.

Large-scale demolition associated with the pedways attracted vociferous protest from conservationists, such as SAVE, which, alongside unfeasible maintenance costs, ultimately halted the project.[74] In 1970, an elusive planning drawing, *no. 3400B*, was somehow released to the public and reproduced for the first time in an article by architect-planner and journalist Jim Antoniou, revealing the full scale of the intended thirty-mile network, which would cover the entirety of the City of London, including the historically sensitive Bank junction.[75] When faced with criticism from heritage groups, the Corporation acted defensively. "It is a very dangerous thing to create a situation where you forget the prime function of the City and think of it in terms as a nice 'olde worlde' tourist attraction," Chandler argued at a RIBA conference in 1975. "The fact remains that if you want something that is efficient as a great financial centre then it is almost impossible to carry it out on a major preservation basis."[76] Despite his plea, by 1978 the pedway scheme was reduced to a "minimum network," comprising existing sections that might be viable with a few added links and bridges.[77] This was primarily due to a lack of use, as most of the raised walkways were in areas with a full network of streets and alleyways, rendering them mostly redundant. By the time of the City building boom of the mid-1980s, barely a fraction of the pedway network had been completed: it was a failed urban experiment.

Pedways represented an attempt to rationalize and make knowable the financial center's informal spatial traditions at a time when the underlying financial system was becoming more and more unknowable. Heritage and the historic streetscape had for centuries come to act as a symbolic marker for this system, but the growing abstraction and global nature of financial markets increasingly severed the entanglement between the financial center and its urban form. Its preservation therefore was unsurprisingly viewed by many as a hindrance to progress in the City, even if the resilience of its built heritage to modernization was not mimicked by its social traditions.

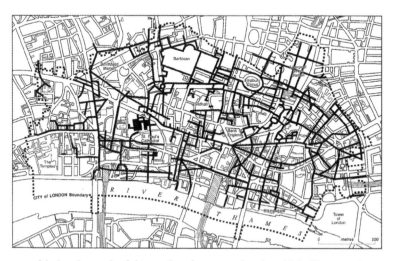

Map of the largely unrealized thirty-mile pedway network, 1963. Published in J. Antoniou, "Pedestrians in the City," *Official Architecture and Planning* 31, no. 8 (August 1968): 1036. Courtesy of Alexandrine Press.

Throughout the 1970s, the City's gentlemanly practices were gradually overhauled by an uncompromising deregulatory impulse underpinned by monetarist experimentation. The power cuts, three-day week, high unemployment, and uncontrollable inflation that had plagued the Heath government (1970–1974) were met by an IMF rescue in 1976 bearing the caveat of adopting monetarism. Now the money supply, not state funding, was the primary concern, and the Bank embraced monetarism, adopting the ideas of Friedman and the Chicago School even before the Treasury.[78] Such a shift was paralleled by the slow formalization of its internal systems of self-regulation, including the closure of the Discount Office in 1976, which meant that the Bank's paternalistic mode of management was replaced by the creation of a specialist Supervision Division.[79] In addition, the enforcement of the 1979 Banking Act, in response to the decimation of smaller banks in the secondary banking crisis of the 1970s, codified banking supervision in law, requiring all regulatory bodies to report to central government and enshrining the Bank's role as a regulator of the City in statute.[80]

Although policy changes had a substantial impact on the geographical rituals in the City, such as the cessation of the daily visits to the discount office, rapid technological innovations caused the most spatial disruption. In particular, the absorption of computer technology into most offices brought a shift in the pace and nature of exchange that was incommensurate with face-to-face operations. There was initial reluctance to abandon the much of the old City's ceremonial conduct, with persistent participation in activities such as the visceral spectacle of messengers running to and from the Bank every Thursday to communicate the bank rate, notwithstanding an operational CCTV network.[81] Despite the increased automation of clearing systems and telephone usage, even late into the 1980s many firms preferred to retain the human infrastructure of the messenger-operated clearing systems to preserve the social structure and psychological security. "One of the reasons people had concentrated in the Square Mile was so that they could be part of this system," a stockbroker recalled. "Messengers were an important part of all City businesses. ... I have a feeling that [they] may have been more secure than the electronic technology we have now which can be hacked into."[82]

Aside from the threat to the City's value system, of face-to-face meetings and ritualistic displays, there were concerns surrounding the economic viability of electronic methods.[83] Paper-based

Photograph of the scene at the Bank of England as messengers dash from the Bank of England in Threadneedle Street, London, with the news that the bank rate has been reduced by half a cent to 5.5 percent, 1960. Courtesy of PA Images / Alamy.

systems, which had emerged due to the geographical organization of the City, had become so ingrained into operations of the economy that faster new technology seemed problematic. Despite the potential profitability of quicker settlement times with computer-run systems, it was feared that "if any improvement is achieved in the speed of payments transmission ... they will be faced with a loss of the interest normally earned on money in the course of collection," which for checks could take up to three days.[84] Electronic payment systems threatened the spatial practices of the club system through temporal distortion, and so the question remained: How could electronic programs reproduce the self-regulatory club-like arrangement that had long protected the City's independence?

In 1968, the first electronic transfer system of payments, known as Bankers' Automated Clearing System (BACS), was implemented, a development underway since the 1950s, overseen by the Association of Clearing Banks electronics subcommittee.[85] BACS was the first system to exist whereby clearing banks grouped together to take advantage of the reduced costs provided by electronic data interchange, and it would grow to be the biggest automated clearing house in the world, operated by around two hundred staff and handling around 262 million items by 1976.[86] However, it was not until 1972 that attempts were made to devise a similar system to accommodate the high-value, same-day, multisector settlement in town clearing, which had been at the core of the City's morphological arrangement and pedestrian activities for centuries.[87] One prototype developed by the Interbank Research Organisation (IBRO) entitled SOVEREIGN was conceived to emulate the spatial form of town clearing, which, it argued, had been "developed to fit the requirements of their users, the convenience of their operators and the restrictions of their geography."[88] The hypothetical payment system was designed as an electronic version of the City's club-like organization. Those who wished to use the system were obliged to be "members of a suitable club. The clubs provide services to their members by accepting and retransmitting their messages, by acting on the contents of the messages and by vouching for the good standing of their members."[89] Clubs were digital versions of existing institutions like Lloyd's and the Stock Exchange, acting as informal modes of surveillance to ensure "the authenticity, credit worthiness, honesty and integrity" of each "player" in the payments game.[90] Although this plan was never executed, the official Clearing House Automated Payments System from 1984 was run along similar lines, providing settlement services for offices within the town clearing area (the one-mile radius of the Bankers' Clearing House on Lombard Street), subsequently renamed the CHAPS area.[91]

Despite the widespread use of electronic clearing technology from the mid-1970s on, it wasn't until 1995 that the messenger-run town clearing officially ended, and the final "dematerialisation of money market instruments" took place.[92] Pedestrian trading persisted alongside CHAPS for over a decade, partly out of habit, and partly due to the belief that the old system, which was surprisingly efficient in handling literally tons of paper with almost zero error, would render the economic benefits of automation too insignificant to bother with.[93] It was the perceived risk of human error in the manual system—which had grown more significant with the increase in transaction amounts—that put an end to the employment of messengers for clearing and settlement in the City. In May 1990, a financial messenger was robbed at knifepoint of £292 million worth of bonds he was delivering in a City side street, following which the Bank of England switched its Central Money-market Operations Office to a digital system entitled CREST, allowing assets to be held in dematerialized, electronic form.[94]

It is tempting to view the financial revolution of the 1980s as a product of such technological inventions. After all, one of the implications of the Big Bang was the normalization of electronic dealing and the abolition of open outcry trading on the floor of the Stock Exchange. City firms became almost instantaneously and directly connected to banks and markets at every corner of the world, and the City became one of the most contained, interconnected hubs anywhere. But the Big Bang was as much a cultural revolution as an economic or technological one. In the City, the struggle to acclimatize to electronic clearing, for example, was largely an ideological aversion to the political consequences of modernization. Historically, paper had been at the core of the operations of the Square Mile, which had, in turn, constructed strong allegiances to spatial practices and rituals. As German sociologist and philosopher Georg Simmel wrote in his great treatise on the social psychology of money, "Only in a stable and closely organized society that assures mutual protection ... is it possible for such a delicate and easily destroyed material as paper to become the representative of the highest money value."[95] Faced with the obliteration of the last concrete abstraction of the money form, older members of the City were also confronted by the breakup of the temporal regime that had cemented its tribal delineations. In the traditional City, the boundedness of time was conflated with the boundedness of space via the creation of physical markets and institutions, operating according to the daily timetable, and it was this temporal-territorial stronghold that gave the City its political independence.[96] The Stock Exchange, Lloyd's, the Clearing House, and the Bank of England were not only nodal points in the daily ritual of banking, but also bastions of the City's self-serving containment, while the daily walks between them were the spatial affirmation of its self-regulation. Consequently, the messenger system coexisted alongside its electronic counterpart for many years, even after it was superseded technologically.

As financial instruments grew more abstract, regulation more overt, and the labor market more mobile, the economic function of the City's streets began to shift from one that visibly facilitated the circulation of money, central to a Keynesian system, to one that implicitly embodied the ideas of individualism, competition, and consumption, underpinning Thatcher's brand of neoliberal financial policy. With quickening transaction speeds, the pedestrian pace became more leisurely. Throughout the next decade of deregulation and technological momentum, the City's planning approach became more focused on the quality of public spaces rather than their quantitative capacity, catering for the rhythms of lunchtime strolls over the mad dash of the messenger.

Psychic Profits

Businesses flock to the City from all over the world just because, in addition to superb efficiency and competitiveness, they can find a unique environmental character: the Wren churches, the livery halls, places like Amen Court and Wardrobe Court, surviving backwaters with their cellar bars and restaurants—attractions which New York and Tokyo cannot offer. To use the jargon: as a world financial centre, the City of London is user-friendly, to a unique degree. In plain English, business people like it. So why spit on your luck? Even the great free-market economists, like von Hayek and von Mises, recognise the importance of what they refer to as "psychological profits."
HRH the Prince of Wales, Speech at the Corporation of London Planning and Communication Committee's Annual Dinner, Mansion House, 1987[97]

When Prince Charles made his epoch-defining speech at the Mansion House in 1987, he not only exacerbated a growing divide between the historicists and the modernists in the British architecture profession, as is well documented, but also drew attention to a fundamental contradiction emerging in planning rhetoric in the Square Mile: to go forward as a leading global financial power, the City would need to harness the symbolic power of its past. "People too easily forget that the London of Wren's time was the greatest trading empire the world," claimed the prince, "yet it was of such a splendour that the vista Canaletto painted surpassed ancient Rome and even rivalled that of his own native city of Venice." He argued that the architects and planners responsible for rebuilding the City should not just embrace this tradition simply for tradition's sake, but instead use the architectural "good manners" of the past to "capitalise on many people's desire for an environment of character and charm, which is also more conducive to productive work because the surroundings make you feel better." In other words, architecture could be a generator of what Ludwig von Mises referred to as "psychic profits" (not psychological, as the prince mistakenly stated): gains that cannot be measured, only felt, experienced, sensed.

In between the more reactionary provocations in the prince's infamous speech was thus a call for a pragmatic, commonsense approach to planning the financial center. Speaking just one year after the Big Bang, the prince's Mansion House address was directed at halting the Paternoster Square redevelopment scheme surrounding St. Paul's, which had been initiated by the Corporation as one of the many projects to meet the new requirements of companies after the financial revolution. His famously provocative comparison of the City's postwar development with the Luftwaffe bombings was indicative of the increasingly preservationist sentiment that had underpinned much of the criticism of the Corporation's planning department for over a decade. Yet the prince's call for a more user-sensitive historicist approach, somewhat paradoxically, also became the basis upon which major commercial redevelopment and privatization occurred in the coming decades. As deregulation increased competition among financial centers globally, the City's built heritage became a key selling point in its marketing strategy.

Despite heavy criticism of the speech in the architectural press, the prince had a marked impact on the Paternoster scheme. Developed under Holford as one of the compulsory purchase areas after the war, the site was designed as a large raised pedestrian plaza built over a car park, accessed by steps from St. Paul's churchyard. Organized as a grid of low- and medium-height slab blocks with one slim tower, all by Trehearne & Norman, Preston & Partners (1962–1967), it was intended as a pioneer testing ground for the pedway system. Holford's scheme was prefigured by Hugh Casson's sketches in the *Architectural Review* townscape plan for reconstruction, aiming to combine a sober modernist aesthetic with picturesque glimpses of St. Paul's between the blocks. Yet despite being praised by Pevsner in 1973 as "outstandingly well conceived" in this regard, by the 1980s it had become vilified as an example of stark and insensitive postwar planning, which flagrantly disregarded Wren's cathedral and the national significance of the site—or, in the prince's words, it was "the continuation of war by other means."[98] His speech was a response to the competition-winning master plan by Arup Associates, awarded by developer Stuart Lipton of Greycoat, by whom the prince had been invited to view the seven finalists. Finding it "deeply depressing that none had risen to the occasion," he commissioned historicist architect Léon Krier to draw up a new lower-density brief, for which John Simpson's firm put together an initial neoclassical scheme, including traditional materials and Georgian accents, countering Arup's stripped classicist design. Simpson's scheme won general favor, and when the site was taken over by an international developer consortium, Paternoster Associates (including Greycoat, Park Tower [US], and Mitsubishi Estate Corporation [Japan]), a new group of architects were employed to develop the neoclassical scheme, including Terry Farrell as master planner and architects Simpson, Thomas Beeby, Robert Adam, Quinlan Terry, and Allen Greenberg. This plan rejected modernist planning and design in favor of historic street patterns and eclectic historicist facades. It was accepted in 1993, only to be superseded by William Whitfield's stripped classical master plan in 1996 due to another change of site ownership, finally realized in 2003.

Although the complex narrative of the site is well known as a formative episode in the history of British architecture, it also represented an important change in the attitude toward public space in the City. Perhaps the most evocative and compelling illustrations of this shift were the projective oil paintings of the historicist Paternoster scheme by Carl Laubin. Laubin began his career as an architect who painted as a hobby, but became known for his romantic canvases of new historicist developments in the 1980s, making his name with the highly publicized depictions of Jeremy Dixon's Royal Opera House in 1986. Hovering somewhere between the tradition of architectural perspectives, capricci, and English landscape paintings, Laubin's oil studies brought character and liveliness to the standard repertoire of architectural media, combining realism and romanticism in oils. The artist was recommended to John Simpson by Leon Krier after working on his Atlantis project in Tenerife. His first *Paternoster Square* painting in 1988 introduced a completely different concept of public space in the City, countering the rather uninspiring brief of providing one

Paternoster Square, City of London, 1965. Architectural Press Archive / RIBA Collections.

million square feet of office space and "a bold concept for retailing" with a scene that foregrounded public life over floor space. Bathed in golden light, a composition of historic facades was the backdrop to a bustling scene of daily activity surrounding the cathedral, peppered with choristers, tourists, and business men interacting and moving through. Laubin's use of oils, rather than the traditional watercolors, added texture and what he called *realism* in his depiction of the building materials, aiming to highlight the passing of time and show "where things would go wrong, where brick would stain for example." Furthermore, oil paint could be modified as the project progressed, claimed Laubin, "scratching out and painting over," rendering the painting a kind of active surface that reacted to change, much like the spaces that Simpson and the prince were advocating.[99]

Whereas traditional architectural projections privileged the building as object, Laubin's paintings portrayed buildings as a stage set for small everyday spectacles of human contact. In his compositions, edifices are simply a product of history, and the space in front shaped from centuries of use and ritual. Thus, as much as Laubin was striving for realism in his mode of representation, it was in service of fantasy: the creation of a fictional

Carl Laubin, *Paternoster Square*, 1988. Oil on canvas. Courtesy Carl Laubin.

present based on an imaginary past, in which the built environment worked in perfect harmony with the activities of its users. Modernism, it implied, had blighted this synergy. Of course, the entire rationale for the Paternoster competition was predicated on the antithesis of this idea. Office buildings in the City were outdated and could not accommodate the changing needs of City workers and international businesses. What was needed was innovation, not a return to a less complicated form of working. Yet what is striking about these paintings is the extent to which business activity seems to be there at all. In his second painting, produced for Paternoster Associates in 1992, under the looming dome of St. Paul's Laubin depicts tourists, lovers, clergymen, casual wanderers, but only a few businessmen (almost no businesswomen), who seem to be engaged in lighthearted conversation rather than work, surrounded by shops and cafes rather than office entrances. In this version of history, the traditional City gent disappeared and the function of the square became recreation.

Simpson and Laubin were set on creating a *place* rather than a site focused on commercial space. As the prince put it in his call to arms, "Surely here, if anywhere, was the time and place to sacrifice some profit, if need be, for generosity of vision, for elegance,

Carl Laubin, *Paternoster Square*, 1992. Oil on canvas. Courtesy Carl Laubin.

for dignity; ... and prove that capitalism can have a human face ...
On such a site, market forces, I would suggest, are not enough."
Yet ironically, it was this very idea that would soon become the
guiding mantra for real estate development in the City. The human
face, the historic facade, the iconic dome, and the leisure spot, all
were essential ingredients for promoting a unique global financial
center in a new economic paradigm.

First indications of this change emerged between the late
1970s and the mid-1980s, when the rhetoric behind the City's
planning strategies became increasingly preservation-oriented
and concerned with the visual aspect of the City's streets. By the
time the draft local plan was published in 1984, pedestrian movement had been removed linguistically from the realms of business efficiency and repositioned within two additions to the City's
planning lexicon: environmental quality and townscape.[100] Introduced into City planning documents for the first time in 1979, the
term *environmental quality* was defined as the "degree of pleasure
or displeasure experienced in living and working in, and in moving about, the City of London."[101] "While the design of individual
buildings is important," the 1979 background study claimed, "so is

the treatment of the spaces between and the settings within which they are seen."[102] Far removed from the statistical emphasis of the pedestrian surveys a decade earlier, the City's "distinctive urban form and 'grain,'" "close-knit building pattern," and "strong general sense of enclosure" would now provide spaces of entertainment between office hours, as opposed to functional appendages to the workplace.[103]

Emphasizing the qualitative dimension of the City's public spaces occurred in tandem with a changing attitude toward the relationship between vehicular and pedestrian traffic. Where Buchanan had called for the separation of cars and people as the way to ensure a safe urban realm, by the late 1970s planners were reconsidering this approach, looking toward integration and coexistence as an alternative.[104] Central to this new attitude was the understanding that pedestrians and drivers had distinct yet interrelated experiences of the city, and therefore the street took on different functions and meanings for each party. For pedestrians, the priorities were communication, orientation, and leisure; for drivers, its main purpose was to facilitate movement. The problem, it was believed, was that the City's streets had been designed when people's movements were simpler, and that more thought was needed to reinstate pedestrian priority over such places through concepts like "pedestrianization" and limiting vehicular access to smaller streets.[105] Such ideas were closely interlinked with conservationist groups; the belief that planners ought to reuse, rather than reconstruct, the urban environment fed into the realm of infrastructure. Restoring/preserving the historic character of an area was a way to enhance the pedestrian experience, thereby transforming the street's role from a facilitator of movement to a scenic backdrop.

By the late 1970s, the City's policy on streets and public spaces had largely adopted the townscape principles that had been put forward two decades earlier, but was more focused on conservation than Holden and Holford had been. Its attitudes toward the pedways, for example, shifted dramatically. Despite persisting with a reduced scheme, the City's planning department now conceded that the walkways did not fit an environmentally sympathetic approach to urban design. "Few would deny that some areas in the Barbican are bleak, draughty and uninviting when the weather is inclement," the department commented in its 1978 walkways and pedestrians background study. "What is needed, therefore, is a choice and variety rather than uniformity or excessive standard-isation."[106] Focusing on the City as the site of a "picturesque street network," the publication was prefaced by a quotation by Samuel Johnson proclaiming that "if you wish to have just a notion of the magnitude of this city, you must not be satisfied with seeing its great streets and squares, but must survey the innumerable little lanes and courts. It is not in the showy evolutions of buildings, but in the multiplicity of human habitations which are crowded together, that the wonderful immensity of London consists."[107]

This study was part of a set of preparatory reports for the ill-fated 1984 DLP, written largely to appease conservation groups and with few concessions toward the floor space and infrastructure concerns of the City's business activities. During this period, the outward focus of the Corporation's planning department appeared to be glorifying the City's historic infrastructure, rather than pro-moting anything new. In 1975, the City took part in European Heritage Year, offering two "heritage walks" in which the City's historic alleyways played a prominent role, including only a few recent architectural achievements.[108] The report reflected a general mood against the perceived alienating properties of modernism that per-vaded the postwar period. It responded to the pleas of critics like Jane Jacobs and Lewis Mumford in eschewing motorways, raised walkways, and any forms of planning that revolved around infra-structure, as opposed to the quality of environment for citizens.

Much of the 1978 study was hence dedicated to celebrating the smaller streets and courtyards as pieces of urban scenery.[109] Churchyards and small public spaces were represented as moments on a picturesque journey, rather than backdrops to working life. "One of the delights of exploring the City on foot is the discovery of small gardens and spaces approached from narrow alleyways leading off busy thoroughfares," the report explained. "It will be seen that no two open spaces in the City are alike and it is this that makes them so interesting, as well as the seasonal and daily changes of light, shade and colour. Variations in paving and plant-ing also contribute to their individual character, as do fountains, sculpture and occasional live entertainment."[110] In this new plan-ning discourse, pedestrian activity was removed from the realm of the office worker to that of the everyday tourist seeking pleasure in the sensorial qualities of the City's public spaces.

Emphasis on leisure and public space was one of the most strik-ing cultural changes that took place in the City in the following decades. The 1969 pedestrian survey showed that only 38 percent of workers actually used open spaces. Reasons given included lack of time; unsuitableness of open spaces; not knowing any open spaces existed; and, most significantly, distance from public spaces. In fact, the latter was "stated on a number of forms and many respondents were totally unaware of any reasonably sized open spaces within walking distance."[111] Furthermore, the study also revealed that there was little demand for increased retail, with just 6 percent desiring more clothes and food shops. Despite the latter, the DLP advocated for a dramatic increase in retail and catering units, claiming that the City was short of seating for around one-fifth of the workforce (assuming that everyone wanted to eat out rather than take away their food).

Contrary to the widespread criticism of the Corporation's emphasis on retail, catering, and preservation—over the provision of office space—in the DLP from developers and both British and international businesses, the new American-style developments of the 1980s made a point of embedding such facilities into their schemes.[112] Whereas previously shopping establishments were

Office "girls" take their lunch break al fresco in a "continental style table and umbrella" on the pavement outside a public house in Milk Street, London, 1962. Copyright Picture Kitchen / Alamy.

Chapter 2

located in five main areas—Bishopsgate, Cheapside, Moorgate, Leadenhall, and Fleet Street—in the form of high streets and markets, in developments like Broadgate they were subsumed as part of the wider public space provision, lining squares and forming part of the flexible ground-level accommodation. One reason for this was the changing entertainment and dining culture of the City with the arrival of international firms. In particular, the integration of eating and drinking into business practice contrasted substantially with the American work ethic. Charles McVeigh III, the vice-president of Salomon Brothers who arrived in the City in 1973, described the clash vividly:

> When I first came to the City ... everyone broke at around twelve-thirty for lunch, which became a major part of the day, whereas Americans tend to eat early and quickly and never drank anything at all. At Salomon in New York we would offer a drink to be courteous but by and large people never took it. People like Morgan Guaranty never even served a drink, it was against their internal rules. Lunch was over in an hour whereas in London it took two to two-and-a-half hours. People had at least one or two drinks before lunch, wine with the meal and thought nothing of having port and at least one cigar afterwards. Interestingly, no business was done over lunch, which, again, was completely different from America. You would wait until the end when you might, over a glass of port or as the dessert was being served, turn the conversation to some business area of mutual interest. Before that, one was positioning oneself socially with one's counterpart.[113]

With deregulation, British drinking culture was gradually replaced by American sobriety, and lunches became matters of brevity and efficiency. New eating habits were a by-product of an attitude to work that favored longer hours and faster transactions to be competitive in the deregulated marketplace. This change was hard for older members of the City: "they came and they had lots of money, and lots of dining rooms, and they drank water" said one. "It was the big thing about the Americans, you know. They did exercise and goodness knows what else. And it took us a while to settle into that."[114]

In many of the 1980s office complexes, cafes and restaurants were included for convenience, enabling business lunches to take place. In-house canteens weren't new, since some buildings in the 1960s incorporated such spaces for their workers. Similarly, the lunch rooms of the merchant banks held legendary status in the City, but were only accessible to those with connections, or by invitation.[115] Those of a lower status were often given luncheon vouchers to buy sandwiches from one of the many smaller cafes, which had proliferated along with office employment.[116] The spread of firms to the City's peripheries in the 1970s and 1980s involved moving to areas less well catered for, and as such, cafes provided within developments became popular. In addition to new eating and drinking patterns, American enthusiasm for fitness and recreation also became significant, which was noted in the Corporation's significantly revised 1986 local plan, claiming that "in general, the amount of leisure time available has increased. There is increasing demand for cultural activities and ad hoc lunchtime events, and a growing awareness of the benefits of sport, especially to people working in high-pressure business environments."[117] Leisure and the wider attraction of the financial center as an extension of the workplace became key to attracting workers in the global labor-force marketplace.

Such transformations were arguably part of a more general shift in the nature of work in the new neoliberal corporation, in which the workplace became an essential attractor to talent. The rise of the service sector and the *knowledge worker*—a term coined by influential organizational theorist Peter Drucker in the late 1950s—required a shift in the perceived status of the worker within the organization, and in turn the manager-subordinate relationship. As Drucker explained: "Knowledge workers ... own the means of production. That knowledge between their ears is a totally portable and enormous capital asset. Because knowledge workers own their means of production, they are mobile."[118] As such, companies had to go out of their way to stop employees taking their capital asset, knowledge, to other firms, replacing command-and-control management tactics with motivation, employee freedom, and fostering interpersonal relationships. The shift to knowledge work repositioned the employee in the overall accounting structure of the firm from an *expense* to an *investment*, in turn augmenting the relative value of the office environment as part of that investment. As Drucker noted, whereas "economic theory and most business practice see manual workers as a cost, to be productive, knowledge workers must be considered a capital asset. Costs need to be controlled and reduced. Assets need to be made to grow."[119] In effect, the worker had become human capital, rendering any action that increased the worker's capacity to earn income or boost satisfaction—such as a training course, a gym, or a pleasant work environment—an investment in human capital.

Hence the 1980s saw a shift in cultural values and morphological preferences in the City. Unlike the office plaza model adopted in the US, its existing small plots and narrow streets did not afford room to provide decent public spaces. Yet the City's spatial deregulation in the 1980s and the introduction of air rights meant that peripheral schemes could build American-style offices centered around a quasi-public square. Broadgate was the prototype for such developments, offering three public spaces on completion: Broadgate Square (enveloped by phases 1–4), Finsbury Avenue Square (bordered by phases 1 and 2, as well as 1–3 of Arup's earlier Finsbury Avenue development) and Exchange Square (surrounded by phases 5, 8, and 11). These spaces were landscaped to include softer finishes such as trees and plants, large steps and planter ledges that doubled as benches, retail facilities, and eateries.

Until this point, the plaza had been relatively unwelcome in the City. Whereas attempts had been made to introduce open spaces previously, such as GMW's Commercial Union and P&O or Holford's Paternoster Square, public opinion was largely negative,

Broadgate development, with farmer's market, photographed in 2010. amc / Alamy.

condemning such spaces as windswept, unappealing, and out of character. The objections were partly ideological, as the plaza represented the destruction of the City's traditional sociospatial system based on the intimacy of its tavern-punctuated alleyways and intimate public spaces. Nowhere was this resistance expressed more vehemently than during the furor surrounding Peter Palumbo's proposal to build the Mansion House Square tower and plaza scheme, designed by Mies van der Rohe and William Holford. Having secured provisional planning permission in 1960, Palumbo took twenty years to acquire the necessary lease agreements to the site, by which time the mood against comprehensive replanning had become entirely unsympathetic; the scheme was ultimately rejected by the Corporation. Palumbo's proposal, which would have consumed an entire wedge of the Bank intersection (a space made a conservation area in 1971), bounded by Poultry and Queen Victoria Street, encountered bitter resistance from conservationists and City firms because it involved destroying Victorian buildings and the old street network. As journalist Brian Appleyard wrote during the public enquiry, "The specific buildings to be demolished may not be brilliant but they are supremely characteristic of that type of Victorian urban development, and they keep faith with the medieval street plan. In any case, the whole Mies development is essentially un-English, redolent of Chicago rather than Cheapside."[120] The "un-English" jibe was key to the Corporation's rejection of the proposal, which, as Jane M. Jacobs argues, was based on the "impulse to preserve a built form that celebrated a fading City (and Britain) of Empire," resulting in its replacement by James Stirling's more environmentally sensitive intervention, No. 1 Poultry (completed 1985).[121]

In the mid-1980s, the Corporation drew up guidelines intended to be sympathetic to the City's existing urban texture. The 1986 local plan declared:

> Because of its heavily built up nature, the City requires a "finer mesh" in the provision of open space than that laid down by the minimum GLDP guidelines. The Corporation considers that no-one in the City should be more than about 200 metres from an area of open space and thus intends to encourage the provision of additional public open space where appropriate. It is important that new open space

should enhance the character of its surroundings. It is also important that there should be a natural soil depth to allow for planting; piazza areas with flower tubs are not usually an adequate alternative.[122]

Broadgate was designed along this model, with the additional integration of retail/hospitality units as "attractors." Despite being located away from the historic core, and sandwiched between the City's main traffic thoroughfares—London Wall, Moorgate, and Bishopsgate–its squares were viewed as successful additions to the urban fabric. A study by the Space Syntax Laboratory at University College London proclaimed Broadgate as "the best used public open space in and around the City of London."[123] Commissioned by Lipton, this study was asked to evaluate the scheme (determined by continuous use) and the extent to which design was a determinant. Space Syntax's statistical and computational analysis (i.e., quantitative rather than qualitative) concluded that the triumph of Broadgate's spaces was the ability to attract people from elsewhere, claiming that "81% of the people spending time (i.e. stopping, as opposed to simply passing through) in Broadgates open spaces come from outside Broadgate"—with each person walking "on average 439 metres to get there, farther than for any other space studied in the City."[124] The process of "creating life" was thought to stem from a combination of facilitating "natural movement," allowing "unprogrammed activity" (provision of physical places to sit, eat, and drink), and providing attractors (e.g., high-end retail, restaurants, and bars). These attractors were considered to be key to ensuring Broadgate's economic success. Heritage, leisure, and environmental quality were no longer simply gestures toward preservationists, but rather became central to a market-led development strategy, involving the financialization and subsequent privatization of public spaces.

Broadgate and other public-private developments in Cutlers Gardens, St. George's Churchyard, Spitalfields, and the City's other markets represented a shift in the City's streets' explicit business activity to supporting leisure spaces. Yet paradoxically, the Corporation's effort to increase open spaces actually reduced the amount of *public* spaces in the City, as squares, plazas, and atriums were part of the wider developer-led strategy of urban development, which began in the 1980s. Within such private-public spaces, the

Social life after work in the City, 2009. Copyright Horst Friedrichs / Alamy.

picturesque approach to urban design became a tactical means
to regulate the demographic within them. Place-making features
were implemented as attractive landscape additions and instruments of control: plants doubled as disguises for security cameras, public art became entry barriers, terrorist barricades were
dressed as benches and fountains. "Unprogrammed activity" was
thus highly programmed.

Many of the strategies employed in these public-private plazas were drawn from 1970s techniques used to design out crime,
such as Crime Prevention through Environmental Design (CPTED)
and the defensible space theories of Oscar Newman.[125] Such measures increased dramatically in the City following the bombings
of the Provisional IRA in 1992 and 1993. The so-called ring of steel
security cordon limited vehicular access via armed checkpoints
and was reinforced by the widespread installation of security cameras across the Square Mile. In the years that followed, security
measures were implemented at the architectural level, creating
a patchwork of corporate citadels throughout the Square Mile
via confine and control techniques.[126] Methods used to control
involved reducing the number of entrances to buildings and adding a security filter (either through barriers or guards), implement-
ing no parking areas in the immediate vicinity, restricting access
to subterranean car parks, and employing private security guards.

At the material level, alongside architectural features like shatter-resistant window film, safety glass, and internal shelters, tactics to "design out crime" were appropriated as antiterror devices, including planters, bollards, and the demarcation of territorial boundaries using metal studs and changes in floor material.[127]

Ironically, strategies to soften the environment, such as the landscaped pedestrian spaces outside buildings, tree-planting, and traffic reduction, were appropriated to harden the City against terrorism. This was particularly true of the traffic reduction strategy of the ring of steel, which had in fact been proposed a few years before in the City of London local plan (1986), then revised in the subsequent unitary development plan as a way to rejuvenate the Square Mile.[128] Previously, the Corporation was reluctant to endorse and finance street "improvements" that restricted access due to opposition from City firms worried about the inconvenience caused.[129] After the 1993 IRA bombing, however, businesses demanded overt protection. Peter Rees, as chief planning officer, remembers: "This helped the funding and roll-out of the environmental measures already planned." He explains: "Prior to the terrorist actions, City businesses had been vociferously opposed to any reduction in road space or traffic routes. After the bombs, they were more amenable to closing and narrowing roads. The business leaders got their 'improved security' while the planners were able to achieve their 'environmental enhancement.'"[130]

In short, the heavily conservative values underpinning the surveillance turn became a catalyst for a radical form of urbanism far in advance of environmental urbanism by pushing through the pedestrianism agenda. By the 1990s, the Corporation's townscape strategies of the previous decades were enabled by the militarization of public space, quite in contrast to the heavy-handed, car-centered approach implemented at Canary Wharf.

This was reflective of the compromises made by the Corporation in the wake of the Big Bang. Negative reactions to the heavily conservation-oriented DLP by businesses and developers required the Corporation to rethink its environmental strategy. In order to make available the floor space required for the surge in business, it altered its conservation policy to one focusing on "the character of areas, rather than individual buildings."[131] This approach prioritized the facades and entryways of historic buildings, enabling these to be retained while entirely replacing the interiors to accommodate the new technological infrastructure required. Conservation became a reductive operation aimed at reinforcing the historic image, while actually keeping very little of the original substance of the building.

By the early 1990s, conservationism had been subsumed into the City's broader strategy to reinstate itself as the world's leading financial center. Throughout that decade, a number of alleys, such as Pope's Head Alley and Ship Passage, were realigned/reinstated because "the relatively short walking distances between firms, institutions and other services located in the City is seen to form a unique and valued feature of the City's business environment."[132] Yet where decades earlier these interlacing channels were a concrete manifestation of the money markets, they were now more significant as symbols of tradition, their eclectic facades and narrow forms showing the patina of a bygone era that underpinned the unique branding identity of the City in a global marketplace. As the neoliberal economy placed more emphasis on the individual knowledge worker, the City's streets had to attract the consumer-employee. Public spaces became spaces of leisure and well-being, the essential counterparts to work in a twenty-four-hour global economy. Thatcher's opening up of the financial system had in turn provoked an internalization of its mechanisms. The work of exchange now occurred deep within the large finance factories emerging all over the City, closing down the notion of trading as a pseudopublic activity that once spilled out from cavernous exchange floors and banking halls into the streets. Simultaneously, the politics of regulation were now concealed far below the City's surface, descending from the ostentatious monumentality of neoclassical institutions like the Stock Exchange and the Bank of England, to a messy network of telecoms cables, junctions, and tunnels threading between tube stations, sewers, and Roman ruins.

Underground Citadels

A manhole cover, gently raised, gives access to one of the Post Office's thousands of sub-surface cable chambers. But this one is different. A stout grey-painted waterproof door leads through the side of this chamber. Open it, and you are standing on the top platform of a shaft one hundred feet deep. Climb down the rung ladders, and you stand poised at the entrance to the secret network. A long ribbon of

lights and cables extends into the distance as you look into Tunnel L
(St Paul's to Bethnal Green). No bustling commuters or noisy trains
here, just a pleasantly warm and enveloping silence. ...
Riding down Tunnel L, one passes side shafts and alleys en route
to the first interchange, directly below Postal Headquarters close to
St Paul's Cathedral. Here, tunnels shoot off in all directions: three
rise to join the ordinary London underground Central Line, and
the Post Office's own underground mail railway. Tunnel R and
Tunnel A grandly circuit round St Paul's Cathedral—they lead to an
underground complex with six shafts below the Post Office's Citadel
telephone exchange. Citadel's workings, and shaft, are hidden behind
seven foot thick concrete walls.
Campbell, "A Christmas Party for the Moles," 1980[133]

In December 1980, investigative journalist Duncan Campbell exposed a government cover-up and infrastructural megaproject hiding deep under central London. "Implausibly disguised as a touring cyclist," wearing a tracksuit and armed with a fold-up bike and camera, Campbell descended sixty meters below the capital's chaotic urban crust to discover twelve miles of secret tunnels, clandestinely running between the highest seats of power in the land. These vast, highly engineered spaces were built as shelters during World War II and subsequently purchased by the Post Office, which extended and repurposed the tunnels as defense infrastructure during the Cold War to protect the personnel and machinery of the British state from aerial assault, including the atomic bomb. Perforated by vertical shafts rising to the surface in unassuming telephone exchanges and manholes, the quiet channels traversed the City and Westminster, including *tunnel Q,* "Post Office jargon for 'hush hush,'" which contained entry points for the Ministry of Defence, the Old War Office, the Admiralty, No. 10, and the Treasury.[134]

During one of his many cycling tours through the underground system, Campbell discovered the Kingsway Telephone Exchange sitting below the then abandoned Chancery Lane tube station. Buried beneath the rambling medieval Inns of Court on the western edge of the City, it was one of the most sensitive and elaborate telephone exchanges in Britain. Built to house London's growing telecommunications network, the exchange was also the terminal for the first transatlantic submarine telephone cable, TAT1, in 1956, which would revolutionize cross-border trading in the City.[135] It contained an office complex, a canteen, and a bar for its workers, amounting to a huge complex—dubbed by Campbell a *citadel*—for the powerful state-owned Post Office.

Despite the playful overtones of the *New Statesman* article, which positioned the tunnels as a wacky venue for the magazine's Christmas party, Campbell's subterranean exploration was politically motivated. Labeling himself and his colleagues Mole Force *NS*, the undercover operatives tunneling both literally and metaphorically underneath Britain's most powerful institutions, Campbell's article was one of many written to expose the security and surveillance infrastructure of the British state. "Mole is now British for 'Whistleblower,' an excellent innovation," wrote Campbell, who had just two years earlier evaded thirty years imprisonment for alleged charges of breaking official secrecy laws after revealing the existence of the British Government Communications Headquarters (GCHQ) electronic communications agency and publishing evidence of its wiretapping activities, including photographs and maps of radio masts, office buildings, and telecoms equipment.[136] For Campbell, Kingsway exchange and the tunnels were symbolic of the extent to which the military-technological complex of the British state was being concealed in plain sight. Prior to Campbell's revelations, the subterranean complex had been erased from public knowledge and underground maps, despite a 1951 article in the *Daily Express* leaking the "secret network of tunnels" as front-page news. Campbell's article was also dismissed by the Post Office as nothing more than a hoax, claiming the photographs were shot in studios, a slur that was subsequently disproved by the rush of urban explorers following his directions.[137]

Campbell's investigations drew attention to the ways that communications infrastructure was becoming an increasingly insidious tool for governments, as the digital age was dawning. The subterranean channels that enabled new technologies occupied a liminal space between public and private, evading the scrutiny of citizens. In the City, the interconnection between political power, economic policy, and technological development that fueled the great financial changes of the 1980s was largely played out underground. Debates over where telecommunications infrastructure should go, how it should be supplied, and why it should be installed were critical to the conversations around urbanism and central to the process of financial deregulation. Telecommunications became prominent in the City in the 1960s when existing telephone/telex systems were merged with computing. Initially they were used to keep up with the increased volume and speed of trading in the Eurocurrency and interbank markets, and to process data—that is, to filter, sort, and analyze information.[138] Yet over the next two decades, computers shifted from being a helpful aid to businesses, to being a fundamental part of the financial transaction. Computers were implemented in City firms to take advantage of deregulation in the foreign exchange markets. Rapid cross-border trade and access to share prices in seconds didn't simply change the method of trading, but rather gave rise to entirely new kinds of online marketplaces and financial consortia, such as the well-known NASDAQ, which by 1985 grew to be the third-biggest stock market in the world following New York and Tokyo.[139] By the early 1980s, all major financial institutions in the City were using electronic systems for securities trading on the Stock Exchange. All this required the installation of miles of subterranean infrastructure on a scale unseen since the construction of the London Underground over one hundred years earlier.

Such a complex technological transformation was made possible due to equally convoluted political shifts. Although the quantity, speed, and volume of transactions transformed the financial services industry before the Big Bang, Thatcher's 1986 ruling to open up markets to outside interests and to erode the jobber-broker division, paired with the switch to on-screen and telephone trading, ensured an unbreakable symbiosis between technology and financial practice. Financial deregulation could only occur if the telecommunications industry underpinning it was also restructured to operate in the new competition-driven economic milieu. Until this point, in America and Europe, public-owned postal, telegraph, and telephone administrations held the telecommunications monopoly. Such a structure worked well for what was a relatively standardized, well-established analogue system. But as digital technology became commonplace, the nature of demand among corporations also became more variable and was constantly evolving. In the eyes of Conservative politicians, the cumbersome state-run monopoly simply wasn't nimble enough to keep up and needed to be replaced with a more competitive, market-based alternative, which combined large corporate users, equipment suppliers, and privatized service providers. In other words, financial deregulation could only be supported by the deregulation of the telecoms sector.[140] The US and UK took the lead in privatization, with the divestiture of the American Telephone and Telegraph Company occurring in 1984, followed by British Telecom in Britain later that year.[141] Britain became the first country to entirely break the monopoly by licensing Mercury Communications, a competitor, to operate in the City.[142] In 1990 the duopoly formed by Mercury and BT was abolished and over forty licenses were given to competitors to operate across Britain— with two targeted specifically at the City, representing the complete deregulation of the sector.[143]

In physical terms, these regulatory changes had a dramatic impact on the City's subterranean environment. In the 1980s and 1990s, hundreds of miles of optical fiber grids were laid underground to overcome the lag caused by copper wires in the telephone system.[144] Such an invasive process was not only hugely expensive, but also logistically complicated on account of its densely built up historic core and the deep layers of heritage underneath the modern Square Mile. Archeological exploration in the City had been well documented since the seventeenth century, and thanks to the continual process of excavating and rebuilding, Roman London was one of the best understood ancient cities. Postwar reconstruction in particular gave rise to several important discoveries, including the Roman Temple of Mithras, dated to around AD 245, which was uncovered during the construction of Bucklersbury House (1953–1958, Owen Campbell-Jones & Sons). Originally standing on the east bank of the River Walbrook, from which votive offerings (including some human skulls) and domestic refuse were also discovered, the temple was moved to a new open-air site above a car park north of Temple Court and shifted from a north-south axis to an east-west orientation—a practice that would now be deemed as insensitive as the crazy paving installed in the temple's former nave.

Deep historical time was thus at odds with the rapid service delivery required by telecommunications companies. Dubbed by the industry as the problem of the "last mile," the greatest challenge was to get the networks through the expensive "local loop" by interlacing optical fiber from historical underground citadels, up through pavements and traffic-laden streets, and into the historic and modern buildings.[145] In a context where millimeters and

Aerial view of visitors queuing to see the Temple of Mithras excavation site in the City, 1954. Copyright Illustrated London News Ltd / Mary Evans.

milliseconds could mean great financial losses, these material barriers were all the more significant.

Due to the difficulties in installing the infrastructure within the City's historic urban fabric, only a handful of service providers adopted the local loop of the City as their target area, including Mercury, City of London Telecommunications, Energis, and Metropolitan Fiber Systems (MFS).[146] In fact, rather than establishing nationwide networks, most of these companies focused their investment on the City, on account of the high proportion of telecommunications traffic concentrated there.[147] To facilitate the process, service providers appropriated existing underground infrastructure, like former canal channels, old London Underground tunnels, sewers, and other utilities ducts, rather than construct new pathways.[148] In order to overcome the barriers of distance and time through faster digital networks, paradoxically the new telecommunications coalitions were reliant on a host of existing historical infrastructures underground as well as an incredibly burdensome process of installation. In other words, as radical geographer David Harvey articulated, "space can be overcome only through the production of space, of systems of communication and physical infrastructures embedded in the land."[149] Such a paradox was described in the plans for SOVEREIGN two decades earlier, which likened the system "to a road or railway" which "rather than being a response to a known demand, is in fact a resource whose supply generates a demand."[150] The latter was certainly true of new digital networks: by the 1990s, the City was second only to North America with regards to its global telecommunications capacity.[151] Armed with this incredibly powerful instrument, the Square Mile sought to align itself with, or even trump, the status of New York as a financial center, while also making a bid for occupants against the emerging Docklands redevelopment in the capital.

More than a financial tool, telecommunications was thus part of a bigger branding strategy for the City. In 1994, the City Corporation commissioned the London Business School to prepare reports into "the competitive position of London's financial services"—one of which considered specifically the role of telecommunications in boosting the City's position. "As a major international financial centre London is an attractive target for telecoms providers," the report argued. "[Financial] firms can now choose between providers in all three segments—the local loop, long distance and international traffic."[152] Infrastructure became a selling point; but implementation was certainly not seamless and the services were by no means accessible straightaway. Enormous up-front investment ensured that initially only large companies had the means to use such systems. Furthermore, early versions were precarious and required extensive contingency and backup procedures, which were costly.[153] Security caused its own problems, as each payment had to go through authentication processes run by software only accessible by a select group of individuals, and it would self-destruct if any other person interfered with it. One of the critical hurdles was locating parts of the City where unintentional disruptions could be avoided, such as roadworks, which might otherwise be systemically perceived as an attack.[154]

Unsurprisingly, the Corporation was initially underprepared for the infrastructural impact of deregulated telecommunications.

Fleet Sewer, Blackfriars, interior view, 1971. London Metropolitan Archives (City of London). London Picture Archive, ref 215381.

The 1984 DLP contained just two pages on telecommunications, despite being published in the same year that BT was privatized, CHAPS was implemented, and on-screen trading was well underway. It argued that while it would do everything possible to provide space for the "era of cabling," the department had little to do with such services; it provided no specifics for how to deal with the new infrastructure.[155] Below the surface, the application of the optical fiber grids was somewhat chaotic. Market operators, rather than municipal regulators, grew to control telecommunications apparatus in the City, often leaving the Corporation in the dark about the nature and location of the infrastructure being implemented.[156] In his book about telecommunications and globalization in Paris and London, Jonathan Rutherford cites two members of the Corporation's Economic Development Unit, interviewed in 2000, who described the systemic incoherence: "The Corporation doesn't even have a confidential map or model of what's underground ... It's a bit of a sort of a Holy Grail. ... We don't really know about the quality of the telecommunication infrastructure. ... We can't tell you how many fibre optic cables there are underneath the ground. [You] just have to take our word for it. ... We know its true, but we've just got no evidence."[157] A 2009 report into the laying of pipe subways showed a similar level of unintelligibility below ground, describing cabling installations to be "very disorganised and chaotic where take-offs occur," arguing that "in some cases, little thought has been given to ... other services and their needs and future requirements."[158] Poor control over infrastructure provision was the result of the early phases of deregulation; the failure to coordinate the "telematic coalition" or plan for the boom in telecommunications infrastructure was arguably a symptom of the City's inability to predict the fallout of the Big Bang.

Architectural provision for this technology was also almost entirely absent from the 1984 DLP. In public consultations of the document, around eighty of the City's leading institutions in financial services, property development, and land severely criticized the lack of foresight where technological change, economic growth, and property development were concerned.[159] Under pressure from conservation groups, the emphasis of the plan was on the preservation of the historic environment. It lacked a clear program for facilitating what DEGW described as "development and redevelopment to meet the changing requirements of the City's financial services industries" and "to retain [the City's] international financial position."[160] Following the consultation, and the appointment of the new planning officer, Peter Rees, serious revisions were made to the document. In its republication as the local plan in 1986, the planning document revealed a change in attitude, stating its intention "to encourage office development in order to maintain and expand the role of the City as an international financial centre" and "to encourage office development which meets the requirements of new office technology and which is flexible to cater for variations in office layout and use."[161] By 1993 some 7.3 million square meters of office space, amounting to 71 percent of all City floor space, was dedicated to offices; most of it was achieved through the provision of peripheral developments outside the historic core where the subterranean intervention required for new technology was easier.[162]

On the streets and squares of the City, the effects of the underground transformations appeared gradually but were palpable. Pedestrian business traffic between institutions dramatically reduced as much of the street activity was subsumed into large, flexible, multifunctional developments. As Graham and Marvin noted, "superblock" sites like Broadgate and New York's Battery Park provided all the necessary amenities for business executives in "single bundled complexes," adding "an architectural dimension to the selective local disconnection of global city cores from their immediate urban contexts."[163] Developments like Broadgate were intended as work-life factories, within which quasi-public areas offered extraneous appendages to the work environment, accommodating lunchtime or after-hours leisure, rather than the physical transmission of messages and money. However, rather than dehumanizing the urban realm, telecommunications gave rise to new forms of mobility and pedestrian life. For example, when the new Stock Exchange building opened in 1972, the floor was installed with a telephone system that could withstand up to 1,200 calls per minute, with one of the fastest connections then in the world.[164] The system required jobbers and brokers to wear pocket-radios called "bleepers" so they could be contacted on the floor, replacing the bellowing call of the "waiters." A contemporary observer pointed out that the devices meant the members of the Stock Exchange could now "be reached anywhere on the Floor or ... in neighbouring pubs and cafes," enabling them to be more mobile than before.[165]

New technology also shifted the synergy between place and self-surveillance in the City. Inbuilt security in digital trading removed the need for *Dictum meum pactum*, as well as the trust-based physicality of the marketplace. Previously, the timetabled, public, and predictable nature of exchange made it easy to police, allowing mutual surveillance in banking and financial markets. Digital trading platforms internalized security, which purported to make the market fairer but often had the opposite effect. As one former jobber explained, whereas before trading was face to face, "with the advent of technology everything is recorded, so you no longer trust each other ... That should take a lot of the fear out, but it doesn't. People easily find ways round that." In particular, in the 1990s, mobile phones increased spatial freedom to such an extent that they initially caused regulatory problems. "When it first started," he recalled, "everybody had their mobile phone in the office ... and they'd never go on the landline because they could be traced. So we had to ban that, and then people went outside to have a fag and get on their phone."[166] Mobile phones produced a more disparate and disorganized kind of activity that no longer conformed to the spatial and temporal norms of the City.

Time in the City was entirely reconfigured by digital technology. Inventions such as the automated teller machine (ATM) enabled simple banking activities to be carried out at any time of day, anywhere in the City. Digital trading platforms ensured dealing was now on a twenty-four-hour basis, exploiting the time zone advantages. Increased transaction speeds also initiated changes in the spatial organization of firms, particularly with regard to the decentralization of back-office activities. In 1988, the world's first fiber-optic cable was laid between London and New York, and many large firms began investing in private networks to secure their own high-speed connections. In the same way that companies had purchased private telegraphic lines in the nineteenth century at great expense to quicken transaction times, so City firms chose to purchase private fiber-optic networks with multiple channels in case the service failed. Investment in such networks meant it was now much easier for large firms to relocate more menial, back-office tasks such as accounting to satellite regions outside the City. Furthermore, increasing continuity planning against failures in the system led to the construction of secondary offices outside the historic core, ready at a moment's notice should there be a City power shortage.[167]

Despite the potential of telecommunications, the material limitations of finance continued to persist. Paradoxically, as technology improved throughout the 1990s, the geographical proximity of institutions grew more important, as distance could cause microsecond losses in high-frequency trading; hence firms tended to cluster in the same area.[168] Financial historian Ranald Michie argues that "there has been no 'end of geography' or 'death of distance' because time is relative when dealing in financial products where margins depend on fractions of a second when orders are placed."[169] Simultaneously, face-to-face business meetings continued to occur, despite technological improvements, keeping the City important as a financial center. It was, however, the nature of this place and its public image that changed radically. Business practice in the postwar years transformed the street from an instrument for the act of exchange—a type of technology in itself—to the visual backdrop for the theater of high finance.

Concrete Realities

From one angle, it therefore appeared as though technology reduced the need for physical proximity and thus stripped the Square Mile of its morphological raison d'être. Security and surveillance had become part of the public hardware of the City, both above and below ground, in turn removing the imperative for self-regulation via eyes—and bodies—on the street. But from another angle, the social role of public space appeared to be more important than ever. Exchange may have been removed from public view, but the outward performance of business life became a critical marketing tool to attract potential employees and ultimately potential corporate occupiers. Eclectic alleys and small squares punctuated by bars and restaurants were no longer channels for messengers and top-hatters to funnel money through the system. But this "architecture of the short view," to quote Holden and Holford once again, continued to provide the setting for business entertainment and after-hours socializing, which acted as a main draw for City talent.

Although the method of use may have changed, there has always been a synergy between the formal character of the City's streets and the essential narratives that underpin its operation. Walter Bagehot understood the money market as a concrete reality, not simply because it had a precise geography, but because that geography was entrenched with long-standing ideas about gentlemanly codes of conduct and spatial rituals, which in turn affected the nature of the market it contained. Shortcuts, boulevards, and quiet corners were the tools with which social traditions were created, which in turn reinforced the illusion of historical permanence in an industry that was frequently subject to change. Throughout the postwar decades, whatever the reigning architectural ideology—be it preservation, modernist traffic segregation, or crime-prevention techniques—mythologies were created to synergize form and function, and in particular attributed a high level of importance to the City's smaller streets and historic facades. As Bagehot noted, "Commerce is curiously conservative in its homes, unless it is imperiously obliged to migrate."[170] Great changes in economic structures and technological development did force specific elements of what Bagehot described as "that money world" out of the Square Mile into cheaper or larger sites elsewhere. But the symbolic and economic value of the ant heap remained intertwined, as collaged street frontages continued to be the stage set for the spectacle of *haute finance*.

3   Facade

The structure looks solid enough but the foundations
are mysterious. ... You can't see it, but they've got it.
You don't know them, but you trust them.
"A Question of Confidence," *Men and Money*, BBC 2,
originally broadcast April 28, 1964[1]

A Question of Confidence

Alingering shot of Lutyen's weighty neo-mannerist
Midland Bank headquarters facade offered the ideal image for Paul
Ferris's characteristically theatrical script in BBC 2's *Men and Money*,
released in 1964. Narrated by film producer Tony Garrett, the second episode of this documentary series focused on the mechanisms and personality of the City's biggest financial houses, the
clearing banks. But here, architecture isn't simply used as a visual
cue. Rather, it is evidence of Ferris's central argument: "Money in
the modern sense means credit, and the one thing that sustains
the system is *confidence* in this credit." This, it is implied, can only
be achieved by an appropriately unabashed architectural display.
Cutting to Lutyens's lavish and ecclesiastical banking hall, the
camera shifts to an emphatically slow-moving upward angle into
a forest of green African verdite Corinthian square columns. "People trust banks, and the banks trust the Government," explains the
narrator, "but bankers maintain the safe, respectable and almost

Midland Bank, Poultry (1930), by Sir Edwin Lutyens in association with Gotch & Saunders, 1965. London Metropolitan Archives (City of London). London Picture Archive, ref 275859.

religious trappings that have come to be associated with financial prudence and foresight." If the visual associations aren't explicit enough, the next scene lays them bare. In a long interview with the chief general manager of the bank, H. H. Thaxton, Ferris himself asks, "How aware are you as a clearing banker of the need to build confidence? One looks at the head offices of banks, sort of marble halls and thick carpets—is this something that you consciously think of?" "Oh yes indeed," replies Thaxton, "there is a very real vital need for us to continue building up in the eyes of the public a sense of confidence."

It is not surprising that Ferris selected the Midland Bank as an emblem of self-assurance for the documentary. In the decade after the war, the majority of deposits in Britain were held by five main clearing banks known as the Big Five: Barclays Bank, Lloyds Bank, National Provincial Bank, Westminster Bank, and the Midland Bank. Each had grown substantially after World War I, with a series of mergers taking place in 1918, causing a surge in new headquarters buildings for the newly expanded institutions.[2] These interwar structures were reflective of their status in the public eye: large, Portland stone blocks dominating the streetscape, with the simplified massing and trappings of neoclassicism required to convey strength and wealth. Built between 1924 and 1939, Lutyens's headquarters for the Midland Bank was lauded by the architectural establishment, and its unprecedented scale had made it an icon in the City. Sitting proudly on Poultry at the Bank intersection, the new head office continued a tradition of the grand neoclassical facade in the City, which was brought up to date by the steel frame, affording its voluminous mass. It was the culmination of a massive expansion of the bank in the decades prior, whereby hundreds of new neo-Georgian branch banks were built across the country to draw in new business, opening up finance to the masses. As Thaxton claims in the interview with Ferris, "I think you'll agree that we are doing everything we possibly can ... by way of advertisement ... to let the public see that we are rather ordinary people, anxious to an ordinary job, for relatively ordinary people." Yet whereas the more domestic-scale bank branches aimed to engage the everyman, its City headquarters was the symbolic architectural figurehead, placed in direct conversation with its competitors. As Ferris retorts, "You can't be too ordinary ... or you'll lose your special advantage," to which Thaxton replies, "Oh undoubtedly, undoubtedly."

Watercolor perspective showing the New Change bank buildings (1960) by Victor Heal built to accommodate the Bank of England's Accountants' Department. Courtesy of London Metropolitan Archive.

However, in architectural terms, confidence was not abundant after World War II. In fact, the fashion among banks for neo-Georgian facades rendered the City a frequent victim of vitriol in the architectural press for its perceived meekness. Perhaps the most famous targets were the Bank of England superstructure and its collection of new outbuildings. Ian Nairn teased, "If the law concerned itself with aesthetics, Herbert Baker should have been indicted for his work at the Bank of England."[3] Victor Heal's redesigns of the war-damaged bank buildings on Princes Street (1952) and the accountancy department at New Change (1953–1960) were also met with dismay by Nikolaus Pevsner, who claimed it was "almost beyond comprehension how a design that would have been reactionary twenty years before could have been put into execution in the 1950s."[4]

Elsewhere, buildings became the subject of public protest. On January 15, 1959, a mock funeral procession was held outside the foundation stone–laying ceremony of the new Barclays Bank headquarters on Lombard Street by a group of students self-titled the Anti-Ugly Action group. Forty students gathered, wearing somber attire and bearing a cardboard coffin with the inscription "RIP Here Lyeth British Architecture," which was subsequently lain outside the entrance with candles and strewn with rose petals. They argued that the building, which was designed by the late Herbert Baker and executed by his successors Alexander T. Scott and Vernon Helbing between 1959 and 1964 was "abysmally ugly, little better than a stone slab in a mortuary" and "just another

Anti-Ugly Action Operation Three: Janet Allen leading a funeral procession down Lombard Street, January 15, 1959. Courtesy Gavin Stamp.

unimaginative Neo-Georgian edifice that will keep this street a dark cavern." Closely following another demonstration by the group just two months earlier, which had included Albert Richardson's Bracken House for the *Financial Times* and Heal's New Change buildings, the group drew attention to a general feeling among the architectural community that the financial center was a fortress of conservativism that was perpetuating second-rate architecture instead of innovation. Or, as one of the placards expressed, "The City is Ugly Enough Already."[5]

From one view, this reaction clearly chimed with the general outrage expressed by Ian Nairn, Nikolaus Pevsner, John Summerson, and their contemporaries against the perceived mediocrity and homogenization of the British townscape after the war.[6] These writers-cum-public intellectuals continued a tradition of architectural commentary in Britain, which combined the satirical wit of the *Architectural Review* and the *Architectural Journal* in the 1930s—through the unforgettably droll lyricism of J. M. Richards, John Betjeman, and occasional inputs from Evelyn Waugh and D. H. Lawrence—with the moralizing tendencies of John Ruskin. For them, the battle between modernism and traditionalism after World War II was not simply a formal or aesthetic concern, but rather called into question the conscience, well-being, and prosperity of the British nation. Yet despite the seriousness of the message, it was only through humor that observation and argument could be elevated from the ungentlemanly ranks of criticism and placed among the well-respected British lineage of public parody.[7]

Nairn, a peacetime RAF pilot and mathematics graduate, became well-known for his polemical attacks on the mundane "subtopia" surrounding postwar British cities, beginning with "Outrage," first published with Gordon Cullen as an essay in the *Review* and later republished as a book. In the latter, Nairn plotted a line from Southampton to Carlisle and traveled along it, using roadside photography and aerial views (taken himself) to show the best and worst of Britain, condemning the lack of coherence and car-dominated planning. But his commentary was loved and venerated by a broader public than the architecture community. Nairn's prose had what Gillian Darley has called "the breadth and brinkmanship of Dickens at his best, attuned to a mid-twentieth century idiom."[8] It was broadcast in regular architecture columns in the *Observer*, the *Sunday Times*, and the *Daily Telegraph*, and later in a popular BBC television series entitled *Nairn's Travels*. In 1966, Nairn published *Nairn's London*, which he purported to be "simply my personal list of the best things in London," but was in fact a sometimes potent, often hilarious manifesto on the good and the bad of postwar urban design and architecture. The City held a special role in the book as what Nairn termed "the real metropolis," the genius loci of London, which was under particular threat from developers and the Corporation's lack of a coherent urban planning approach. For Nairn, "Westminster and the West End are just hangers-on and could have been built anywhere, but the City needs this particular site. We are squandering its essence without a thought."[9] His antipathy towards the neo-Georgian was thus a rejection not simply of traditionalist tendencies, but of the rash parochialism that characterized its postwar redevelopment and undermined the City's historic and contemporary significance in British life.

Beneath the general disdain for the neo-Georgian seemed to be a more complex concern with the inappropriateness of architectural display in the City, in particular the idea that its buildings failed to outwardly articulate its contemporary role in public life. Holden and Holford noted in 1951 that the City "is functionally disciplined, although its physical apparatus is not always directly representative of its true character." They continued:

> For many years now, in order to impress on investors and the general public the stability and importance of the great commercial houses, architecture has been called into service. Thus the great banks ... are grander than they need be for purely functional purposes. On the other hand a large part of the commercial machine is operated in premises that make no attempt whatsoever at high standards of physical provision and have simply one asset in their favour, convenience. Just as there is no truth in the idea of the City as a centre of wild speculation, so there is no wild display in its architecture, but one finds cheek by jowl impressive buildings complete with columns and cornices, small badly-lit and narrow buildings housing professional and commercial firms of great antiquity and reputation, and large office buildings of monotonous appearance.[10]

Holden and Holford believed that the speculative building traditions of the twentieth century had disrupted the coherent visual message of the Victorian City, in which a clear symbolic relationship was established between grand architecture and its status as the national and imperial center of commerce. The rise of industrial capitalism and the global reach of Britain's trade had instigated the growth of financial institutions, necessitating larger and bolder architectural statements to compete. Within this context, a prominent neoclassical frontage became a crucial defining emblem for banks, exchanges, and other establishments, demonstrative of the City's inflated self-perception.[11] Like the postwar planners, Nairn argued that the unimaginative developer-led rebuilding in the twentieth century created discord with these grand edifices, going even further to suggest that it rendered them caricatures. He quipped: "The character is shrinking away from a

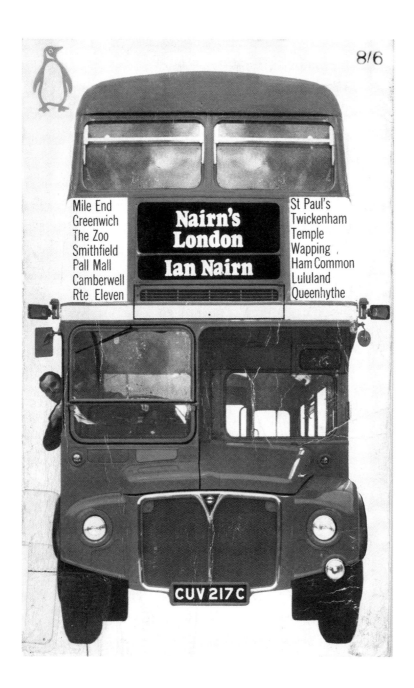

Cover of Ian Nairn, *Nairn's London* (London: Penguin Books, 1966). Courtesy of Penguin Books.

whole city-pattern into isolated attractions which will eventually become as phoney as the Tower [of London]."[12] Ugliness seemed to hover between unpredictability and monotony.

At the root of such critique seemed to be the idea that City buildings lacked decorum. In *Georgian London*, for example, Summerson stated that the majority of nineteenth-century architecture in the City was "absurdly ornate for its function and situation."[13] These attacks on the City's architectural judgement were not necessarily new. Historically there had been no aristocracy living in the City, which, coupled with its geographical distinction from the royal court, meant that there was nobody to "direct the course of taste, and many of the City's leading figures maintained a robust independence from such fashions."[14] As such, the financial center didn't appear always to understand the styles it adopted, leading to criticism of somewhat eclectic and overdone exteriors. For its postwar critics, neo-Georgian facades were indicative of the City's lack of cosmopolitanism and of the alienation of the Square Mile from the rest of the country, which Nairn claimed was "still as insular as if it were walled and gated."[15] In reality, there were many high-caliber architects employed in the City, both by financial institutions—including Herbert Baker and Albert Richardson, among others—and by the Corporation itself, to create such buildings as the stately Wood Street police station by McMorran & Whitby and the Guildhall extension by Giles Gilbert Scott. McMorran & Whitby's unusual building for the Corporation's private police force was widely and intentionally ignored by the major architectural publications on completion in 1966, despite being one of the most arresting edifices to be built in the financial center, and one of the few public buildings. In Nairn's critique for the *Observer*, entitled "Architecture against Crime," the subtlety and sensitivity of the building's unusually restrained take on Italianate classicism and minimalist Portland stone tower were disregarded outright as "repressive" and a "disaster," rather than a unique alternative to the prevailing modernist discourse.[16]

The idea that City institutions adopted certain architectural styles out of ignorance, apathy, or timidity disregarded the local architectural customs of the financial district and disparaged the long-standing importance of the classical facade as a carrier of meaning within the financial community. In architectural terms, one problem for City institutions after the war was how to embrace the conflict between modernist architecture—which renounced

Front facade, Wood Street police station by McMorran & Whitby, Wood Street, 1966.
Courtesy of McMorran Family Archives.

the facade as communicative device—and the expression of traditional values. Historically, street frontages had enabled the clarification of status and function, whereas the holistic form of modernist office blocks primarily conveyed expression in height and silhouette. In essence, the removal of load-bearing facades in modern architecture put at risk the "face" of the building, in turn stripping architecture of its most individualist and communicative element.

For businesses in the postwar City, there was what Anthony Vidler has called a tension "between classical humanism and modernist antihumanism, between faced buildings and faceless ones."[17] A facade, like a face, determined character and individuality—a matter essential for the City's *Dictum meum pactum* mythos, where deals rested on the strength of a name and durability of a reputation. This was the case in particular for banks, which were the main perpetrators in these trials of taste, particularly where neo-Georgian architecture was concerned. Comprising the largest workforce and physical footprint, banking was the main growth sector in the two decades after the initial building boom of the late 1950s, representing over one-third of new floor space.[18] While a proportion of this new space was built speculatively, most new offices were commissioned and developed by banks in conjunction with in-house architects.[19] As such, a good number of new flagship buildings under scrutiny in the postwar City belonged to banks.

Contrary to the pervasive critique of the neo-Georgian as inappropriate for the modern City, banks were wedded to this style specifically because of its perceived appropriateness. Georgian revival first emerged as the branch bank vernacular during the reign of George V, thriving in the interwar years. In addition to being relatively cheap in material terms thanks to the prominence of brick, it was thought to be sufficiently domestic for the scale of a British town, while also expressing the dignity of the banking houses first established in the eighteenth century. As historian of bank architecture John Booker notes, "In a society still structured by class, where a bank account for non-business reasons was a mark of the bourgeoisie, it was impossible in bankers' eyes to find any formula of derivative design which expressed sentiments more proper and at the same time more domestic."[20] Whereas Victorian neoclassicism repeated and replicated specific Greco-Roman motifs, neo-Georgian architecture was an abstraction of an implied order, thereby lending itself to historical association and contextual assimilation. Sitting comfortably between formality and informality, between the proper and the domestic, neo-Georgian thus also became a style that was bound up with mythologies about British tradition. As traditionalist Robert Byron, founder of the conservationist Georgian Group, articulated in a BBC debate titled "Farewell Brunswick Square" in 1938, "It corresponds, almost to the point of dinginess, with our national character. Its reserve and dislike of outward show, its reliance on the virtue and dignity of proportions only, and its rare bursts of exquisite detail, all express as no other style has ever done that indifference to self-advertisement, that quiet assumption of our own worth, and that sudden vein of lyric affection, which have given us our part in civilisation."[21] In short, it was a style that the self-described "young Fogey" and Georgian enthusiast Gavin Stamp once described as "English, gentlemanly and polite."[22]

Connotations of decorum and historic continuity were not lost on the banks. Heal's New Change building, so vilified by Pevsner and the Anti-Ugly group, was specifically designed to be "polite" to its context, providing the backdrop to St. Paul's Cathedral. Clad with red brick and Portland stone dressing, the curving facade was conceived by Heal—the Bank of England's in-house architect—as a "backcloth" to Wren's ensemble, in order to achieve "one large harmonious whole."[23] Likewise, at the much-protested Barclays headquarters foundation stone ceremony, Baker's design was described by its chairman as "a building which we may hope will stand and serve successive generations of customers, staff and stockholders for unnumbered years to come."[24] It was a design valued for its links with the past.

In other words, although the majority of the neo-Georgian buildings going up were unadventurous, unpopular, and unfashionable, in the financial district they a were safe bet. They embodied the values and tradition of the banking sector and the City at large, which in turn made them a secure investment. When the first modernist glass buildings were erected in the City, many developers expressed uncertainty because they were concerned that the banks would see a nontraditional building as too great a financial risk—as was the case with one of the largest postwar developments, Bucklersbury House and Temple Court (1953–1963), designed by architect firm Owen Campbell-Jones & Sons. According to Oliver Marriott, the developer of the scheme, Aynsley Bridgland, was vehemently against the design throughout the planning process "on the grounds that … being new and untried, it was less likely to be readily acceptable to the institutions which lent money on security of the buildings."[25] Despite protests from the LCC and Royal Fine Art Commission, which even had Giles Gilbert Scott submit a Portland-stone reworking of the proposal, the original design went ahead and Bridgland "reaped the glory as the promoter of the first glass box" as well as the economic benefits of uninterrupted floor space.[26] But the fact that the building caused such a public furor in the City highlighted the role that traditional facades had played in public life. The architectural history of the City had until this point been dominated by the idea of the facade, in part due to confined building plots built up on three sides, and in part because the uniformity of office buildings inherently prohibited expressive design and thus relied on an elaborate frontage. As a result, cladding materials, which could be carved, molded, or decorated with more identifiable characteristics, continued to be popular well after the arrival of steel and glass, despite the economic efficiencies associated with the latter.[27] In the 1950s, Gresham Street and Cheapside were reconstructed with various developer-led structures that amounted to an almost continuous facade of cavity-filled Portland stone cladding known as "roach," which decked pseudomodern facades by the likes of Ellis, Clarke & Gallanaugh and Trehearne & Norman, Preston & Partners, among others. Grander buildings were adorned with various types of polished stone, which were commonly used in bank facades in the 1950s and became particularly fashionable in the 1970s for their ease of cleaning and reflective qualities.[28]

Although neo-Georgian architecture was the most common architectural idiom for banks, conventions of outward display varied across the banking sector, which in the City had a very specific structure. On account of its mercantile roots, the City had developed a unique set of banking institutions, each dealing with the different needs of each industry. In addition to foreign banks, in the postwar period there were three types of bank within its boundaries: merchant banks (private houses established to finance overseas trade, which became specialists in mergers and acquisitions and corporate finance in the postwar period), discount houses (intermediaries in the money markets working closely with the Bank of England to regulate liquidity levels), and the clearing banks (now known as retail banks, originally emerging as joint stock banks in the mid-nineteenth century, dealing with the finances of the general public).

These three strands of banking had distinct personalities, which were expressed architecturally. For example, unlike the monumental, public-facing approach of the clearing banks, merchant banks opted for a more domestic scale, based on early banking house architecture, to reflect their private status and familial structure. During their ascendency in the nineteenth century, the merchant banks adopted a mixture of styles characteristic of the age; the restrained grandeur of their buildings evoked self-assurance and decorum. Richard Norman Shaw's Queen Anne–style design (1881) for Baring Brothers—described by Pevsner as "very domestic, and not at all for display"—evoked the family house with its red brick facade; Hambros adopted a simple neo-Wren frontage; whereas Morgan Grenfell opted for a "chaste frenchified Palladian style."[29] Rothschild bank adopted an enclosed courtyard to further emphasize its inwardness and discretion, a spatial motif that was repeated in subsequent premises on the site. The meaning of

59-67 GRESHAM STREET E.C.2

Embracing 27-36 WOOD STREET and having
important frontages to
ALDERMANBURY AND LOVE LANE, E.C.2

Joint Architects : *Sir John Burnet, Tait & Partners and Felix Wilson & Partners.*

A New Office Building with Every Modern Convenience now under Construction
by Messrs. Holland & Hannen & Cubitts Ltd. To be completed by December 1955

CENTRAL HEATING • ELECTRIC LIFTS • EXCELLENT NATURAL
LIGHT • PUBLIC RESTAURANT IN BASEMENT • CAR PARK
AT GROUND LEVEL

TOTAL NET FLOOR AREA 211,500 SQUARE FEET

Basement	30,270 sq.ft.	Fourth Floor	24,350 sq. ft.
Ground Floor	16,680 ,, ,,	Fifth ,,	19,925 ,, ,,
First ,,	25,300 ,, ,,	Sixth ,,	19,925 ,, ,,
Second ,,	24,350 ,, ,,	Seventh ,,	14,825 ,, ,,
Third ,,	24,350 ,, ,,	Eighth ,,	11,600 ,, ,,

Sir John Burnet, Tait & Partners, 59–67 Gresham Street, London, 1955. From Jones Lang
Wootton, *Post War Office Buildings in the City of London and Its Environs* (London: Jones, Lang,
Wootton & Sons, 1955). Courtesy of Jones Lang LaSalle Limited.

CLEMENTS HOUSE
14-16-18 GRESHAM STREET E.C.2

Contractors : *Harry Neal Ltd.*　　　　　　　　Architects : *Trehearne & Norman Preston & Partners.*

AN OFFICE BUILDING NOW UNDER CONSTRUCTION
ELECTRIC PASSENGER LIFTS　　　CENTRAL HEATING
EXTENSIVE STRONG-ROOM ACCOMMODATION

Basement	12,910 sq. ft.	Fourth Floor	14,960 sq. ft.
Ground Floor	14,200 ,, ,,	Fifth ,,	14,960 ,, ,,
First ,,	14,580 ,, ,,	Sixth ,,	14,960 ,, ,,
Second ,,	14,960 ,, ,,	Seventh ,,	11,960 ,, ,,
Third ,,	14,960 ,, ,,	Eighth ,,	8,550 ,, ,,

TOTAL NET FLOOR AREA 137,000 SQUARE FEET

Trehearne & Norman, Preston & Partners, Clements House, London, 1955. From Jones Lang Wootton, *Post War Office Buildings in the City of London and Its Environs* (London: Jones, Lang, Wootton & Sons, 1955). Courtesy of Jones Lang LaSalle Limited.

this smaller scale was linked to the merchant banks' line of work, which relied upon close relationships with their customers and an emphasis on privacy. As Paul Ferris wrote in 1960, "Without exception the merchant banks share a distaste for publicity. Their reputation is what counts, they say—and that, they argue, involves the exercise of absolute discretion."[30] Consequently, most merchant banking houses relied on their domestic appeal. At Lazard's bank on Poultry, designed by Gunton & Gunton in 1927, for example, the use of red brick was "deliberately informal" on the suggestion of the directors, who thought the building ought to look like a provincial bank transported to the capital.[31] As Ferris pointed out, the frontage reinforced its exclusivity: "With a coat of arms and two night buttons, one for the porter and one for the caretaker," it doesn't *say* "Lazards."[32]

Discount houses, on the other hand, made little attempt to visibly brand their workspaces; there was no need for a public image, as their business was with a few important institutions within the Square Mile. Aside from the largest and most influential house, the Union Discount Company (which commissioned its purpose-built headquarters at 39 Cornhill in 1890), almost every other discount house resided within rented accommodation. Discount houses were required to be reactive to the state of the market, facilitate the movement of cash throughout the City, and assist the Bank of England in regulating the money supply. This was reflected in their geographical development within the triangle bounded by Threadneedle Street, Gracechurch Street, and King William Street; as agile intermediaries, it was vital that the houses were located in between the major banks, the Stock Exchange, and the Bank of England. In place of a prominent facade, the brand of each house was articulated through the face-to-face meetings held ritualistically every day and by their defiant sartorial signifier: the top hat. When Union Discount sought to refurbish its headquarters, initial plans were to entirely demolish the building, including the facade, in favor of a more flexible interior that could accommodate the changes in the London money market in the 1970s. The priority was maintaining a central location on a prestigious street, which was "very important for physically accomplishing business day by day in the busier, more varied markets now operating," rather than retaining its historic architectural image.[33] For the other houses, rentable dwellings were efficient as they not only

Morgan Grenfell merchant bank offices, 23 Great Winchester Street, 1926 by Mewes & Davis. London Metropolitan Archives (City of London). London Picture Archive, ref 51322.

offered the maximum flexibility, but to a certain extent also provided the cover of conformity, thereby enabling a visual assimilation with the City establishment. Discount houses were entirely reliant upon the cartelized composition of British banking. These institutions were unique not only to Britain, but to the City of London in particular, a place where location had currency.[34] A generic, speculative facade on Cornhill offered a number and street name that was more important to the discount houses than any visible architectural ensemble.

Quite in contrast to the discount houses, clearing banks historically retained the most visible banking presence in the City of London. Established as joint stock organizations in the mid-nineteenth century, these vast institutions were the first to accept deposits from middle-class individuals and emerged as a public alternative to the private banking houses that dominated the capital.[35] Challenging the elite and privileged world of private banking, as well as the Bank of England's monopoly, the clearing banks grew to become public symbols of security and stability in the British economy. Operating through a vast network of branch banks extending to the provinces, the geographical reach and quantity of clearing banks ensured that their architecture was more varied and visible throughout Britain, behaving explicitly as a marketing device.[36]

Facades were thus a self-conscious and explicit form of advertising for clearing banks. Where giant orders and monumental classicism were employed to invoke strength and permanence during the nineteenth century, these features also acted as expressions of the banking hall inside, which had been obsolete in the private houses that preceded them and were thus a symbol of the new democratic approach to finance.[37] National Provincial's headquarters at 15 Bishopsgate, designed by John Gibson in 1862, were demonstrative of such grandiose displays adopted by the clearing banks at the height of Britain's imperial heyday. As the banking sector expanded, the design of bank facades also had to negotiate two conflicting factors that came with a City location: the desire for an imposing street frontage and the necessity of a prestigious address. Space requirements for the clearing banks were not paralleled by other sectors in the Square Mile and thus presented difficulties within awkward, medieval sites, such as Lombard Street, surrounding the Bank of England.[38] The solution, demonstrated by the Barclays Bank headquarters at 54 Lombard Street, was to separate the facade from the spatial arrangement of the interior, such that the building took the form of a screen with a warren of rooms and connecting corridors behind.[39] This approach was reinforced by the fact that almost all banks in the City employed different architects for the interior and exterior of the building—usually commissioning external practitioners for the exterior shell and in-house designers for interiors, as the latter were knowledgeable about the working methods and practices of the institution.[40]

As clearing banks increased in size due to mergers after World War I, giant art deco structures with "wedding cake" setbacks entered the Square Mile, epitomized by the designs of Edwin Lutyens and Herbert Baker. Inspired by the civic architecture of American cities, this genre of financial building—referred to by Pevsner as "big-business classicism"—became the norm in the City of London since it also conformed to building height regulations.[41] However, prejudice against the perceived crassness and greed of American banking meant that many banks adopting this style denied its transatlantic origins, while others opted for neo-Georgian. As Booker notes, the acceptance of the American style was not connected to any change in banking ethics in London, but rather due to the economic benefits of that mode of design. This was particularly true for banks that were their own developers, meaning that "the taller the building, the more lucrative the return from rented offices, and the greater the temptation to following American styling."[42]

Height and its attendant associations would add a literal and representational dimension to City facades after World War II. High-rise towers of glass and concrete slowly began to proliferate from the 1960s onward as the financial sector and its architecture was increasingly internationalized. New forms and a new customer base triggered a shift in the mode of architectural communication for banks and other financial institutions, as buildings were valued less for what they could express in local terms and more for what they could narrate globally. Towers had a graphic, symbolic power that could speak without being read or interpreted, as the neoclassical face had demanded. Of course, this supposedly universal language required translation in the context of the City, and the next decades were fraught with cultural and legal battles to bring the tall building into the gentlemanly fortress.

Union Discount, 39 Cornhill, 1890 by J. Macvicar Anderson. London Metropolitan Archives (City of London). London Picture Archive, ref 38814.

Expert Packaging

In the main, we require from buildings, as from men, two kinds of goodness: first, the doing their practical duty well: then that they be graceful and pleasing in doing it.
John Ruskin, "The Virtues of Architecture," in
The Stones of Venice, vol. 1 (London: Smith, Elder, and Co., 1886),
quoted in National Provincial Bank Ltd. Press Release, 1964

When the nineteenth century writer and art critic John Ruskin wrote his epoch-defining treatise, he could hardly have imagined that its moralizing prose would have been used to justify the demolition of a historic edifice in favor of a steel and glass tower. Even less so given that the quote was used for a London bank building. Ruskin, who when asked to speak to the Bradford city council members in 1858 on the Gothic proposal for their new wool exchange famously told them, "I *do not* care about this exchange of yours," argued that good architecture should be "an expression of national life and character," which did not extend to the realm of commerce.[43] In *The Stones of Venice*, he claimed that one dimension of a building's "practical duty" was to "talk," "to record facts and express feelings; or of churches, temples, public edifices, treated as books of history, to tell such history clearly and forcibly."[44] It expressed the Victorian preoccupation with visual communication, predominantly through style—which for Ruskin could only be Gothic—to which the ideology of the modernist tower was vehemently opposed.

Yet when National Provincial Bank invoked *Stones* in its press release, the equivalence of style, morality, and national character was at the core of the message. Advocating for the demolition of John Gibson's banking hall and the City of London Club by Philip Hardwick (1833–1834) to make room for its new high-rise headquarters, National Provincial Bank's statement was published prior to a public inquiry initiated by the LCC in an attempt to save both structures. It argued that neither had sufficient merit to remain and were both a hindrance to progress; Gibson's hall was unsuited to the bank's space requirements in a changing age, and demanded costly and specialist maintenance.[45] It went on, "Architectural merit is not merely a question of what a building looks like. ... 15 Bishopsgate can no longer be said to do its practical duty well and is quite incapable of being adapted to modern conditions."[46] Modernity was, for the bank, the crux of the issue. Written in the same year that Baker's neo-Georgian Barclays Bank HQ was completed, the institution wished to communicate its desire to be a forward-thinking bank in the new age of consumer banking. Quoting "an eminent architect, who had no part in the design," the statement described the building as "a really remarkable creation, a great tower standing in its own piazza in the very centre of the City of London. No other age could have produced this solution; it is one that arises from and overcomes the effects of congestion; it is the outcome of many minds bent on the same problem; belongs utterly to us; and can be seen, as I would like you to see it, as a significant hostage to our own future as a nation. ... It will flood the old canyon streets with sun."

For National Provincial, the modernist tower was a technology and a style that precisely encapsulated the spirit of the age as well as the "national character" that Ruskin espoused. But it also indicated a radical shift in the associations between style and attitude in banking, and more specifically the role played by the building facade in communicating the social functions of the bank in a changing economy.

Despite the spread of modernist office buildings after World War II, the head offices of the major clearing banks remained on the sites on which they had existed for over a century, still mostly in premises from the interwar period. However, from the mid-1960s, the architectural approach of clearing banks altered with bigger shifts in financial and property spheres. In keeping pace with the regulatory changes and internationalization of banking in the City, banks took on extra staff and expanded their operations to various sites throughout the Square Mile. Moves included Barclays leasing part of Holford's Paternoster Square, and the Midland sending departments to Mariner House on Coopers Row (completed in 1963), a speculative development designed by Carl Fisher & Associates for Metropolitan & Provincial Properties Ltd. By the late 1970s, 32 percent of floor space in the City was taken by banks, half of which was occupied by Barclays (6 percent), Midland (3 percent), and the newly formed National Westminster Bank (9 percent).[47] The latter, formed by merging National Provincial and Westminster banks in 1968, represented the first major amalgamation between clearing banks.[48] The merger was a defensive strategy to prevent either establishment being taken over by competitors amid a hostile period of takeover mania in the City during the 1960s, causing banks to grow larger than ever.[49]

In the decade prior to its merger, National Provincial Bank had already been making provisions for expansion and modernization in the form of the tower on its existing site at 15 Bishopsgate. Designed in 1959 by its in-house architect, Frank Norman James, whose Canterbury branch for the same bank (1957) was later Grade II listed, the scheme covered two acres of land, which the bank had purchased in eighteen parcels over its 130-year occupation of the site.[50] James's design was radical for the City, although a poor imitation of American precedents. Taking the form of a 120-meter tower, the scheme comprised three eight-story glass cubes with service layers in between, bound on two sides by oversized vertical bracing, and a large plaza in front. With echoes of Skidmore, Owings & Merrill's (SOM's) headquarters for Chase Manhattan in New York (1957–1963) and GMW's putative design for Commercial Union and P&O in the City, the National Provincial scheme was designed to bring together its 1,100 employees, who were then scattered across three separate buildings, and provide room for growth.

While National Provincial was the first bank to adopt the glass tower, it was not the first institution to do so, nor the first building of its kind in the City. Following the abolition of building controls in the mid-1950s, developers looked to American glass curtain wall buildings and their modular techniques as models of cost- and time-efficiency. The City of London Real Property Company, which employed in-house architects, started to produce buildings around this period that mimicked SOM's buildings in New York, including Fountain House (by W. H. Rogers and consulting architect Howard Robertson, 1954–1958), which was based on Gordon Bunshaft's design for Lever House (completed in 1954), whose modular systems and shell-and-core structure enabled economies of scale. Anonymity permitted by the rationalized grid also added value, as demonstrated by one of the biggest lessor scheme developments in the City, London Wall (1960–1964), planned by City architect Anthony Mealand in collaboration with the LCC, and conceived as the commercial counterpart to the Barbican residential development to the north. Compulsory purchase powers enabled the Corporation to utilize a strict set of building regulations based around a modular curtain wall system to produce five eighteen-story blocks standing obliquely to a six-lane highway. The result was total visual uniformity despite

F. Norman James's design for the National Provincial headquarters, 1959. Printed in "Bank and LCC Battle over Plans for City Skyscraper," *Evening Standard*, February 18, 1964. Courtesy of *Evening Standard*.

Fountain House (1957) by W. H. Rogers for the City of London Real Property Company, 1957. London Metropolitan Archives (City of London). London Picture Archive, ref 39291.

Photograph showing five new postwar office buildings along London Wall (1960–1965). Copyright William Gordon Davis. Courtesy London Metropolitan Archives, ref. SC/GL/PHO/A/368/1.

being designed by five architects each working with one to five developers.[51]

This scheme won the Corporation high praise, likely because of its association with the LCC and its status as one of the few "planned" schemes in the financial district. Nairn celebrated the development as "the only consistently modern part of the City," with "moments of brittle magnificence," while Pevsner agreed it was of "high aesthetic value and London's most advanced concept of central area development."[52] Over the next decade the glass curtain wall became more widespread as the language of commercial architecture in London. Modular and systems building was advocated by the government for use by local authorities, particularly under the Labour prime minister Harold Wilson in the 1960s, part of the enthusiasm for technological and scientific innovation as a path for bolstering Britain's position on the global stage. As historian Alan Powers notes, "Images of modern architecture formed a natural backdrop for his vision of Britain's future," an opinion also voiced by the City Corporation, which introduced a "high buildings policy" in 1962 advocating for "clusters" of "well-related and well-designed" towers, provided they were "designed to a common idiom": the curtain wall tower.[53] Several high-rise buildings emerged in the financial center as a result of the new policy, including GMW's Commercial Union development, and the proposal by Mies van der Rohe for developer Peter Palumbo's doomed Mansion House Square scheme.[54] However, as the glass curtain wall became more commonly used among developers over the next decade, critics found fault with its derivative style. As a former practitioner of the LCC Architects' Department, Rodney Gordon, later commented: "To us at the LCC the private commercial sector ... represented the antithesis of creative architecture. ... They were bastardising the Miesian philosophy ... producing crude, ill-proportioned, naive, matchbox buildings, taking the elevations and whatever else that was pre-designed by manufacturers straight from their catalogues."[55]

Qualitative distinctions between the Miesian original and the "bastardized" copy were common among critics of postwar commercial architecture, despite the fact that, as Reinhold Martin notes, "the status as a singular artwork generally attributed to Mies's Seagram Building, for example (as distinct from its many 'copies'), is rendered obsolete by the very idea of the curtain wall as a generalized technological system."[56] What Gordon and his LCC colleagues were lamenting was the lack of an "idea" in the production process and the privileging of noncerebral skills—such as valuation—over the academic and "creative" processes typically associated with the profession.

National Provincial's tower had less to do with cost calculations—though as a bank, these were of course of paramount consideration—and more to do with the changing function of the bank. From one perspective, this meant the accommodation of practical changes that the bank was already experiencing with new technology. In its press release, National Provincial explained that, in addition to staff provision, the existing building was unsuited

Model of the proposed tower block for the Mansion House Square scheme, 1 Poultry, City of London, at dusk, 1981. John Donat / RIBA Collections.

to the use of telephones, typewriters, adding machines, and book-keeping machines as the acoustics rendered it all but impossible to keep noise to a reasonable level, while the banking hall was becoming increasingly problematic "to light, to heat, to ventilate and to keep clean."[57] It also claimed that the demolition of these two buildings would allow for the widening of Bishopsgate and Old Broad Street, which was deemed to be of commercial interest to the bank as a main thoroughfare through the Square Mile, and enable the tower to be connected to the City's much anticipated raised walkway scheme.

But the building also had symbolic value at a moment when the social function of the bank was being reconfigured. After World War II, the relaxation of wartime economic controls insti-gated mergers, expansion, and the formation of international banking consortiums, which, alongside advances in comput-ing, enabled banks to offer a more diverse array of services for customers and to capitalize on the newly available surplus cash of the aspiring working and middle classes. As the commercial operations of British banks became more publicity focused, many began to reconsider their built appearance as part of a bigger pub-lic relations policy.[58] The goal was to attract the new, wealthier demographic, who began to conceive of money less as an inert possession that should be stashed in a vault, and more as an operational commodity that could be invested and cultivated. By the 1960s, banks had recognized that their Victorian and interwar banking halls were an insufficient architectural tool for engaging its new public, and they thus sought more open models that replaced Portland stone with glass curtain walls. Confidence was no longer expressed in the thickness of a vault door, but through transparency. Customers would put their faith in bank employees to use their money effectively, not simply in the strength of the building to protect it.[59]

Unfortunately for National Provincial, their rhetoric was not convincing enough for Housing Minister Keith Joseph, who concluded that the Gibson banking hall was "a fine building and a good example of Victorian classic bank architecture," well worthy of preservation.[60] Demolition of the City of London Club was granted, and so the architects reluctantly drew up a new scheme incorporating the nineteenth-century banking hall. Finally, on November 5, 1964, five years after the project was conceived, the Corporation gave outline planning permission, but within weeks the Labour government imposed a stranglehold on commercial construction via office development permits for all developments over 300 square meters. Planning permission was ultimately rescinded, forcing them to find alternative office space, the urgent need for which made them susceptible to higher rents.[61] Frank Norman James was perturbed by the new legislation: "It cramps our freedom of planning very seriously," he argued. "We shall have to do some serious rethinking of the disposition of the departments."[62] Inconvenience was exacerbated by the fact that in the five years since the redevelopment plans were conceived, National Provincial had expanded substantially, acquiring North Central Finance (1958–1959), Isle of Man Bank (1961), and District Bank (1962). The latter alone added 550 branches to the bank's network, making its total 2,240.[63] The increased scale and complexity of its organization forced the bank to seek temporary rented accommodation while reapplying for ODP permission. Architect Richard Seifert and developer Harry Hyams's latest high-rise project at Drapers Gardens was one of the few substantial new developments available for leasing, and despite the exorbitant rent of £5 per square foot—the highest then ever paid in the City—National Provincial agreed to lease the entire building.[64]

Drapers Gardens became an unanticipated marketing opportunity for the bank. The design, credited to partner Len Watson, was sensitive to the complex nature of demand in the City, whereby tenant preferences were intimately connected to changes in financial markets.[65] Whereas the initial proposal accepted by the Drapers' Company had taken the form of four low-rise blocks (by architect Milton Cashmore), Seifert, through his manipulation of the plot ratio, was able to recommend a singular and imposing glass tower. Projecting high above the cornice line in between the Bank of England and the London Stock Exchange, the building was clad with curved precast concrete horizontal fins (actually projecting air-conditioning ducts) and displayed a rhythmic horizontality, and a "pop" edge, tiled in lustrous white mosaic. At ground level, the entrance was approached via a sunken courtyard garden, with steps leading up to a podium level, soon to be connected to the City's anticipated raised pedway scheme, so that the building would hover above the dense streets below. Seifert and Hyams may have been a bold choice for National Provincial given the numerous, often unfavorable press reports about their Centrepoint project and the pop nature of Seifert's aesthetic. However, Seifert's buildings were becoming increasingly prevalent in the City, with other schemes including Royex House on London Wall and Guinness Mahon on Gracechurch Street. His work was loud enough to capture the public eye but safe enough that their gaze wouldn't linger too long—an ideal combination for a long-standing institution that desired a new image while simultaneously sending the message of business as usual.

Seifert's building became an emblem of efficiency and technological innovation. These themes were particularly important for the bank to convey to its customer base as it sought to promote itself as up to date with the latest in banking techniques in an age of computerization. Over half of the floor space in the building was dedicated to automation, with the top nine floors given over to computer rooms and clearing (also enabling efficient cooling via proximity to the plant rooms), and a sculpture named *The Spirit of Automation* by Fred Millet in the entrance hall. In organizational terms, the building's section revealed a sliding scale of importance. Occupying the next highest floors were the executive boardrooms and entertainment spaces, positioned to receive the most prestigious views over London, with floors for legal, advances, accounting, stock department and communications, messengers

Drapers Gardens, 1967, by Richard Seifert & Partners, branded with the National Provincial logo during the final months of construction. Reproduced by kind permission of NatWest Group © 2023.

and engineers, respectively, below. The building was received favorably by the business community. Heralding the tower as "just about the only aesthetically pleasing skyscraper in the City," the *Stock Exchange Gazette* described the building's "considerable grace" and sculptural form, praising "its success, as many of New York's skyscrapers do, in having a sense of proportion which is so lacking in the majority of Londons upturned matchboxes."[66]

National Provincial's move to Drapers Gardens represented the first time that any bank, or indeed any major financial institution, within the City had adopted a tall building for its headquarters. The Stock Exchange itself had two years to go before commissioning its concrete monolith, and Commercial Union was still in progress. Cashmore and Grosvenor's thirty-five-story Britannic House (1967) was perhaps the only comparable purpose-built headquarters in the City, but it was built for its tenants, British Petroleum, well beyond the City core, northeast of the Barbican. By appropriating Seifert's modern pop aesthetic, National Provincial Bank not only aligned itself with progressive banking but also indicated a change in the function of architecture in the process of image-making for financial institutions in the City.

The vertical silhouette of the tall building became a convenient graphic motif for publicity. By 1967, National Provincial had fully adopted Drapers Gardens within its own branding strategy. Such an approach was becoming increasingly common among the clearing banks as their shifting commercial strategies placed emphasis on public relations, of which their buildings formed a key part. In 1964, Midland Bank was the first to implement such a scheme, setting up a design panel in 1964 to enforce a consistent appearance in all elements, ranging from stationery to premises.[67] National Provincial bank followed suit in 1967, producing themed headed stationery and advertisements, alongside a commemorative publication about the new headquarters, entitled *A New London Landmark*, to be circulated to clients. Using bold colors and slick graphics, the pamphlet aligned Seifert's use of futuristic curves and stark lines with the bank's forward-looking, fast-paced business ethic. "Even a cursory tour of the new National Provincial Bank head offices gives one an insight into the future world of banking," claimed the pamphlet, "for quite obviously, this is not only a handsome building: it is also a business machine on a very large scale."[68]

Despite the time and money spent on Drapers Gardens, the "new London landmark" was quickly rendered obsolete as the

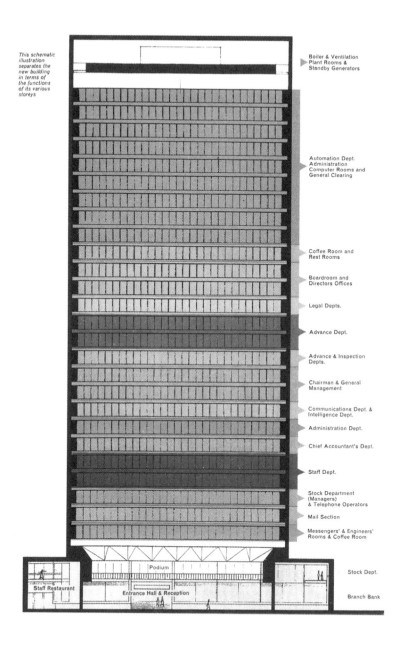

This schematic illustration separates the new building in terms of the functions of its various storeys

Boiler & Ventilation Plant Rooms & Standby Generators

Automation Dept. Administration Computer Rooms and General Clearing

Coffee Room and Rest Rooms

Boardroom and Directors Offices

Legal Depts.

Advance Dept.

Advance & Inspection Depts.

Chairman & General Management

Communications Dept. & Intelligence Dept.

Administration Dept.

Chief Accountant's Dept.

Staff Dept.

Stock Department (Managers) & Telephone Operators

Mail Section

Messengers' & Engineers' Rooms & Coffee Room

Podium

Staff Restaurant

Entrance Hall & Reception

Stock Dept.

Branch Bank

Section of Drapers Gardens showing the organization of departments in National Provincial Bank Ltd., *A New London Landmark* (London: National Provincial Bank Ltd., 1967). Reproduced by kind permission of NatWest Group © 2023.

Pages from National Provincial Bank Ltd., *A New London Landmark* (London: National Provincial Bank Ltd., 1967). Reproduced by kind permission of NatWest Group © 2023.

merger with Westminster Bank took place less than a year after moving in, demanding a larger building and a new unified image. In a fortuitous turn of events, just six months after the merger, the ODP for the Bishopsgate site was granted to National Westminster, but Norman James's designs were now out of date.[69] Furthermore, the increased stringency of building controls in London now required a more ambitious set of tactics to get through planning. A number of practices were invited by the bank to submit proposals for a new building, including well-known architects such as Seifert, Basil Spence, Hugh Casson, and Frederick Gibberd. Seifert was, perhaps unsurprisingly, given the commission, partly because his proposal was unfeasibly cheap—mistakenly proposing to build it for £10 per foot rather than £100 per foot, as he'd intended—and partly because of his skill in getting around planning regulations.[70] "It needed to be somebody with much more experience than we had," explained Brian Burns, chief architect of National Westminster. "He had a big selling job to do to get things off the ground."

Seifert was popular among corporate clients due to his skills as a businessman and negotiator. He worked directly with every client and operated as a mediator between occupiers, developers, and local authorities, viewing himself as a problem solver who used economic restrictions and planning regulations as the design framework. As Seifert noted, "The chemistry of the architect is creative—he is a natural artist. He rarely has the calibre of a businessman, lawyer or accountant, but the successful practitioner of today has to be all these things."[71] Whereas the former head of the RIBA Lionel Brett had condemned the so-called developer's architect, perceiving commercial architects to be experiencing "crises of conscience" for their lack of artistic honesty, Seifert believed his straightforward, businesslike approach was the most ethical mode of working with a client.[72] Transparent communication was particularly important to Seifert, who prided himself on adhering to the cost specified in the initial contract.[73] One fundamental instrument in the firm's process was a written pre-design brief that would be circulated to clients and contractors, detailing "the functions and design intent of the building with suggested forms and materials ... as well as the organization and inter-relationship of component parts, costs and finishes, forms of construction, systems and timing," ensuring that the writing was "in a form which others are able to understand." Seifert believed this written format enabled the design process to be open rather than hidden behind "mystifying layers of verbiage and the dazzle of beautifully finished perspective drawings which are dramatically presented after the architect emerges from his studio following a suitably long delay, while his unrevealed research is subjected to the marvelous alchemy of the creative art."[74] While the architecture establishment labeled Seifert a philistine, the firm's pragmatic approach was popular with corporate clients and developers. As Brian Burns commented, National Westminster selected Seifert on the basis that "he knew his way through the legislation."[75]

Seifert also understood the branding potential of the high-rise building. At 185 meters, the final design for the National Westminster Tower went beyond the rudiments of the slab block and curtain wall, with a triangular footprint formed by three chevrons or *leaves*, cantilevered from a central concrete core or *trunk*, characteristic of the architect's sculptural approach to form. Richard Seifert & Partners was the first British commercial practice to experiment with reinforced concrete for office buildings in the 1960s.[76] Like the steel frame, precast concrete was a relatively cheap material that could be systematized, yet it also allowed for surface variety with a conventional slab skeleton. Critics frequently lambasted the firm's emphasis on the exterior shell as a form of "facadism" and a poor mimic—aesthetic and not ethic—of the socially conscious new brutalism. "The correct attitude in London is to ignore Seifert buildings, which run to circles, lozenges, zippy curves, sweeping angles and zigzag precast frames that make them look wrapped in rickrack, knitted on giant needles or baked in piecrusts," Ada Louise Huxtable wrote in 1971. "Seifert is an expert packager of commercial space."[77] Yet Seifert was openly in the game of "packaging." Prefiguring the landmark buildings that would proliferate in the 1980s and after, the sculptural facade was designed to be an independent icon that might easily be reproduced in the media or the minds of the public. In the case of the National Westminster Bank, this strategy was almost farcically overt, as the three-leaf format of the floor plan mimicked the three chevrons of the bank's insignia; when viewed from above, it became apparent that the tower was a three-dimensional extrusion of the company logo. Although Seifert never explicitly admitted to this, brushing off any similarities as mere coincidence, he did admit that the bank wanted the building "to be their emblem of advertising themselves all over the world."[78]

Emphasizing silhouettes, rather than facades, represented a marked shift in attitude toward the design of bank headquarters, and toward commercial architecture more generally in City of London. Where the face put forward by neo-Georgian buildings communicated a set of established values within a community, high-rise buildings expressed a competitive, individualist message to an international market. Such a shift was not simply a product of the changing aspirations of the financial institutions, but also of the City Corporation and its zealous implementation of the 1962 high buildings policy.[79] In the decade following its announcement, the strategy generated silhouettes like Drapers Gardens (99 m), Stock Exchange (100 m), Winchester House (74 m) and Commercial Union (118 m), and others such as Ethelburga House (98 m) and Angel Court (85 m) were in the pipeline.[80] Aligning itself with New York and other European central business districts like La Défense, the Corporation saw the high-rise tower as an international signifier of progress and success, and thus used plot ratios and consultations to encourage more vertical construction. "We had the impression all along that we were supposed to produce the focal point to that cluster of towers," claimed Burns. Seifert's associate Mike Byrne, confirmed "the idea of a tower of something up to 600 ft came from the City Corporation, certainly."[81]

Among the British clearing banks, American high-rise architecture was emulated for its associations with Wall Street, the leading international financial center that was paving the way in deregulation and innovations in commercial banking. Following several exploratory trips to the US during the project, Seifert brought back a number of techniques used in American construction to improve the technical and structural capacity of the building, as well as the building schedule. These included the facade's futuristic skin of aluminum mullions, which doubled as rails for automatic window cleaners, the tower's centrally controlled lift system, and the system of red polished cantilevers and concrete core, which enabled faster construction.[82] However, unlike the American real estate sector, British commercial property was yet to adopt the fast-track techniques that would appear in the next decade, rendering construction costly and slow. Furthermore, within the City of London, the system of appointing architects, contractors, and engineers

Model of Richard Seifert's first proposal for the National Westminster Tower, 1969. From National Westminster Tower press pack, 1971. Reproduced by kind permission of NatWest Group © 2023.

was entirely embedded within the old boys' network, often hiring on recommendation rather than through competitive tender. In the case of the tower, until 1972 project management was done by National Westminster's Premises Committee, usually used for day-to-day estates management, which was unable to cope with a project of such complexity.[83] In addition, all of the main contractors had a close relationship with either the bank or the architect, such as engineering company Pell Frischmann, which had worked with Seifert on numerous projects, including Centrepoint, and the main contractors John Mowlem & Co., loyal customers of National Provincial "for over half a century."[84]

Comparisons with the US became less than favorable in the coming decade, as the building came under frequent attack in the press. In the 1970s, financial commitment and the scale of the project in tandem with the difficult economic and political climate in Britain caused problems for National Westminster. Higher wage claims from building industry, energy crises, inflation, and planning obstacles meant severe delays and financial difficulties for the redevelopment scheme.[85] Initial reports in 1969 had estimated a total development cost of £43 million, but by 1977 this had reached £83.8 million, with a completion date of 1979, five years after the original deadline.[86] The *Daily Telegraph* called it "a damning indictment to our construction industry," comparing the project to Sears Tower in Chicago, which, despite being well over twice the height of the National Westminster Tower, was built in under three years, costing a total of £68.2 million.[87] Whereas in New York skyscrapers were increasingly emblematic of the power and innovation associated with finance capitalism, in the City of the 1970s, tall buildings seemed to encapsulate the long-held criticism of the financial center as a retrograde and insular community.

On its completion in 1981, the NatWest Tower projected an image of cosmopolitanism and internationalism in the City. Acting as an international brand icon, Seifert's media-ready silhouette was imprinted on the London skyline, prefiguring the rush of towers that would be built in the City's "eastern cluster" two decades later. However, the bank's reputation did not live up to the architectural statement. In an effort to salvage the project by cutting expenses, in 1976 National Westminster decided to overhaul its occupational strategy and use the building to house its growing international division rather than the head office. The idea was that the latter would remain at its nineteenth-century building at 41 Lothbury, thereby saving around £4.83 million in adaptation costs, while the location of the international division within the new tower "would give prestige and added importance to the expanding International operation" and symbolically align the new building with the new ambitions of the bank.[88] NatWest vigorously promoted the tower as part of its international branding strategy, releasing publications and press releases and even making a film about the building.[89] But by the early 1980s, National Westminster—like many other British financial institutions—had not made much headway globally, nor reviewed its organizational structure to align with the requirements of the global market. As one *Financial Times* journalist later remarked, "[National Westminster's] profitability is the envy of commercial banks all over the world, yet its UK management is wholly in-bred and often less than sparkling."[90] British retail banks paled in comparison to the enormous commercial banks in America, where deregulation had taken place six years earlier.

The architectural shift from secure neoclassical fortress to efficient and transparent machine to international symbol embodied by National Westminster was symptomatic of the broader transformations and struggles experienced by the British banking sector after the war. If neoclassical facades had once represented the face of banking in the local context of London, the vertical projection of the high-rise head office was a gesture toward a new consumer-focused approach to banking, communicating to a wider public beyond the capital. But the biggest changes were yet to come. In the next decade, deregulation led to the rapid erosion of distinction in British banking. Through mergers and acquisitions, clearing banks diversified their services into investment banking while retaining their retail function. This process of homogenization rendered the architectural demands of banks more generic, resulting in the proliferation of speculative architecture throughout the City, and across London, to the financial island of Canary Wharf and the shores of Southwark. Developer-led architecture came to dominate the City, where the building envelope had a function that extended beyond the representational into the contractual and economic calculations of the project. As banking became more complex in the post–Big Bang world, all that was solid in its graphic facades would soon melt into air.

Layers of Longevity

Take the cross-section of the SOM phases [of Broadgate]. ... Within lies the simplest form of construction imaginable—steel frame, metal decking, prefabricated lavatory units, packaged air-conditioning. At the perimeter is a veneer, no thicker than 10 cm, which transforms this utterly paradigmatic, international, interior world, into what purports to be localized, urbane, London respectability—stone balusters below, echoes of Louis Sullivan's Chicago above, Edwardian lushness everywhere. It does not matter too much what the skin itself represents because that too can be changed—and no doubt will be changed.
Duffy, *The Changing Workplace*, 1992[91]

When Broadgate first arrived in the City, it was admired universally for its adoption of advanced construction, engineering, and financing techniques, all of which were based on American precedents. Like the Big Bang itself, the financial center's architectural revolution of the 1980s was a product of the so-called special relationship between Britain and America, whereby the Chicago School's market capitalism transformed commercial buildings and the processes underpinning them. It was perhaps the acute awareness of the internationalism pervading the City's redevelopment that caused the City's then chief planning officer, Peter Rees, to intervene in Peter Foggo's design of the first phases of Broadgate for Arup Associates (1986–1987). Whereas Foggo had originally designed the complex with a robust steel exoskeleton, Rees insisted on using marble cladding "because we believed [the buildings] wouldn't be accepted as part of the City."[92] Seemingly continuing the old preconceptions about the stone facade emanating trust and legitimacy, or, as Rees put it, "the sense of permanence and solidity that you expected from a bank," Broadgate was wrapped in a protective layer of traditional "British values" to achieve commensurate market value.

Yet looking closer at the design, Broadgate's exterior subverted the conventional relationship between the facade and the building. In Foggo's design, thin slices of marble were attached to an exposed steel frame, interspersed with chunky bolts, brackets, and glass, as if to highlight the elevation's superficiality. As Rees himself commented, "If you look at Broadgate the facades look like you could just unbolt them. It's a very cynical use of stone."[93] Here

Photograph of 100 Liverpool Street, Broadgate, 1987 by Arup Associates, showing a thin layer of detached stone cladding. Courtesy of Danielle Willkens.

the facade was not simply distinct from the building, in the way that the Dutch architect Hendrik Petrus Berlage had so brilliantly expressed in the glazed tile curtain wall of Holland House on Bury Street (1916). Rather, it implied a reconceptualization of the facade as a component in an entire building system.

If the high-rise building of the 1960s communicated through a graphic impression of unity and wholeness, the groundscraper of the 1980s was defined by precisely the reverse. As architect and space planner Francis Duffy observed in his analysis of the later SOM phases of Broadgate, what made the new groundscraper remarkable was that it exploded the singular mass of an office building into an assemblage of layers, serviced by an assemblage of specialists. In this new architectural schema, the facade became the skin: the outermost envelope of the building, comprising the continuous surface of walls and roof. As just one element in a broader financial and infrastructural assembly, it became a mediating layer in the relationships between architects, developers, investors, and users.

Of course, the concept of the building envelope as a distinct financial component had existed since the uptake of shell-and-core construction methods during the first postwar property boom. Originating in the US, the practice entailed the developer and contracted architect providing the shell (structure and cladding) and core (the services, including washrooms, base plants, etc.), leaving the interior spaces for the occupier to finish during a "rent-free" tenancy period, by means of a contract furnisher. It meant that for developers, commercial buildings could be subdivided according to the number and size of tenants moving in rather than on a prelet basis, while occupiers could determine the organization and style of their offices.[94] By the 1980s, this model was used in almost all new construction in the City, both occupier-led and speculative, in part due to the increasing requirements of tenants to have good quality, bespoke interiors, and in part due to the need for adaptability with the changes in technology.[95]

Shell-and-core construction maximized the profitability of office building in both spatial and temporal dimensions. In spatial terms, the role of the shell was to wrap the building in the thinnest layer possible; architects and engineers devised lucrative ways to maximize floor area through minimizing the floor space taken up by heavy stone frontages, using pared-back steel frame structures with slender curtain wall facades. Universal open plan space was made possible through modular steel frames, which were valuable to the architect and the developer for their repeatability and easy legibility of cost/space relationships. But the appeal of shell-and-core buildings, like Fountain House or the London Wall development, wasn't simply floor area and economy. Performance over time was a less explicit but important factor of profitability. Occupiers could continually remodel the arrangement of their office throughout their occupancy cycle, while developers could accommodate an unlimited number of tenant combinations throughout the real estate cycle. Shell-and-core was commercially successful because it extended the building's economic productivity beyond the point of construction.

Indeed, the necessity for adaptation over time, or *flexibility*, had become a prominent subject within modernist architectural discourse in the postwar decades. Adrian Forty has claimed that the term offered "a way of dealing with the contradiction that arose between the expectation ... that the architect's ultimate concern in designing buildings was with their human use and occupation, and the reality that the architect's involvement in a building ceased at the very moment that occupation began."[96] Designing flexible buildings therefore enabled a semblance of future control beyond the point of completion. By the 1960s, the temporal dimension of architecture was being widely and critically explored across the professional spectrum. Neofuturist projects by groups like Archigram and the Metabolists implied architectural worlds in which nothing was fixed and anything was possible. Structurist architects like Herman Hertzberger, Piet Blom, and Aldo van Eyck designed limitless building systems comprised of "linked identical spatial units," which, in theory, could be repeated, extended, used, and reused ad infinitum.[97] Pragmatists like John Weeks, Richard Llewellyn-Davies, and Peter Cowan, in Britain, and Ezra Ehrenkrantz in the US, acknowledged the economic merits of planned obsolescence and indeterminacy through their experiments in state-led hospital and public school design.[98] Proposed during a period of widespread sociocultural upheaval, all of these groups to some degree elicited the sociopolitical value of responsive, rather than prescriptive, design, positioning the architect as the creator of continually changing environments rather than static buildings.

Within these experiments, the facade—as a representational elevation—became a redundant concept as the exterior of the building was simply an extension of the systemic logic of indeterminacy underpinning the entire building. As Llewellyn-Davies wrote in an article entitled "Endless Architecture," the goal was to create "loose fitting and extendable building envelopes."[99] Here the modular Miesian shell was taken to its logical extreme, as the outermost layer of the building was the element that permitted its intrinsic extendibility in all directions, rather than simply marking spatial (and thus financial) limits of the floor plate. *Envelope* thus implied a reconceptualization of the facade as a three-dimensional layer that was simultaneously an integral part of building *performance*—a term that became common parlance in both architectural and business fields at this moment, indicating an intertwining of the temporal and economic aspects of the new architecture.

Shell-and-core office buildings in the postwar City embodied a rather limited definition of the term *flexibility* in comparison to these radical experiments in structural adaptability. While the modularity of the curtain wall building theoretically offered continual change, the realities of stringent planning regulations in the 1950s, limited building plots, and a seller's market restricted the adaptive potential of this technology to the provision of universal space. Here the shell continued to act as a container for space. Developers exploited the flexibility of the steel frame module only to the extent that it enabled them to achieve the maximum floor space area in any given plot ratio framework; there was, as yet, no financial advantage in having a stake in the structural life of the building after completion. The somewhat superficial level of flexibility permitted by the open plan was at this point sufficient enough to ensure substantial profitability, as the needs of financial firms were relatively straightforward, in terms of technology and personnel organization.

It wasn't until the 1980s that a more profound detachment of the building envelope took place. As shifts in the nature of organizations and the economy necessitated more readily adaptable buildings, so a more structurally integrated conception of flexibility entered into the mainstream of office design. Growth and the instabilities caused by financial deregulation and the rapid expansion of the service sector meant that organizations became increasingly volatile and susceptible to fluctuations in staff numbers. After the Big Bang, mergers between merchant and foreign banks, jobbers and brokers gave rise to the new investment banks of a scale hitherto unseen in Britain. By the end of the 1980s, investment banking was the largest financial sector in the City, employing approximately 20 percent of the City's workforce and operating in multiple fields such as corporate finance, capital markets, corporate lending, and pension funds.[100] Such exposure rendered these firms susceptible to market fluctuations, which in turn demanded more responsive buildings, thereby putting a premium on the flexible use of space.[101] These banks were not only large but highly sensitive to shifts in the market, and therefore subject to changes in scale and personnel. Adaptive layouts were thus appealing on economic grounds and essential in organizational terms. With the ever-increasing value of financial transactions, the rising cost of better-qualified staff, and growing investments in IT and property, corporations were looking to cut down occupancy costs where possible. *Churn*—the industry term for staff turnover and subsequent reorganization—was potentially an extremely expensive and regular occurrence.[102] Furthermore, the uptake of in-house dealing floors meant that the same companies were now highly dependent on information technology, which not only had certain infrastructural requirements but also was in a constant state of flux. These features of the new financial environment put a premium on highly adaptable buildings, yet for the most part existing building stock in the City was incapable of accommodating such indeterminacy.

According to the outcomes of the highly influential ORBIT report by DEGW and Eosys, the high rate of obsolescence in existing

City office buildings had been caused by their complete lack of adaptability, revealing that several large banks with buildings only ten years old were out of date due to their incapacity to accommodate change and technological innovation.[103] Redundancy was caused by limitations in scale alongside the interconnectedness of the structural and cosmetic elements of the building, which prevented the constant updating of service provisions required in the electronic age. The report—or more accurately, Francis Duffy, who had been working on this solution since completing his doctoral thesis in the 1960s—claimed that the way to overcome these shortcomings was to break down the static office building, with its immovable central service core, into an assemblage of independent, temporally defined layers: the *shell*, incorporating the main structure, with a lifespan of fifty years; *services*, including elements such as ducting, air conditioning, and plumbing, lasting fifteen years; *scenery*, the internal partitions, large furniture, and so on, lasting five to seven years; and *sets*, including plants, paper, smaller furniture, and so on, changing every day.[104] In practice, these layered buildings took the form of deep-plan structures with atria and dispersed cores to enable easy service maintenance; generous slab-to-slab heights for cable and ducting cavities; and steel-frame shells with detachable facades.[105] Through this process of dismantling, Duffy reconceived of the office building as slices of time, each calibrated to ensure the maximum profitable outcome for both developer and user. This way, the shell could be built and let quickly and efficiently, and interiors could be maintained and updated more easily and economically than ever before.

In DEGW's approach, the open plan gave way to the open building, redefining architecture as a *process* rather than a fixed form. "Our basic argument is that there isn't such a thing as a building," wrote Duffy. "A building properly conceived is several layers of longevity of built components."[106] Like Llewelyn-Davies, John Weeks, and Peter Cowan before them, for DEGW the core argument for this mode of deconstruction was economic; in most cases, expenditure on the updating of buildings usually outweighed the initial cost of construction, rendering the life of a building after completion just as important, if not more important, than the original structure. As Duffy noted: "It proves that architecture is actually of very little significance—it's nugatory."[107] DEGW became successful because it claimed to consider the performance of the building throughout its entire lifecycle in order that it retain value for

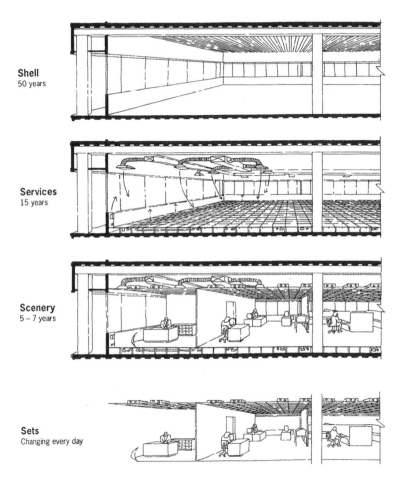

Shell
50 years

Services
15 years

Scenery
5 – 7 years

Sets
Changing every day

DEGW diagram breaking down the building into temporally defined layers: shell, services, scenery, and sets. From Francis Duffy, *The Changing City* (London: Bulstrode Press, 1989). Courtesy of AECOM.

the user and the investor. In turn, the layered building eventually became the standard for high-specification commercial structures in the City of London because it eased the architectural and economic burden of organizational change for the occupier—be it personnel-oriented, technological, or cosmetic—while also acting as a highly effective financial instrument, which was continually *productive* in real estate terms by virtue of enabling its workspaces to be continually *reproduced*, ever renewing and reinstating the building's profitability.

Within this context, the building's envelope was configured as a responsive layer, rather than a fixed form. Prefiguring the "membranes" of blob theory and the "skin" of so-called intelligent buildings, which would emerge in the coming decades with the prominence of computation in architectural design, Duffy's shell (which he would later call a skin), was conceived as an interface among the user, the designer, and external conditions. Yet whereas these biomorphic conceptualizations of the skin would be designed with environmental and atmospheric externalities in mind, Duffy's shell was primarily sensitive to economic conditions. Here the facade was a framework for change within a context of financial instability and business volatility. The success of Duffy's deconstructed office was not predicated on making the future conditions of an organization *knowable*, but rather based on constructing an environment in which anything could happen.[108] In this formulation, the building shell actively provided the conditions for change. As Duffy explained, rather than "attempting to use buildings to exploit behavior patterns, it is sanest to try to design buildings and organizations which permit all possible behaviors to coexist without coming into conflict."[109] In effect, DEGW adopted a systems design approach in order to resolve the longstanding temporal conflict between architectural longevity and organizational flux. For Duffy, the organization was a complex, self-regulating system, which functioned most effectively when unfettered by architectural impositions. "The building," Duffy wrote, "is the framework that permits technology, organization and communications to exist," and the study of work is "the investigation of complex relationships."[110] In order to enable the organization to function effectively, the building would need to become part of its operational process.

Within DEGW's process of "shearing layers," as Stewart Brand would later label it, the architect's role therefore became to design a framework that the user could adapt in order to perform their part within the continually changing market, and in some sense to speculate on what form that future adaptation might take. As Duffy noted of DEGW's practice in the 1980s, "The unit of analysis for us isn't the building, it's the use of the building through time. Time is the essence of the real design problem."[111] The reconceptualization of the building as an ongoing process—or rather, the reconceptualization of the architect's involvement with the building as extending beyond the point of completion—in turn affected the operation of the architecture firm. Writing in 1984, Duffy argued that market shifts had necessitated a reconsideration of practice in relation to time, calling for a reorientation of the architect's relationship with the client from one that was *synchronic*, where "each transaction is separate and comes at a unique moment in time," to one that was *diachronic*— "that is, continuing and developing through time."[112] In effect, Duffy was calling for architects to adopt a consultancy model, whereby architectural labor was reconfigured as a process that was ongoing, rather than bound by a contractually fixed end point.

Duffy's call for operational innovation was driven by a high level of precariousness and competition in the marketplace, caused in part by the rapid increase of commercial practices working in Britain the 1980s. The Thatcher government's cessation of funding for public housing toward the end of the previous decade, and general emphasis on privatization, caused a rush of public sector redundancies for the many architects previously employed by the state. To add to an already competitive environment, the deregulation of the architectural profession ensued, beginning with the ruling of the Monopolies and Mergers Commission to abolish architects' fee scales in favor of a free market approach, and culminating in the overhaul of the RIBA rulebook in 1981. The latter finally allowed practices to advertise, to "go public" on the London Stock Exchange, and to engage in property development and the construction business.[113] With jobs scarce, a surge of firms entered the private sector. Without the protection of fee scales, architects were forced to lower their rates and develop significant areas of specialization.[114] In addition, the familiar City firms like Richard Seifert & Partners, Fitzroy Robinson & Partners, GMW, T. P. Bennett & Son, and Sheppard Robson, Renton Howard Levin Wood (RHLW) Architects, Rolfe Judd Group Practice, Sir John Burnet, Tait & Partners, Covell Matthews Wheatley and Partners, and YRM continued to be highly active in the City, with many expanding with the new opportunities of the Big Bang building boom. By the mid-1980s, Fitzroy Robinson and YRM had over 250 employees, and even the smaller practices such as Elsom Pack & Roberts had around one hundred staff, with Rolfe Judd employing over fifty.[115] Newer firms brought with them specialist expertise, particularly in the realm of architectural fit-outs, as in the case of Whinney Mackay-Lewis, or space planning, with the likes of DEGW taking center stage.[116]

In response to the increasing complexity of user needs, the market demanded that architectural practices develop departments capable of managing different elements of the lifecycle of the building in order to remain competitive. The deconstruction of the office building led to the subdivision of the architecture and construction industries into a spectrum of specialist professions, ranging from mechanical, electrical, and telecommunications experts to space planners, interior designers, and facilities managers, which in turn threatened to limit the creative (and professional) remit of the architect to the shell of the building.[117] As Duffy lamented, "Architecture has retreated from the plan form, ... from services, ... from the design of interiors. ... The only area of architectural discretion in artistic or financial terms is the skin. The architectural imagination has allowed itself to be well and truly marginalised."[118] DEGW avoided marginalization by developing a consultancy, or diachronic, model of practice, which offered research-based services that extended into the pre- and postconstruction lifecycle of the building, such as postoccupancy studies, building appraisals, and sectorial studies to evaluate change for users, developers, and investors.[119] For Duffy, this model of practice required not only innovative approaches to construction but also a reimagining of corporate style, calling for a "totally new aesthetic based not on the bright, sterile and peopleless moment of move-in but on the gradual adaptation of space through time, an aesthetic of process and maturity."[120]

It is perhaps unsurprising that the high-tech style, with its embedded aestheticization of process and movement, became the lingua franca of office design from the late 1970s onward. Firms such as Richard Rogers Partnership, Foster & Partners, and Arup Associates produced large, deep floor plans by externalizing all cumbersome service elements to the facade and reducing them to a network of lightweight precision components, expressing temporariness and mobility. With a strategy commensurate with Duffy's deconstructive approach, high-tech architects dissolved the building into a series of restless, maneuverable parts, visibly extending the flexibility of the open plan from the horizontal plane to the entire building envelope. On the surface, the appeal of this style in the newly deregulated City was, perhaps paradoxically, its monumentality. Rogers's radical redesign of Lloyd's of London was a case in point, a building that was essentially an exercise in Baroque theatricality for one of the oldest and most conservative institutions in the City. As Peter Buchanan noted in an article in the *Architectural Review* in 1983, unlike its more radical original formulation in the works of Archigram and Cedric Price, which sought to do away with any sense of the monumental in favor of mechanistic assemblages, the sleek high-tech productions emerging in the corporate sphere were "no longer anti-art but high art," striving "to be not so much pragmatic and playful process as refined and elegant thoroughbreds."[121] Buchanan's argument was that architects like Rogers and Foster were more fixated on the visual representation of high technology than its actual functionality, resulting in the production of iconic sculptural forms—building-as-object—rather than pure structural assemblage—building-as-process.

Buchanan's critique overlooked the economic and technological underpinnings of the style in use. But there is no doubt that the notion of monumentality, or rather the landmark building, was an essential component of the London real estate market in the 1980s. The early part of the decade had witnessed a general loss of faith in property as a good investment on the part of financial institutions. Rising unemployment, high inflation, and climbing interest rates resulted in a slowdown in the growth of rents and low returns for property.[122] Following the opening up of international markets after the removal of exchange controls in 1979, insurance companies and pension funds began to invest in overseas securities, rather than in real estate, as property became increasingly less attractive relative to these new markets. Property had sizeable disadvantages as an investment medium on account of its illiquid nature, high management and transaction costs, and the fact that it was only available in large blocks.[123] In addition, the rapidity with which technology was changing meant that the shelf life of office buildings was measurably decreasing. These issues, in combination with the continued threat of decentralization and high interest rates, ensured that between 1980 and 1985,

Lloyd's building elevation drawing by Richard Rogers. Courtesy of RHSP.

the net institutional investment in property fell by 47 percent in real terms.[124] Within this context, developers had to be competitive by providing high-quality attraction developments to allure tenants.[125] Facilitated by the deregulation of planning laws, the latter gave rise to large prestige developments, spread around the outer edges of the financial center: for example, projects such as 1 Finsbury Avenue (1982–1984) by Arup Associates utilized the high-tech genre to create a sellable building in an area that had been formerly considered too far from the Bank intersection (the City core) to be legitimately considered part of the financial center.[126]

On the other hand, the appeal of the high-tech building could also be found in its propensity for assimilation and the provision of generic interior forms. In an essay about Norman Foster and his adoption of a systems-based method, Duffy argued that the genius in Foster's approach to design was a "severe, puritanical kind of ideology" that privileged the consistent provision of the generic deep plan, allowing the "rationalist, corporate orthogonal" to prevail.[127] High tech was appropriate for the new corporation because it simultaneously rendered the building equipment, which could be tailored to meet the needs of any organization due to its standardized, unencumbered interior, while also providing a visually arresting, if somewhat unreadable, exterior. In other

Finsbury Avenue building by Arup Associates, photographed in 1984. Heritage Image Partnership Ltd / Alamy.

words, it was a style that was servile to the occupier and the investor, rationalized to maximize productivity. As with Duffy's dismantled building, the high-tech style was commercially viable because of its inherent flexibility. This flexibility operated through a distinct delineation between the building as a precision-engineered envelope, which could be calibrated and adjusted as required, and the interior as pure space, which could be subdivided as required. High-tech architecture was the ideal instrument of deregulation as it removed the temporal inconveniences of the building-as-object, enabling its continual manipulation to complex and fluctuating demands of the user.

The pliable exteriors of the new corporate architecture were also exploited to reactionary ends in the City. Unlike the policy changes that were enacted overnight in 1986, the cultural shift from gentleman's club to global financial center was slow, and consequently approaches to architectural modernization on the part of developers were cautious. In some cases, this led to buildings that embraced tradition via inflated postmodern neoclassicism, as in Beaumont House on Aldgate by RHWL Architects (1988). Encasing over 55,000 m² of floor space within a bombastic

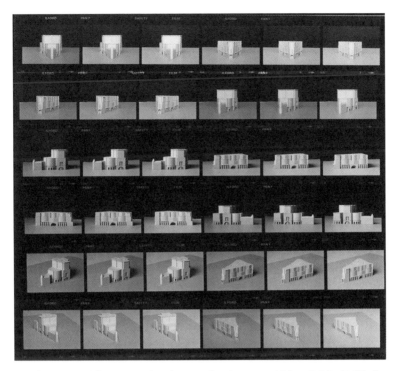

1 Poultry, James Stirling, Queen Victoria Street elevation. James Stirling / Michael Wilford fonds. Canadian Centre for Architecture. Copyright CCA.

pseudo-Mannerist shell, its heavy projecting pediment and bow-fronted facades emulated the American corporate classicism show-cased in all its splendor at Canary Wharf. Some buildings drew upon the area's built heritage, producing postmodern versions of Victorian corner wedges, such as Terry Farrell's Landmark House on Fenchurch Street and James Stirling, Michael Wilford & Associates' much-publicized No. 1 Poultry. Stirling's design broke the decades-long spell of Mies's internationalism with which the site had become associated. Instead, the exaggerated tripartite structure of a heavy striated base, rhythmically fenestrated midsection, and mansardesque setbacks pointed directly to its Victorian predecessor, J. & J. Belcher's Mappin & Webb building (1870–1871).

Retained facades also facilitated the co-opting of heritage into the new system of architectural equipment. This method of construction—the practice of building a new structure inside an existing shell—had been used in the City since the onslaught of building restrictions in the 1960s as it didn't require an office development permit. Furthermore, following the sustained attack by heritage organizations in the 1970s, the Corporation considered it a strategic way to continue building. While this approach was often criticized by conservationists for its superficiality, the heritage organization SAVE (one of the Corporation's biggest critics), in its well-known 1976 report *Save the City*, actually advocated "facadism" as appropriate for the City. Claiming that the footprints of most Victorian office buildings were uneconomical, as grand staircases and reception rooms wasted up to 40 percent of gross floor space, which could easily be salvaged by internal reorganization to "offset the costs of conversion and modernisation," the report argued that facades had "prestige value," which would influence lettings.[128] Fitzroy Robinson had been particularly prolific in this activity, pioneering the technique at 13–15 Moorgate in 1966. By the 1980s, practices had somewhat perfected the art, particularly in the treatment of side and rear elevations (where properties had been merged) and in the addition of extra stories, such as Fitzroy Robinson's addition of a fourth story to William Tite's Royal Exchange (1843).[129] The City of London's planning department advocated such compromises, positioning them to developers as an opportunity to maximize floor space while avoiding costly debates with the central London planning authorities that a new building would entail.[130] Retained facades were absorbed easily into the architectural assemblages of the deregulated City, in the sense that they offered simply an alternative and preexisting shell in the system of layers.

In some senses it is clear that the emphasis on the future performance, and thus deconstruction, of the building was intrinsically related to the shifting dynamics of real estate in a deregulated system. The value of a building after the point of construction became increasingly significant as real estate became integrated into financial markets through strategies such as *securitization*, which transformed property mortgages into tradable securities, and *unitization*, which made it possible to trade in small units of a building.[131] Within this context, developers and financiers adapted accordingly. The former became more focused on property trading, while property investment banking became popular among the new financial conglomerates, using capital markets and a range of financial instruments to fund developments.[132] The office building became a financial instrument, and as such, the economic worth of corporate buildings was inseparably tied to

Mellon National Bank and Trust Company in Moorgate, 1970. London Metropolitan Archives (City of London). London Picture Archive, ref 48592.

future property values in the City. It is unsurprising then that architects would also be working toward developing buildings that had the capacity to be continually productive in the future, or even that they visually embodied this with styles like high tech. As Fredric Jameson has noted, "Time and a new relationship to the future as the space of necessary expectation of revenue and capital accumulation ... is now the final link in the chain which leads from finance capital, through land speculation to aesthetics and cultural production itself, or, in other words ... to architecture."[133]

Performance, Reviewed

As finance became more unstable under the new neoliberal regime, the temporal dimension of architecture was repositioned at the center of commercial practice. The need for organizational agility in the new economy, and the necessity to adopt ever-updating IT systems, demanded offices that were not static forms but flexible frameworks for change. As the thinking, consuming individual— what Foucault called the *homo economicus*—emerged as the protagonist in the market-based economy, the worker, and by extension the organization, became an increasingly complex and important driver of design.

Here the external layer of the building shifted from a representational elevation, or a monolithic high-rise symbol, to a distinct aspect of architectural production. Whereas in the postwar decades this meant the packaging of commercial space in the most efficient and economical manner, by the 1990s the building shell had been fragmented from the building both literally and economically, as financial imperative demanded an increasing division of labor between those involved in architectural output. Where previously the maximization of floor space and manipulation of planning regulations had been the central concern of the commercial architect, now their dominant responsibility was to devise an architectural image sellable to the occupant.

Yet the meaning of these images had also fundamentally changed. After World War II, facades were still considered to be an architectural manifestation of a bank's reputation. It was an assurance of trust, a statement of confidence. Architectural image-making was thus a moral act based on the classical notion of decorum. A bank should look like a bank, and transmit its core values.

In the fifties, this meant classicism. In the sixties and seventies, this began to shift toward an open, international language with the growing consumerism of the banking sector. This does not mean that all were agreed on what this meant in stylistic terms; neo-Georgian and high-rise modernism were equally and oppositely critiqued by the architectural establishment, not least for their associations with developer-led design. But the notion that a bank had an architectural specificity and an active, operational image was widely accepted and adopted.

By the 1980s, debates about the visual function of a bank's architecture disappeared because banks, in their traditional form, ceased to exist. The mergers occurring as a result of deregulation created new multinational, multifaceted financial conglomerates unparalleled in scale and scope. At once, the long-held distinctions that had previously characterized London banking were, on the surface at least, eradicated. Space and technological prowess were prioritized, and so the facade dissolved to make way for the new technical-financial assemblages. Now the building skin was judged by its temporal-economic performance, rather than measured by its rhetorical showmanship. As developers and architects became the custodians of image-making in the City, so the new investment banks—the users—focused their attention inward, toward the spectacle of the new corporate interior.

4   *Interior*

The noise of the screech-owl ... the howling of the wolf, the barking of the mastiff, the grunting of the hog, the braying of the ass, the nocturnal wooing of the cat, the hissing of the snake, the croaking of the toads, frogs and grasshoppers—all these in unison could not be more hideous than the noise which those beings make in the stock exchange.
Charles Hales, *The Bank-Mirror*, 1795

No sooner did you pass the fake fireplace than you heard an ungodly roar, like the roar of a mob ... the bond trading room of Pierce & Pierce. It was a vast space, perhaps sixty by eighty feet, but with the same eight-foot ceiling bearing down on your head. It was an oppressive space with a ferocious glare, writhing silhouettes ... arms and torsos of young men ... suit jackets off. They were moving about in an agitated manner and sweating early in the morning and shouting, which created the roar. ... There were no partitions and no signs of visible rank. Everyone sat at light gray metal desks in front of veal-colored computer terminals with black screens. Rows of green-diode letters and numbers came skidding across."
Tom Wolfe, *Bonfire of the Vanities*, 1987

In the Roar of the Jungle

Noise. This was the defining experience of a London trading floor. The encompassing, rumbling, reverberating sound of voices. Discordant, overlaid, and, at times, deafening. But noise wasn't simply sound; it had meaning in the City. On the London Stock Exchange's trading floor prior to the 1970s, the loud, raucous din of up to eight thousand bodies under its lofty dome in Capel Court was an essential part of its activities. As initial trades were made in person between jobber and broker on the floor, noise was an indication that the market was working. As a journalist in 1933 astutely put it, "To the untrained listener

Photograph of the trading floor of the Stock Exchange in the 1960s, designed by J. J. Cole, 1885. Courtesy of Mary Evans Picture Library.

the noise will probably sound like senseless babel: and by way of assistance to a more intelligent appreciation of its quality I can only suggest ... the resultant sound may be compared to the steady hum of a dynamo."[1] Here the implication was that the verbal act of doing the trade upheld a set of moral values, which in turn underpinned its role in the national economy. Noise was the sound of a productive marketplace, helping to fuel Britain's industrial and trading activities at home and abroad.

But as with all of the City's mythologies, the cult of the verbal agreement, the conversational mode of trading, the loud familiarity of the club was an invention designed to sustain this important community. According to Juan Pablo Pardo-Guerra, *Dictum meum pactum*—the legendary motto upon which all of the City's values were apparently based—was in fact a twentieth-century construction, introduced with a new crest in 1923.[2] This single phrase gave legitimacy to the system of self-regulation through members' clubs and exchanges, which the City wished to defend at all costs. So important was notion of the face-to-face agreement, of noise, that when the Stock Exchange came to redesign its trading floor in the 1970s, the discovery that it was too quiet triggered mild panic among the Stock Exchange Council. Despite being asked to reduce the resonant sound in the space, its cohort of architects and architecture firms, comprising Richard Llewelyn-Davies, Fitzroy Robinson & Partners, and Llewelyn-Davies, Weeks, Forestier-Walker & Bor, was quickly charged with reinstating the famous reverberation of the existing floor.

The new floor was part of as part of the wholesale rebuilding of the exchange (completed in 1979), intended to rationalize, reorganize, and innovate the institution at a time when it was frequently under attack for its insularity and informality. As the chairman of the Stock Exchange's own PR committee noted in 1965, in the postwar milieu, "the traditional 'couldn't care less' attitude had ceased to be an amiable, if anachronistic, eccentricity, and had become a positive danger."[3] Radically departing from the institutional classicism of the last two centuries, Llewelyn-Davies et al.'s brutalist tower was conceived to reduce overcrowding on the floor and improve its communications technology. In its existing premises in Capel Court, trade was a visceral, chaotic spectacle, involving the constant movement of traders and clerks around the floor and messengers running to and from the Bank of England to communicate changes in the bank rate. All this wore down the wooden

Photograph of the trading floor of the new Stock Exchange building (1967–1979) by Richard Llewelyn-Davies, Fitzroy Robinson & Partners, and Llewelyn-Davies, Weeks, Forestier-Walker & Bor. Architectural Press Archive / RIBA Collections.

flooring "at an estimated rate of 1 3/4 inches per decade," requiring it to be intermittently watered with watering cans throughout the day to settle the dust clouds. In the nineteenth-century trading hall, the buildup of heat and sound was intense.[4] Traders did deals beneath the constant bellowing of the waiters standing on podiums, calling members to the floor, disseminating market information, and often running sideline betting shops from their stands and selling "everything from paintings, to razor blades, to contraceptives, to tins of salmon."[5]

The new building reflected the Stock Exchange's new long-term business strategy to be the largest and most efficient market in Europe.[6] It was a bold and brutalist hexagonal appendage containing 2,200 m² of trading space, connected to a twenty-six-story concrete tower. A key part of this rationalization process was noise reduction: rubber flooring was installed to dampen the sound and reduce wear, the dome was replaced by a low ceiling with hexagonal coffering, and the background roar of the waiters was substituted by almost inaudible personal bleepers worn by each trader.[7] However, initial tests prior to its opening in 1972 revealed that the floor was now *too* quiet: by lowering overall volume in the room, private conversations and verbal agreements between members could be heard. In response, the architects used hard-wearing materials such as concrete, travertine marble, and stainless steel to reintroduce the famous resounding echo.[8]

The fear of losing this sound was connected to a deeper fear of losing the City's traditions, and thus its independence. For centuries, trading floors were the primary mechanism of normalizing and policing the financial district, achieved via the architectural act of assembling bodies in space. Buried deep within blocks, hidden behind both unassuming and grandiose facades, encircled by arcades and galleries, and surmounted by lofty domes, the City's trading floors had constituted the hubs of social and economic life in the financial district prior to the 1980s. Providing a network of semipublic interiors distributed across the Square Mile, these paved, wooden, and later rubber expanses were not simply surfaces on which trade was done, but highly controlled worlds within which relationships were built, cultures were established, and information was exchanged and protected. Built predominantly in the eighteenth and nineteenth centuries, the network of exchanges in the Square Mile emerged to contain and formalize the informal and increasingly specialized markets that grew

Photograph of the Stock Exchange celebrating of the Relief of Mafeking, May 18, 1900. From Elizabeth Hennessy, *Coffee House to Cyber Market* (London: Ebury Press, 2001).

with Britain's industrial and imperial expansion. In addition to the Royal Exchange and the Stock Exchange, which evolved functionally and physically over several centuries, in the nineteenth century a plethora of specialist trading floors emerged in the City, including Edward Moxhay's Hall of Commerce in Threadneedle Street (1842–1844), John Gordon's Wool Exchange on Basinghall Street (1873–1874), the London Metal Exchange on Whittington Avenue (1882), the Baltic Exchange on St. Mary Axe (1900–1903), and the rather dramatic rotunda of the London Coal Exchange on Thames Street, by J. B. Bunning (1848). Although these markets varied in scale and scope, they were linked by the common goal of creating specific communities of exchange via membership and codes of conduct. By the end of the nineteenth century, they were not simply local marketplaces, but were more widely recognized as national institutions, adding further legitimacy to the City's self-regulatory practices.

On the floor, the physical movement and proximity of bodies in space was perceived to reinforce trust. Communicating via gesture, dialogue, and lip-reading, and jostling between each other,

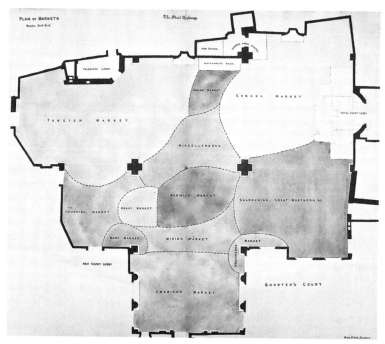

Plan of the markets in the London Stock Exchange, 1880, by J. J. Cole. Courtesy of Guildhall Library, City of London.

the trading floor could be an uncomfortably crowded, chaotic trading space, but as Stock Exchange historian Elizabeth Hennessy notes, "this was not always seen as a disadvantage" because "if you were close to where the leading brokers passed ... this brought opportunities to quote a price and *form a judgment* about the business."[9] Visibility and propinquity enabled traders to assess the validity of the information offered on account of the integrity of the man offering it: on the floor, brokers and jobbers were not merely trading in financial products, but advertising their own personality in order to create strong exchange relationships. Historically, failure to live up to this bond of trust, by defaulting on a deal, would result in immediate expulsion from the exchange "and their characters blasted by the suspension of a blackboard in a conspicuous part of the House on which their names are painted at full length."[10]

The Stock Exchange understood how important these rituals were in retaining the City's independence. Despite its up-to-date aesthetic, the new trading floor was essentially a rationalization of historic and outmoded practices. By the early 1970s, new electronic price-display systems enabling the broadcasting of stock prices via CCTV to television sets in offices beyond the walls of the exchange technically removed the need for a physical floor at all.[11] But the new floor was built because it was understood to be the institution's most important regulatory tool at a moment when the City of London's informal methods of self-monitoring were coming under pressure. "Successful and professional operations must be founded on confidence and trust both between practitioners in the market and their clients," wrote the Stock Exchange Council in defense of self-regulation in 1975. It continued, "The very complex inter-relationships and internal operations of those City bodies which form the financial system, are best regulated by each individual body under the general supervision of the Bank of England."[12]

But while the mythologies surrounding the verbal contract helped maintain the City's internal mechanisms, to critical outsiders this noise represented the obfuscation of market mechanisms. Historically, observers like Charles Hales, in his eighteenth-century publication *The Bank-Mirror, or A Guide to the Funds*, had referred to the noise of stock jobbers on the floor as an audible reflection of the apparent animal disorder within. Audible chaos rendered the performance of products or the integrity of the institution difficult to assess, blurring the boundary between speculation and good judgement. In the eyes of its detractors, the noise of the Stock Exchange trading floor, and its environs, had always rendered it a space of otherness, a spectacle to be observed, feared, perhaps even to be in awe of, but always at a distance.

It was this commotion, and its gentlemanly trappings, that the Thatcher government sought to mute with its restrictive practices legislation in the late 1970s. Despite the architectural attempt at modernization, which totaled over £70 million, the Stock Exchange failed to make organizational changes that went beyond its superficial sartorial transformation, and in 1979 it was listed on the OFT Restrictive Practices Register. Several activities in particular were seen as preventing competition: its reluctance to open up to international markets (such as the Euromarket), its continued insistence on fixed commission rates and single capacity (the required separation of jobbers and brokers), and its two-century-old British-only membership policy, which permitted only jobber and broker firms to apply (within which all partners

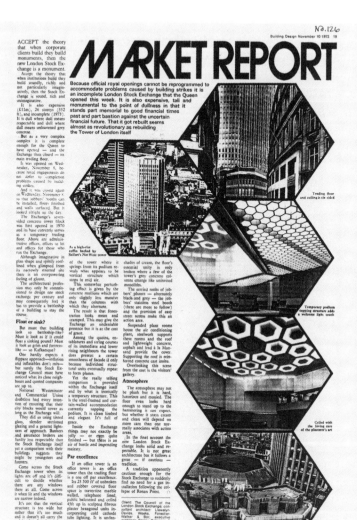

Page from "Market Report: The Opening of the London Stock Exchange," *Building Design*, no. 126 (November 1972): 19. Courtesy of *Building Design*.

had to join and could have no other occupation) and which, until 1967, prohibited members from having seats on any foreign stock exchange.[13] With increasing international competition from the likes of the New York Stock Exchange, the Stock Exchange fell behind in a city where even the biggest institutions were increasingly based upon Japanese, American, or European capital.[14] After almost a decade of investigation from central government, in 1983 the Stock Exchange made a deal with Cecil Parkinson, the secretary of state for trade and industry, to open its market to international investors. Realized in the Big Bang of October 26, 1986, this deal not only transformed the operations of the UK stock market, but also entirely reconfigured the organizational structure, function, and character of the UK banking sector. The introduction of dual capacity (enabling firms to be both jobbers and brokers), the abolition of fixed commissions, and the admission of overseas and large institutional members led to various mergers between its jobbing and broking firms and to the growth of financial conglomerates (predominantly from the US and Japan) combining the activities of dealing, banking, and currency trading.[15]

One of the conditions of deregulation was the adoption of an electronic dealing system that would remove the inefficiencies embodied by the physical marketplace. Launched on October 27, 1986, the Stock Exchange Automated Quotation system aimed to "take advantage of methods of communication that would enable members wherever they were located to see the prices made by market makers and to be able to deal with them on the floor and by telephone."[16] Based on the American NASDAQ market, initially SEAQ was conceived with the idea that it could be used both on the Stock Exchange floor and within the offices of members. However, as Ranald Michie notes, the electronic system "offered the possibility for the first time of replicating the conditions on the floor of a stock exchange," but at a much faster rate, initially handling eight to nine transactions per second.[17] The result was that despite the relative novelty of the Stock Exchange building, only one week after SEAQ was launched the numbers on the floor fell from roughly two thousand to two hundred traders, and it was entirely abandoned by the next year.[18]

Within a matter of months, the Stock Exchange floor had fallen completely silent. Computing and communications technology had ensured that the securities market now transcended location. Traders had dispersed from the exchange to new American-style dealing rooms embedded within offices throughout the City and later Canary Wharf.[19] With this single typological move, an entire cultural reimagining of financial practice in Britain took place. Computerized dealing and new regulatory structures slowly produced a sociological and architectural transformation so dramatic that within twenty years the demographic composition and cultural attitudes within the City were almost unrecognizable. Its interior worlds were entirely reconfigured as the old face-to-face ways of doing business were reduced, patriarchy was destabilized (though not eradicated), and the specifically British networks of gentlemanly capitalism were broken down as more international firms entered the City. Dealing floors became symbols of deregulation—an ideological, as much as a technical, process. Emulating the new "sexy greedy" financial culture of Reagan's Wall Street, these spaces were the macho-masculine machines driving forward Thatcher's market-led economy. And now a new noise— the "ungodly roar" of advanced capitalism, so vividly described by Tom Wolfe—emanated from deep within the new expansive floor plates emerging throughout the City.[20]

Floor space demand and the need for technological infrastructure increased dramatically the expenditure of the new financial conglomerates. Dealing rooms were at the core of such investment. As Francis Duffy noted in 1989, "The cost of providing a trading position can be as much as £30,000, to which back-up computing and communications can add another £20,000, while the cost of buying in information services can total £5,000 per position annually," resulting in an estimated total investment of over £1 billion in 1986 on information services and backup facilities.[21] As most new firms sought dealing floors of between three hundred and five hundred positions, the initial setup, excluding building costs, might total as much as £15 million, which would have been inconceivable for the small partnerships that inhabited the City just five years earlier.[22] New technology also increased energy consumption, and therefore cost, by over a third in the City from 1984 to 1989, while rapid obsolescence of many buildings in the context of technical infrastructure brought with it huge outlays in redevelopment or the acquisition of new properties.[23]

Dealing rooms were expensive in the UK not purely because of the technological equipment required to run them, but largely because the small Victorian or interwar office blocks that characterized City institutions were unable to adapt to the demands of such equipment. The dealing floor itself was not an entirely new phenomenon; the interbank markets, foreign exchange, and Eurodollar and Eurobond markets had always been decentralized without a physical marketplace, and thus were carried out in small in-house departments using the latest communications technology. However, such spaces were usually only built to accommodate tens (not hundreds) of dealers, and usually consisted of one long, continuous dealing desk. Discount house Gerrard & National, for example, had a dealing room with a large H-shaped desk lined with telephones, with small built-in monitors and keyboards with the names of individual banks on them.[24] Similarly, Morgan Grenfell's foreign exchange desk was wrapped around a central pentagon, offering enough seats for just ten traders.[25] Such spaces were perhaps commensurate with the scale and scope of their markets.

It was the American investment banks that were responsible for introducing the new gargantuan dealing room to London, enticed to the City by the new regulatory environment. Whereas these banks had been accustomed to trading areas of around 1,300 m² in sizeable New York office towers, the largest dealing space in the City in 1986 measured just 510 m².[26] In the wake of deregulation, the dramatic growth, internationalization, and multisectoral character of the new investment banks demanded buildings with bigger footprints. Furthermore, the City's existing office stock did not have adequate floor heights to accommodate cabling and air conditioning in large ceiling cavities and under plenum flooring. In some cases, as in the offices of James Capel, City buildings were gutted internally and an entirely new internal structure would be added with adequate floor heights. This rather unsatisfactory approach would often result in floor plates cutting across large arched windows, giving a somewhat shoddy finish externally and odd window heights internally.[27] In response to the lack of adequate spaces in the City, American banks became large investors in property in the 1980s, with many moving to bigger properties on the fringe of the City or outside the City entirely. Electronic trading systems removed the need for proximity, and the City's foreign tenants were not so concerned with centrality as older City firms. Salomon Brothers was one of the first to break through the City boundary, taking an enormous space in Victoria Plaza near Victoria Station for a new dealing room of 1,200 m².[28]

The architectural implications of dealing floors were less straightforward than space provision. Deregulation and

TRADING FLOOR LAYOUT - LONDON

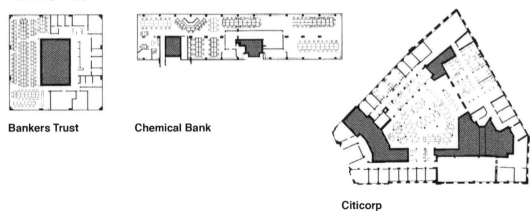

Bankers Trust   **Chemical Bank**

Citicorp

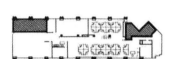

Manufacturers Honover Trust

Salomon Bros.

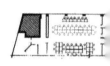

Shearson

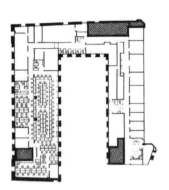

Lehman Bros.

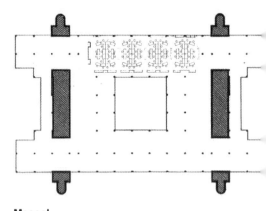

Messel

Comparative floor plans of trading floors in the US and UK, 1986. From Duffy Eley Giffone Worthington, *Trading in Two Cities: Design Guidelines for Trading Floors: A Report for Rosehaugh Stanhope Developments Plc* (London: DEGW, March 1986). Courtesy AECOM.

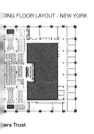

ers Trust

Chemical Bank

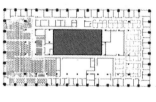

Citicorp

Boston

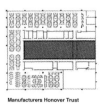

Manufacturers Honover Trust

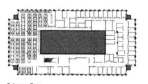

Salomon Bros.

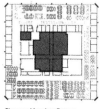

Shearson / American Express

digitalization rendered the marketplace all the more capricious, and the dealing floor was particularly vulnerable to change due to the increased speed and volume of transactions. These spaces required fixtures, and potentially even entire sections of buildings that could be rearranged and manipulated easily. "Trading floors should, if possible, be designed to be reversible into normal office space," wrote DEGW in its 1986 appraisal of trading floor design in London and New York. "It is possible to design buildings ... by using atriums which are reversible to the extent that a big square or rectangular trading floor can be converted back into normal office space by removing a relatively light central structure—and, of course, vice versa."[29] DEGW's collaboration with Richard Rogers Partnership and Ove Arup & Partners on the renovation of Horace Jones's Victorian Billingsgate Market building (1874–1878) for Citicorp Investment Bank in 1985 gave some indication of how an American-style floor might be adapted to the City's existing building stock. Based on a research trip to several well-known US investment banks in Wall Street, the redevelopment used the wide-open market hall to provide 740 m² of continuous open space.[30]

Uninterrupted floor space was a critical characteristic of the new interior not simply for its malleability, but also because it facilitated the continuation of marketplace behavior among traders. Despite the fact that the majority of business was now

Interior

Trading floor dealing in stocks currency, City of London, 1994. Copyright Mike Goldwater / Alamy.

screen-based, dealing still required communication between traders at their desks. A clear line of sight, free of columns and service cores, enabled easy access to information and news appearing on whiteboards and television screens around the room. But this layout also enabled an arguably more important sense to function optimally—namely, the ability of dealers to hear each other at near and far trajectories, or what has since been referred to as *broker's ear*. As sociologist Donald MacKenzie has written more recently of this phenomenon on City trading floors, a key skill is "the capacity to monitor what is being said by all the other brokers at nearby desks, despite the noise and while at the same time holding a voicebox conversation with a client. As one broker put it to me: 'When you're on the desk you're expected to hear everyone else's conversations as well.'"[31] While the open outcry method of trading had been abolished, verbal communication via telephone to some extent continued the auditory tradition of the open trading floor.

In addition to permitting verbal and visual communication, the vast open area also emphasized a sense of unity within the space. In the same way that the Stock Exchange had relied on the containment of the floor to reiterate the wholeness of the organization, so the new dealing rooms used the visual phenomenon of the mass of bodies in a single space to promote corporate unanimity. In Capel Court, a public viewing gallery installed in 1953

Circular dealing room in NatWest's Broadgate premises. Reproduced by kind permission of NatWest Group © 2023.

emphasized the activity on the trading floor as a performance to be watched but not understood. It was largely illegible to outsiders due to the spectacle of oneness; its markets were defined only by the bodies operating within them or by the architectural features of the building, only known to those working there. Within the new electronic dealing rooms, markets were similarly opaque, defined by clusters of desks, each cluster somewhat confusingly referred to as *a* desk, as if to highlight the continuity of the furniture. As the "basic organizational unit of the trading room," the desk in this sense was a byword for the market and the teams of traders it contained—or as sociologists Daniel Benuza and David Stark put it, the "identification of the animate with the inanimate."[32] Like the old exchange floor, the drama of visual continuity was further enhanced by its enclosure from the outside world. A lack of natural light and the use of blinds, in part to avoid reflections on screens (also assisted by uplighting, rather than downlighting), focused the gaze inward. As Duffy noted, because trading has always been conceived as "a public, quasi-theatrical activity," the trading floor must be treated like a theater, in which "no [external] view is a good view ... all attention is within."[33] In some cases, such as NatWest Investment Bank's dealing room at Broadgate, the analogy was approached quite literally. Taking advantage of the scheme's generous floor-to-floor heights, the bank inserted raked seating, with desks organized in concentric circles increasing in floor height from the inside out, to produce a kind of amphitheater arrangement.[34]

Although theatricality had always played an important part of trading on the Stock Exchange, the deregulation and internationalization of the City instigated a cultural shift toward competitive individualism, which in turn heightened tensions in the dealing room. While trading had become an overwhelmingly sedentary activity, the atmosphere became arguably more intense than it had been previously due to the increase in personal gain to be achieved from activities on the floor. To remain competitive with other financial centers, employers increased wages dramatically throughout the 1980s, meaning that employees frequently changed jobs to get them.[35] American banks were more likely to offer lower wages but award exorbitant bonuses for good performance.[36] Where previously the hierarchical structure of firms meant that brokers and merchant bankers would wait to rise to the top of their firms and accrue a civilized wealth on retirement, the new corporate environment incentivized hard work with immediate reward. While the City remained flooded with public school and Oxbridge graduates, the increase in the size of firms meant that employers had to broaden their recruitment strategies to include more middle- and working-class individuals, steering the atmosphere of the securities market away from the gentleman's club to a more meritocratic model.[37] Traders in particular were more likely to be recruited straight from school, rather than university, beginning in the back office and then eventually moving to the dealing floor.

The combination of a more financially incentivized approach and a broader social pool prompted a social divide between the dealing room and the executive office. In particular, as sociologists of work in the City Linda McDowell and Gillian Court note, the dealing floor became associated with "a more macho masculinity of 'guts,' 'iron balls,' and the 'killer instinct' necessary to overcome clients' resistance, to make sales, and to conclude deals." Whereas those working in corporate finance continued to embrace the "staid and sober paternalism" of the City gent, dealing floors became the sites of an aggressive, Americanized financial culture, as depicted in films like *Wall Street*.[38] Such spaces acquired a reputation for primitive, animal-like behavior. As former bond salesman Michael Lewis put it in his famous memoir *Liar's Poker*, the trading floor was mythologized as a "jungle" in which "a trader was a savage, and a great trader a great savage."[39] This performance of brutish masculinity was cultivated architecturally. Most major investment banks viewed proximity between traders as a stimulant to productivity, leading many employers to request that their dealing rooms provide less space than the 3.7 m^2 per person recommended in the Offices, Shops and Railway Premises Act of 1963. As DEGW noted in its report on trading floors, "Salomon Brothers, with an average trader density of 2.9m^2 per person in New York and 3.1m^2 per person in London, openly acknowledge that their high densities promote an aggressive market and atmosphere and hence more aggressive trading."[40]

Women were not integrated easily into such testosterone-fueled environments (where it wasn't uncommon to see a stripper or inflatable female dolls), and would often experience verbal and sometimes physical harassment. As one of McDowell's female respondents described, "It is difficult to be a woman on the dealing floor. It [sexism] is so overt ... I was much more conscious of being a woman to be looked at and ... having to put up with ... a lot of that gutter humour."[41] Salesmen and market makers were cast as young, white, able-bodied heterosexual men with "natural" aptitude for numbers; a good trader worked on instinct and impulse and was apt to take risks. Here the bodily and the intellectual were unified, tapping into long-standing ideas about male sexuality, libido, and virility. The corollary was that women, and men not fitting into such a category, automatically fell into the antithetical stereotype of the subservient, submissive, and quiet *other*, and were frequently chastised when not fitting this role. While the Big Bang may have succeeded in removing the "restrictive" gentlemanly behavior of the old Stock Exchange trading floor, it was simply replaced by a different set of social barriers in the new high-density trading "jungles."

Dealing rooms were designed to invoke the illogical and emotional aspects of exchange—what Keynes had referred to as the *animal spirits*—through the creation of sensorially overwhelming environments: desks pushed end to end, traders shouting down several telephone receivers simultaneously, flickering computer screens (often four or five per desk) and blaring television sets, and air conditioning units blasting cool air to overcome the huge amounts of heat generated by the computers. All this accumulated to produce an intense pressurized space where traders would engage in audacious and fearless behavior. Such a competitive, high-stakes environment inevitably led to incidences of fraud, as in the case of Nick Leeson at Baring Brothers, a talented rogue trader from humble beginnings who brought down one of the oldest and most respected merchant banks in the City. As these incidents increased in number, so the level of monitoring on the floors became more intense. The informal method of surveillance was gradually replaced by the recording of phone conversations, the installation of CCTV, and the implementation of stricter, codified regulations on trading, and consequently eradicated the original function of the floor as a space of self-regulation. Yet outwardly, rather than rationalizing the old system, the new markets appeared to be as chaotic and impenetrable as ever.

Microcosms of Meritocracy

It is no coincidence that the eighties and nineties gave rise to more films, television programs, and novels about the world of high finance than ever before. Lavish executive suites, boisterous trading scenes, sexually charged nightlife, and a conspicuous lack of morality provided a seductive cocktail, as demonstrated by the conversion of novels like Bret Easton Ellis's *American Psycho* (1991) and Wolfe's *Bonfire of the Vanities* (1987) into high-grossing Hollywood movies. Perhaps the most compelling aspect of this world was the paradox of the rich materiality and intense physicality of financial practice with the increasingly abstracted nature of financial instruments. With more complex derivatives entering the marketplace and trades being executed at higher numbers than could have ever been imagined ten years prior, exchange had become an almost fictitious act. Volatile, invisible, and speculative, the new financial products rendered the bullish endeavor of trading exciting in its unpredictability, miraculous in its alchemy, and absurd in its aggression. As Max Haiven has written, "Finance is both dependent on and productive of social fictions," which operate both "at the level of its primary operations, where a financial assets claims to value are essentially fictitious" and in the realm of everyday life, where finance "depends on and produces fictions on the level of lived culture."[42] For the abstraction of finance to make sense, evocative stories of risk and reward had to be produced in business culture and then reproduced in popular culture. The theater of the trading floor and the drama of the boardroom gave meaning to a highly technical, and in some senses imaginary, process.

Nowhere was the absurdity of these social fictions more appositely expressed than in the work of German photographer Andreas Gursky. Bewitched by spaces of global capitalism, Gursky became known in the 1980s and 1990s for his digitally altered large-scale scenes of office interiors and in particular trading floors. In one of his most well-known photographs, *Chicago, Board of Trade II* (1999), Gursky captured the chaos of activity in the raucous trading "pits" of the world's biggest futures and options exchange. A sea of colored jackets, wildly gesticulating limbs, and paper detritus tell the story of the pit as a battleground. Using the technique of double exposure and digital manipulation, Gursky saturates the huge picture plane (1,574 × 2,840 mm) with figures, color, and movement, in the tradition and scale of a great history painting. The Rubens-like cropping of the scene, with no reference to the limits of the architectural container, draws attention to the sheer magnitude of the event, putting the viewer above the fray. But the closer one gets, the less one sees. Bodies and architecture become blurred into one, jackets float without heads, arms and hands are duplicated, people are reduced to smudges of purple, yellow, blue. More Pollock than Delacroix, close up the dramatic narrative of the battle dissolves into abstract expressionism. Just one in a series of photos of from exchanges from all over the world during this period, *Chicago, Board of Trade II* reveals Gursky's fascination with the duality of the spectacle and the specter of finance in the post-deregulatory moment. Unlike an earlier photograph of the Chicago Board of Trade (CBOT) in which a pitch-black framing of walls and screens describes the pit as a kind of theater, Gursky's second photograph seemed to shift the attention away from the human drama of the event toward the fragility of the fiction of trade. Here bodies become an unreadable mass, fading in and out of existence.

Gursky's photographs reveal the contrast between a seemingly high-tech, electronic world and a mode of trading that privileges an almost primal method of communication. Although the floor of Stock Exchange and in-house dealing rooms could be boisterous and intense, the pit was an exercise in physicality and primordial human behavior, in which hand signals, shouting, and jostling to

Andreas Gursky, *Chicago, Board of Trade II*, 1999. Copyright Andreas Gursky. Courtesy Pictoright Amsterdam 2023.

be seen and heard were the way of doing business. The first pits in the City emerged in the commodity exchanges of the nineteenth century, but it wasn't until 1982 that such a trading space was built for the financial markets, in the form of the London International Financial Futures Exchange (LIFFE). Modeled on Chicago's famous open outcry commodities futures markets, the CBOT, and the Chicago Mercantile Exchange ("the Merc"), the concept of a futures market was that of a contained marketplace for speculation on the future price of a certain product (grain, butter, eggs, etc.), using standardized contracts and a third party—the clearing house—to back and settle deals, thereby absorbing credit risk.[43] By the late 1970s, with the academic assistance of Milton Friedman, the Chicago futures markets had expanded to financial products, including currencies, Eurodollars, American Treasury bonds, and the Dow Jones Industrial Average Index and mortgages, rendering Chicago home to the largest futures markets in the world.[44] Its appeal in London was as a method of minimizing risk in a period of great volatility in exchange and interest rates following the recent abolition of exchange controls and the oil crisis.[45] Where previously investment managers had been able to make long-term predictions based on good research, the growing volatility of the money markets now prohibited such accuracy and, as such, new financial instruments (such as hedging in financial futures) were required to help minimize risk.[46]

In both its organizational and social characteristics, LIFFE represented the Americanization of British financial practice in tangible form. Frequently dubbed the "American style" or "Chicago style" of trading, the market was unlike any other in the City for two reasons. First, at the time of opening, LIFFE was the only exchange in the financial district with a membership policy that was both international and multisectoral, offering approximately 100 of its 373 seats to non-UK firms and across the traditional industry divides, incorporating commodity brokers, overseas banks, commercial banks, and stock exchange firms. Unlike the Stock Exchange, which was still restricted by minimum commissions and single capacity, all trades within LIFFE were carried out on commission, with all parties about to act as buyers and sellers on the trading floor.[47] Second, where existing exchanges in London only permitted corporate members, the CBOT and the Merc were heavily populated by independent speculators trading on their own account, a feature that the organizers of LIFFE saw as an asset. These characteristics meant that from its inception, the market existed beyond the traditional hierarchical and cultural limits of the City.

The pit typology and the presence of independent traders (known as *locals*) were viewed as the primary means by which to transport the Chicago-style trading into the City of London, although this proved difficult due to a fundamental misalignment with City traditions and City buildings.[48] With the consultancy of Chicago-based traders, the LIFFE working party chose to self-consciously model the physical exchange on the Chicago trading floors rather than the local commodity markets in London, such as the London Metal Exchange in Plantation House, which was based around a central trading ring.[49] The Chicago style of exchange consisted of three elements: sunken trading pits with steps, an enormous price display board, and low open booths rather than the intimate boxes of the Stock Exchange.[50] Demanding a large, double-height room that could accommodate sufficient techno-logical and communications infrastructure, with decent acoustics and capacity for air conditioning, the requirements outstripped the capacity of most City buildings. Furthermore, the very con-cept of the institution was at odds with the main markets in the City. When initially approached as a possible venue for LIFFE, the Stock Exchange refused on the basis that it preferred not to be associated with the untried, American-style market.[51] After scour-ing six sites, the successful bid was for the Royal Exchange, which was deemed to be ideal in terms of space requirements, offering over 600 m² of eight-meter-high space with another 400 m² of single height space for associated offices.[52] However, while the Royal Exchange made sense as a venue both in terms of its phys-ical capacity and its historic role as a trading space, the building was held back by typical City problems. Hardly used for active trading since the start of the century and closed since 1972 due to the danger of falling plasterwork, the exchange was a scheduled ancient monument with a convoluted series of restrictions and permissions procedures, as well as access problems and a lack of contemporary service routes.[53]

LIFFE solved this cultural-spatial barrier through a crude architectural solution: the American-style trading floor was lit-erally transplanted inside the skin of the Royal Exchange. Con-ceived as "a building within a building," architect firm Whinney Mackay-Lewis in collaboration with engineering firm Ove Arup

& Partners effectively constructed a metal box nestled within the extant courtyard, conforming "to the fundamental stipulation ... that no damage was to be done to the existing structure of the Royal Exchange." Built of steel trusses mounted on steel columns, with wood-wool decking for sound insulation, the lightweight structure was underpinned by the exchange's original brick vaults. Internally there was also a mezzanine built in reinforced concrete on steel decking for sound and fire installation. As the structure could be prefabricated off-site, the market could theoretically be assembled and dismantled swiftly, leaving little trace of its presence. The use of a discreet shell also facilitated the colossal installation of advanced telecommunications infrastructure, undertaken by British Telecom at the cost of £1.5 million. As Kynaston notes, "Involving at least 55 miles of cabling, a Monarch and Herald call-connect system, a Cheetah telex, 2.5 racks of control and signalling equipment, over 300 dealer boards, 650 exchange lines, more than 800 private circuits, a 30-line Datel 600 network for computer data communications, 60 Ambassador telephones, and several public cardphones ... this was the largest single telecommunications project of its kind yet handled by BT."[54] Internally, the new exchange was conceived along the lines of the Chicago markets to enable maximum sightlines in a column-free space, and free circulation with the addition of an ambulatory surrounding the central floor. High ceilings enabled the erection of a large Ferranti price board that could be seen by all, while the mezzanine level provided a public viewing gallery in addition to interview rooms, offices, and a library.[55]

Whereas the dealing floor was a generic space that required constantly changing sets, the LIFFE trading floor was fixed, enabling a visual reading of the mechanisms of the financial futures market. Centered round three octagonal pits, home to three separate markets, each pit was fitted with a pulpit for a member of LIFFE staff to supervise trading. Surrounding the pits were rows of reception booths where deals would be confirmed and accepted, written onto slips and communicated to the member's office via telephone. Trading information would then be displayed on computer monitors distributed throughout the floor and in traders' booths. Diagrammatic and unchanging, pits provided the background for a highly mobile, physical performance of exchange. Based on the visceral spectacle of open outcry, which had defined the Chicago markets, traders in the pit shouted out their offering price to the

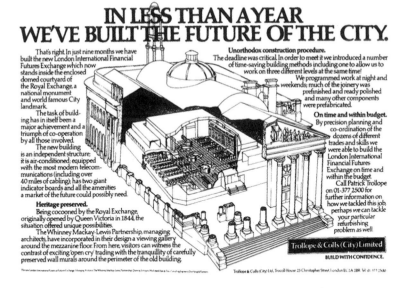

IN LESS THAN A YEAR
WE'VE BUILT THE FUTURE OF THE CITY.

That's right. In just nine months we have built the new London International Financial Futures Exchange which now stands inside the enclosed domed courtyard of the Royal Exchange, a national monument and world famous City landmark.

The task of building has in itself been a major achievement and a triumph of co-operation by all those involved.

The new building is an independent structure; it is air-conditioned; equipped with the most modern telecommunications (including over 40 miles of cabling); has two giant indicator boards and all the amenities a market of the future could possibly need.

Heritage preserved.
Being cocooned by the Royal Exchange, originally opened by Queen Victoria in 1844, the situation offered unique possibilities.
The Whinney Mackay-Lewis Partnership, managing architects, have incorporated in their design a viewing gallery around the mezzanine floor. From here, visitors can witness the contrast of exciting 'open cry' trading with the tranquillity of carefully preserved wall murals around the perimeter of the old building.

Unorthodox construction procedure.
The deadline was critical. In order to meet it we introduced a number of time-saving building methods including one to allow us to work on three different levels at the same time!
We programmed work at night and weekends; much of the joinery was prefinished and ready polished and many other components were prefabricated.

On time and within budget.
By precision planning and co-ordination of the dozens of different trades and skills we were able to build the London International Financial Futures Exchange on time and within the budget.
Call Patrick Trollope on 01-377 2500 for further information on how we tackled this job, perhaps we can tackle your particular refurbishing problem as well.

Trollope & Colls (City) Limited
BUILD WITH CONFIDENCE.

Trollope & Colls (City) Ltd, Trocoll House, 23 Christopher Street, London EC 2A 2BR. Tel: 01-377 2500.

Advert for Trollope & Colls Ltd. showing LIFFE as a "box in a box." Printed in Ann Saunders, ed., *The Royal Exchange* (London: London Topographical Society, 1997). Courtesy of Aker ASA.

seller, gesticulating with codified hand signals between the pit and the trader's colleague back in the booth. Requiring traders to stand, shout, jump, and wave their arms around for hours at a time, the pits provided the optimal conditions for a physically demanding and competitive kind of transaction, encouraging high densities, enabling good sightlines, and facilitating audibility via carefully calibrated acoustics.

Physical interaction in the pits was not simply a method of boosting the animal spirits of the traders, but also facilitated a highly managed form of risk-taking. As anthropologist Caitlin Zaloom notes, the pit is an "exchange technology" in which "traders scrutinize each other constantly. ... The success of a trader can be measured by how the pit watches his movements—whether to emulate or ignore him or to evaluate him as a competitor or a potential ally. The audience is attentive to a skilled speculator's every move."[56] As trades in the pit would take place in an incredibly short time span, doing a single trade within seconds, the pit enabled a form of tacit knowledge that could not be provided through electronic platforms. As Zaloom concludes, in the pit,

Open outcry trading at LIFFE in the Royal Exchange. Copyright Peter Stone / Alamy.

"profit and loss are the measures of successful action—not institutions or theories."[57]

The social fictions told at LIFFE were a dramatic departure from the gentlemanly aural pact espoused by the Stock Exchange. LIFFE accommodated a mode of exchange that was far wilder than anything seen before in the City. Whereas the sound of the Stock Exchange had been loud, it was a product of the sheer number of traders conversing rather than the volume of each trader. In LIFFE, the act of exchange was boisterous, loud and hot, representing competitive individualism. In part, this was based on the concept of the free individual trader working on his own account; to get noticed and thus be a successful speculator, each trader had to be visible and audible. At LIFFE, the process of visibility was assisted by the sartorial requirements of the market, as each member was required to wear a brightly colored jacket, each adorned with a pattern that represented his or her firm. Partly worn for visibility, and partly for durability in the fray of the pits (as beneath these jackets was a strict dress code of shirtsleeves and ties), firms used the dress code "to build a corporate ethos and create an identity."[58] According to Nicholas Durlacher, chairman of LIFFE from 1992 to 1995, the jackets reinforced the exoticism of the market in the Square Mile, as "the vast predominance of people working in the City were wearing grey or blue suits of one design or another. Suddenly these brightly coloured dust jackets were seen right in the core of the City, round and about the Royal Exchange, the Stock Exchange and the Bank of England, and some people thought it was at least as shocking as the new Lloyd's building."[59]

Sartorially speaking, the Royal Exchange served the opposite function to the brightly colored dust jackets. Whereas the jackets enabled traders to transform themselves into aggressive traders far removed from the cultural conservativism of *Dictum meum pactum* outside, the Royal Exchange was a gesture of conformism, rendering the American-style market appropriate for polite society. "Opened by Queen Victoria on the site for centuries London's oldest market place," began the market's promotional video, panning across the facade of Tite's exchange to a soundtrack of classical strings, LIFFE was positioned as a complementary addition to the City, in which "centuries of tradition thrive alongside a business community with its sites set firmly on the future."[60] But inside the metal box, an international and diverse workforce set the market apart from the dominant City culture. Unlike the Stock Exchange, where women had been admitted since 1973 but were still very few in number, LIFFE was open to female members from the beginning, with around 150 women active on the exchange in its first year, although still outnumbered four to one by the men. The energetic dealing culture on the floor didn't make the transition for women easy, and as Kynaston notes, "it was aggressively male, indeed, outright sexist. Nicknames for female traders included 'Boiler' and 'Slapper.'"[61] In general, traders were generally much younger than at other institutions in the City, recruited from outside of the traditional red brick university network and often straight from school. Kynaston quotes a senior commodity broker, who vividly described the situation: "We find the barrow-boy type is best at this game. ... We have our graduates from Oxford, Cambridge and Exeter to talk to clients and write reports, but the best dealer we ever had came straight from Dagenham at the age of 15."[62] A microcosm of meritocratic American values, LIFFE sought traders that were removed from the traditionalist cultures and familial ties of the City to maximize the competitive potential of the new market.

Although in symbolic terms the Royal Exchange performed a helpful assimilative function, in practical terms it soon became redundant due to the growth experienced by LIFFE following deregulation. Despite its otherness, the Chicago-style pits were highly successful over the next decade, and by the late-1980s the market was widely accepted as the City's "fourth pillar" after the Bank of England, the Stock Exchange, and Lloyd's.[63] By 1991 it had become the world's third-largest derivatives exchange, with the number of contracts traded increasing from 6.9 million in 1986 to 101.8 million in 1993, with up to one thousand traders on the floor at any one time. In addition to a greater uptake in the futures market after the Big Bang, LIFFE had attracted a number of American investment banks and Chicago-based brokers to enter the UK market, thereby increasing its turnover. Initially building a third story on the Royal Exchange to accommodate further office space, by the early 1990s the council sought larger premises elsewhere in the City.[64] Requiring enough space to contain two thousand to three thousand traders, potential sites included Canary Wharf and the 1970s Stock Exchange floor, although the latter was quickly deemed to be too expensive (with an annual rent of £3 million) and "tired," rendering it difficult "to project an exciting new image."[65] A space in the new development above Cannon Street station was chosen, with an interior fit-out by Whinney Mackay-Lewis costing around £15 million. A vast expansion on its 750 m² courtyard at the Royal Exchange, the new exchange totaled a dramatic 8,400 m² of floor space, including two 2,400 m² double ceiling height trading floors, with sixteen new trading pits demonstrating the increased breadth of financial products.[66] In the context of postderegulation London, LIFFE's pits were no longer "foreign" and no longer required housing in a protective heritage cloak.

As with most exchanges in the City (the London Metal Exchange being the one exception), the expansion of global markets resulted in a paradoxical withering of the physical space of the LIFFE marketplace. In 1999, LIFFE abandoned its open outcry system, at a moment when digitalization was the only efficient option in a financial world that was becoming increasingly technologically sophisticated. Like the Stock Exchange, which ultimately moved to markedly smaller premises in Paternoster Square

following the redundancy of its trading floor and later the removal of its regulatory capacity by the Financial Services Authority (FSA) in 2000, LIFFE was reduced to the physical status of the offices and electronic dealing floors. Losing the distinctiveness of place associated with an exchange or marketplace, the transition was symbolic of a broader shift from away from the cultural practices that had demanded proximity for so many centuries. Yet where some institutions lost their architectural distinctiveness, others relied on new buildings to reinvent themselves. It was here that the battles between tradition and modernization were waged in the City, where the micromatter of materials, furniture, and objects became the front line in a greater ideological war.

The Coffeehouse Feeling

Hanging in one of the galleries in the Lloyd's of London insurance market is a small series of cartoons drawn by the satirical artist Henry Mayo Bateman. Set within the crowded Underwriting Room—known as "the Room"—each drawing captures an unlikely or humorous episode in the daily life of the institution. "A Little Ray of Sunshine Visits Lloyd's" shows a well-dressed woman standing in the middle of the Room, being stared at by hundreds of men sitting on wooden benches, whose necks have been lengthened for comic effect. In another, entitled "The Underwriter Who Missed the Total Loss," the sketchy classical decorum of the Room is disturbed by a chaotic scene as a ship is lost, with crowds gathering around a grand colonnaded rostrum where the red-cloaked "waiter" vigorously sounds the bell. In a third, a pin-striped underwriter throws a punch at a brown-suited broker for stealing his best client, while the rest of the Room's inhabitants cheer and shout in a rowdy haze.

Commissioned by the chair of the broking firm Stewart Smith in 1946, and subsequently published in a small book for their clients, these cartoons show the internalized image of an institution saturated with its own mythologies.[67] Through parody, the visual coding of the Lloyd's community is made all the more explicit. Rich wooden surfaces, the high shine of brass, sumptuous red cloak, the scandalous brown leather brogue, and the regal neoclassical rostrum transmit the core values of the oldest institution in the City. Objects and surfaces are replete with messages of legitimacy and trustworthiness. But as these values came to be reevaluated, challenged, and even thrown out under deregulation, what became of the City's most prestigious interiors? In the pits of LIFFE, innovation had prevailed over the City's traditional

THE UNDERWRITER WHO MISSED THE TOTAL LOSS
Showing the inside of Lloyd's, and the famous " Lutine" bell, which is rung to announce a total loss

"The Underwriter Who Missed the Total Loss," 1946. Copyright H. M. Bateman Designs Ltd. (www.hmbateman.com).

Chapter 4

working methods and also its design. Yet in most cases, the rupture between old and new was not so definitive; the adoption of technology and new ways of working by institutions was often piecemeal and partial due to a reluctance to relinquish a well-established bond between business practice and social etiquette. These conflicting forces demanded architectural compromises. But these did not always play out through expressive built symbolism. More often was this divergence uttered in intensely heated debates about seemingly trivial decisions over interior decoration and furniture design.

When Richard Rogers Partnership completed the new headquarters for the Lloyd's of London insurance market in 1986, it was met with admiration from some, disgust from others, but always surprise, described as "one of the most artistic pieces of patronage [Britain] has seen," while the client was proclaimed "the most controversial and avant-garde of artistic patrons."[68] One of the first prominent high-tech buildings in Britain, the structure would hardly have been viewed a compromise from the outside as it arguably reset the limits of institutional patronage in the City. Yet viewed from the inside, from deep within its lofty "Room," the Lloyd's building emerged as a negotiation between the spatially and materially ingrained rituals of the oldest institution in the City, and the rapidly transforming insurance industry in the new financial environment.

In the context of the wider insurance market, Lloyd's was successful because of the provision of proximity and diversity of markets it offered in a single space. At this time, Lloyd's was just one of three sectors in the British insurance market, alongside the main company insurance market and the reinsurance market.[69] The company market was the dominant sector, operating through large insurance companies existing independently outside of Lloyd's, such as Commercial Union, Prudential Assurance, and Royal Insurance Co. The advantages of becoming a member (called being a "Name") at Lloyd's or using a Lloyd's broker rather than the company markets were threefold: the efficiency and range of specialist areas covered in Lloyd's, made possible by virtue of the number of underwriters operating in one place; the security of the marketplace thanks to regulation offered by the Corporation of Lloyd's and by the trust network inherent in its club-like form of organization; and the prestige associated with becoming a member of such an elite institution.

As a marketplace, the single Room at Lloyd's had historically facilitated the routine interactions between buyers and sellers. Its economic operations were complex, but the basic concept was simple: Names would put forward capital and accept unlimited liability for insurance risks and in return receive premiums from the insured. As all members were private investors without an in-depth knowledge of the value of such risks, they were grouped into syndicates, each organized by a managing agent. The managing agent then selected an accredited Lloyd's underwriting firm to act on its behalf at Lloyd's, setting its premium rates and deciding the risks it would incur. As underwriters tended to be highly special-ized in narrow fields of marine or nonmarine insurance, members could spread their risk by joining a number of syndicates. The Room itself consisted of two groups of people: the Lloyd's under-writers, who would be seated at tables with high-backed wooden benches, known as *boxes*, each representing a different syndicate; and the Lloyd's brokers, who would shop around the underwriters on behalf of their clients (those wishing to buy insurance), seeking out the best rate for their risk, or *premium*. In most cases, the bro-ker would spread the replacement cost of a given asset between several underwriters, so for the market to operate efficiently, the underwriters needed to be situated in the same room to allow the broker ease of movement between them and also to provide both parties with the necessary administrative services.

Over the centuries, the Room at Lloyd's had come to be cul-turally synonymous with the institution itself. It was a helpful symbol, which simultaneously served to reinforce the rituals of self-regulation for insiders while projecting a defensive aura of mystique to outsiders. The latter was a nineteenth-century con-struction. As Britain's financial sector grew and formalized with industrialization and imperial expansion, Lloyd's reified the pre-viously informal relationships and interactions present in the coffee houses within much grander and more formal premises in the apartments at the Royal Exchange, as rebuilt after the fire of 1838 by architect William Tite. As Lloyd's architectural historian Priscilla Metcalf has argued, these Victorian premises "more fully evolved the idiosyncratic nature of 'The Room'—Olympian title— where the accolade was to be called 'a great man of the Room' or, even better, 'born in the purple of the Room.'" During its tenancy here, several traditions were established, including the addition of the Lutine bell, recovered from the HMS *Lutine*, which sank in

Lloyd's building (1986) by Richard Rogers. Courtesy of Arcaid Images. Copyright Richard Bryant.

1799. The bell was hung in the center of the Room and struck when news of an overdue ship arrived—once if it was lost to the seas, and twice if it returned safely. It was also at the Royal Exchange that the Room adopted its unique hybridity that would become the model for Lloyd's in all subsequent buildings, positioned as "a cross between an exchange or trading floor, with dealers on their feet and an open-plan office with experts sitting down."[70] In architectural terms, this hybrid was apparent in the top-lit, basil-ica- or palazzo-like form of the Room, reminiscent of early Italian banking halls and counting houses that later became a model for open-plan offices, and also not dissimilar to some of the grander European trading floors of the early nineteenth century. At the moment that the familiarity of Lloyd's conversational approach to business was threatened by its own expansion, it fixed this modus operandi into a new institutional floor plan.

This spatial arrangement would form the basis of new myths and rituals of community and practice at Lloyd's for the next two centuries. The Room was aggrandized in Edwin Cooper's purpose-built headquarters on Lime Street in 1928, taking the form of a glass-domed Greek cross spanning over 160 feet, famed to be

Lloyd's of London Underwriting Room at the Royal Exchange, 1886, designed in 1844 by William Tite. Courtesy of Mary Evans Picture Library.

as big as Oxford Circus.[71] By 1945, Lloyd's had become the largest insurance market of its kind in the world, viewed as a bastion of strength in the City, its status rivaled only by the Bank of England and equaled only by the Stock Exchange. The growth of the market—and the availability of bombed land directly adjacent to its current site—required the development of an even larger neo-Georgian complex in 1958, designed by Terence Heysham, successor to Cooper's practice. Heysham's building was the market's largest headquarters to date, with its core space, the Underwriting Room, spanning ninety-one meters in length.

One key rhetoric that emerged from Lloyd's sedentary typology was that it facilitated a more careful and morally transparent way of doing business. Insurance—the business of calculating and managing risk—required time. Whereas the Stock Exchange "floor" was designed to cater for the movement of people over it and act as a platform for the various markets, which were in a continual state of flux, the Room was intended as an intimate container for conversation, in which each broker could outline, in great detail, the intricacies of each risk to the underwriter. At the Stock Exchange, each jobber or broker was dealing in essentially abstract economic concepts. In insurance, each risk was far more distinct and, in a sense, material. As each ship, house, and airport was an entirely individual case, in an absolutely unique set of circumstances, it was—in theory—necessary to know all the details to be able to calculate the risk. As one former broker remarked of his time at Lloyd's in the decades after World War II, "Everything was done in a very correct, and personal, and labor-intensive way." This was bound up with a moral code of conduct that required the broker to be completely honest with the underwriter. He went on:

> I think it's often forgotten that the basis of insurance is not good faith, it's utmost good faith. Utmost. That means not being clever and saying I didn't tell a lie. It's meaning I'm telling you the truth, whether it's to my advantage or not. ... I think utmost good faith is important because otherwise the balance of power is not even. ... If the client has just done five years in jail for grievous bodily harm, [the underwriter] would be entitled to know. Otherwise all an underwriter sees is a slip of paper saying "Miss X wants to insure her jewelry and seems a very nice person."[72]

Such a high level of disclosure was perceived to be paramount to the operations of Lloyd's as a self-regulated market, and as such, demanded an immediate working environment for the underwriters that could simultaneously act as a market stall and yet also mimic the more intimate—if somewhat cramped—setting of an office. Here the Room encapsulated the uniquely informal, club-like system of self-regulation in the City, whereby regulation was a by-product of business activity. The Room *was* the club. And in the club, rules were not written, but they were embodied spatially and verbally through etiquette and social rituals.[73]

In the decades after World War II, the single Room concept came under pressure due to fundamental changes in the calculability of risk. When Lloyd's was first established, insurance risk was the commodification of a specific and knowable event, referring to the fate of a ship on a voyage.[74] Yet by the mid-twentieth century, technological developments in aviation, shipping, oil exploration, petrochemical plants, satellites, and space travel reconfigured the scale and complexity of risks to be insured. The impact of "normal" disasters or occurrences in these new fields incurred replacement costs beyond the limits of the world insurance and even reinsurance market as it then stood.[75] For Lloyd's, such developments brought serious losses in the 1960s, in part due to a strict

membership policy which required all new Names to have a minimum "show of wealth" of £75,000 before joining. Although the
intention of this policy was to ensure that each member of Lloyd's
had sufficient resources to pay out in the event of any disaster,
such restrictions actually limited Lloyd's capital base by excluding thousands of willing investors under the £75,000 minimum.
One incident in particular brought to light the limitations of this
system and ultimately triggered a series of profitable reforms. In
1965, Hurricane Betsy struck the Gulf of Mexico, resulting in mass
devastation to the area's offshore oil industry and historically
unprecedented property damage, resulting in a loss at Lloyd's of
£38 million. Names had to make unexpected, large payouts for
the damage, ultimately causing many to withdraw their funds
and move their money elsewhere, thereby reducing the capacity
of the market even further. In response, Lloyd's lowered the minimum "show of wealth" to £50,000 and introduced a system of
"mini-Names," required to show £37,500 in return for participating in fewer syndicates.[76] The impact was a dramatic uptake of
new Names, with a record 2,251 joining in 1976, making the total
10,617 members.[77]

A defining problem for Lloyd's was the level of unpredictability
that the new landscape of risk introduced—or, as sociologist Ulrich
Beck wrote, "Along with the growing capacity of technical options
grows the incalculability of their consequences."[78] For example,
the greatest ever loss at Lloyd's before the 1980s was caused by
the widespread diagnosis of asbestosis, the disease caused by sustained exposure to asbestos. These new pervasive phenomena
were known as "long-tail" risks, due to the fact that claims could
take a very long time—over twenty years and longer—to be settled.
As the Lloyd's in-house magazine put it in 1986, "One leading rein-
surer recently made a conservative estimate that asbestos-related
claims will still be in the process of settlement at the end of this
century, and could eventually cost insurers $10bn!"[79] Whereas
previously risks could be calculated using standard instruments
like actuarial tables, the unprecedented arrival of highly complex
and environmentally pervasive technologies created more uncertainties than they dispelled, making the future opaque, both in
terms of the risks to be insured and also, by default, in terms of
the form of the insurance market. As sociologist Anthony Giddens
concluded, this kind of "manufactured" risk created a future that
had "few direct lines to it, only a plurality of 'future scenarios.'"[80]

These developments threatened to make the working practices of Lloyd's uncompetitive, both in terms of the lack of space, but also on the basis of the new working methods required to access the breadth and depth of information available for each claim. Lloyd's had a technological deficit where intelligence gathering was concerned. Underwriters were facing an "information gap" due to the inability of punch card systems (housed off-site) to hold the quantity and quality of data required to calculate a risk.[81] Similarly, brokers were also concerned about the speed with which business was handled, receiving increasing numbers of complaints that claims were not being paid quickly.[82] In addition, the growth of two distinct new markets—in addition to the well-established marine and nonmarine markets—in motor and aviation brought with them specialist requirements. Motor was the first sector to install visual display units in 1970 in the basement because, unlike in other markets, Lloyd's syndicates wrote 100 percent of each risk, which in turn produced levels of paperwork.[83] The current building was entirely unsuitable for these new technological requirements, with little opportunity for expansion.

In 1978, the Lloyd's Committee set aside a budget of £100,000 to find an architectural practice with which they could work to cultivate a design for a new building, which could accommodate the potential upheavals of the next decades. Requesting an architect, rather than a building proposal, the institution sought to mitigate the possibility of premature obsolescence, in the knowledge that the projected growth rate of space requirements was in excess of two hundred square meters per annum for the foreseeable future.[84] In a sense, this method was also a calculation in risk management. Lloyd's short-listed firms that had an international reputation to position themselves in the global context during a period of dramatic change in the insurance industry. As the head of administration and Lloyd's redevelopment project coordinator, Courtenay Blackmore, explained in an interview for the *RIBA Journal*, the British public often saw Lloyd's as an old fashioned institution, but "from overseas we are seen as a great international institution; entrepreneurial, innovative and very successful in one of the most cut-throat businesses in the world."[85] Heysham's 1958 building had not been successful in promoting this cutthroat image, receiving attacks in the architectural press for its lack of imagination and heavy, retrograde neo-Georgian aesthetic. Selecting an architect, rather than a proposal, also gave the institution the ability to cultivate a strong working relationship with the architect. Blackmore, who is largely credited as the creative impetus behind the Lloyd's headquarters and with the selection of Rogers, believed that an avant-garde approach to architectural patronage was an important strategy to modernize the insurance market. Having recently overseen the redevelopment of Lloyd's award-winning computer center at Gun Wharf in Chatham, by Arup Associates, Blackmore had a fascination with modern architecture. With Rogers, he took a number of architectural trips all over the world, including to see the Maison de Verre in Paris, which he saw as a model for the client/architect rapport he wished to establish at the Lloyd's building.

Rogers + Partners' proposals appealed to the committee not simply because it accommodated limitless growth, but also because it played into the myths surrounding the Room, placing it at the conceptual and physical core of the design process. As Rogers + Partners wrote in the first full outline report of June 1979: "The efficiency of Lloyd's relies on a single marketplace within which national and international insurance can be handled. Lloyd's place in the complex international market of insurance ... emphasizes the importance of continuing a single room concept."[86] Arguably, of course, Rogers was simply reusing the same "inside-out" formula of flexibility through the unencumbered universal plan as in his recently completed Centre Pompidou (1971–1977) in Paris, designed with Renzo Piano: by positioning all services on the exterior of the building, the interior would remain an economically efficient, malleable space that could expand and morph according to the needs of the institution. At Lloyd's, one-fifth of this interior space would be given over to the Room, comprising 9,500 square meters of underwriting space that would consume most of the ground floor and two galleries, with space above for more gallery extensions that could be built as the market expanded and elegantly connected by banks of intersecting escalators.

Yet while Rogers emphasized the semantic heart of the institution in the plan arrangement, the overall stylistic and structural treatment acted as something of a rejection of its underlying values. In this sense, the building encapsulated the tensions underpinning the reorganization of the insurance market, and indeed the City of London, toward the end of the twentieth century. The Lloyd's commission came about at a moment when its local traditions were being destabilized by the impending deregulation and

The Underwriting Room at Lloyd's, as designed by Richard Rogers + Partners, 1986. Martin Charles / RIBA Collections.

Photograph of the underwriters' boxes, 1961. London Metropolitan Archives (City of London). London Picture Archive, ref 59657.

globalization of the financial system, by the increased use of computer technology, and by the ever-complex landscape of insurance. As Giddens wrote of the new "manufactured" risk environment: "In a world where one can no longer simply rely on tradition to establish what to do in a given range of contexts, people have to take more active and risk-infused orientation to their relationships and involvements."[87] Rogers + Partners' new building embodied the duality of the new economic paradigm. It promised to enable the insurance institution to modernize itself, and thus be future proof, but it also required the organization to relinquish its material heritage, thus threatening to undermine its public image of longevity and tradition.

Until this point, Lloyd's public image was founded on an architectural language of material richness tempered by functionality; in the Room, the deep caramel of the wooden underwriters' boxes was framed by glinting green and white marble, punctuated with flashes of lush cadmium red in the waiters' soft cloaks. These materials not only sustained the illusion of continuity with the coffeehouse days of the past, but, in the case of the underwriters' boxes in particular, played an important narrative role in the construction of the Lloyd's identity. Boxes, in one or another variation, had been part of Lloyd's since its inception and were also integral to the conversational mode of business, and were therefore perceived to be at the core of its self-regulatory culture. When it came to the new building, they were nonnegotiable. As Metcalf wrote: "The box in action is the condition of Lloyd's architects always have to accept. Every time, so far as property boundaries allow, it is the building that has to give. The success of the latest container will be judged by its flexibility in allowing the boxes— that is business to operate, to be serviced, to multiply."[88] Flexibility placed the onus on the modern to accommodate tradition, rather than the obverse. It was in the design of these key pieces of furniture that the conflict between the core values of Lloyd's with the central ideology of the new building and the changing economy of work in the 1980s, was negotiated.

For Rogers + Partners, reconciling the building's radical, high-tech aesthetic with these somewhat archaic objects was critical to the success of the Room. In its outline brief, Lloyd's had made it clear that it was essential that the "Coffee House feeling of the Room be retained," which meant the wooden box.[89] In December 1981, the firm established a Box Redesign Working Party, which would spend the next three years observing and documenting the old Room, carrying out numerous surveys, producing hundreds of drawings and several prototypes, and working with a handful of manufacturers to provide a box that would reconcile the modern complications of computer technology with tradition. In order to manage the development of the box, Czech architect Eva Jiřičná was brought in as a consulting architect to develop the prototype, and she later went on to design other key elements of the interior, including floors, lighting, and the staff restaurant known as the Captain's Room. According to Jiřičná, the central reason for her appointment was her supposed aptitude for working with wood, following her work on an exclusively wooden interior for the retailer Kenzo in Sloane Street. Wood was intended to appease the Lloyd's Committee, which grew increasingly concerned about the use of hard, modern materials in the interior as the project progressed. As Jiřičná noted, "The client had an idea of sitting in a very traditional building, using very traditional methods of working," but the new building was based on hard modern materials such as concrete, stainless steel, and aluminum, "materials which they had never before had around themselves."[90]

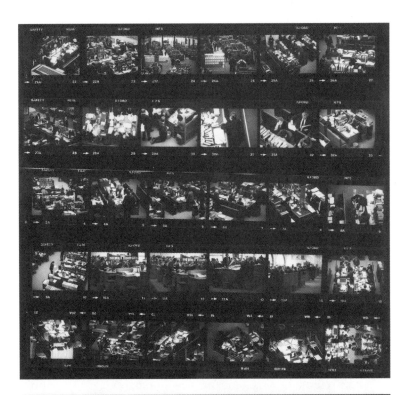

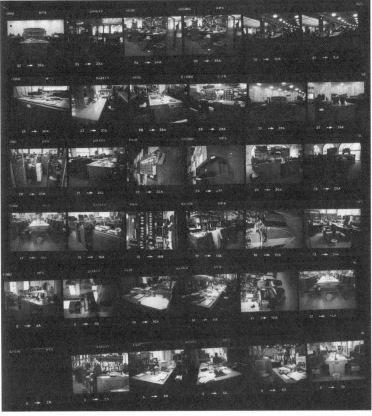

Negatives of the photographic survey of Heysham's Room showing the underwriters' boxes in use, 1982. Courtesy of RHSP and Lloyd's of London.

On the surface, the preoccupation with wood implied a desire for visual and functional continuity. The underwriters' boxes had gone more or less unchanged since the seventeenth century, comprising a long wooden table, originally of mahogany, flanked by benches with high backs for privacy. Some modifications had occurred in the nineteenth century, including the extension of the backs with glass partitions to protect against noise and draughts, the lengthening of the boxes to accommodate more underwriters, and the fixing of wire cages to the end of each table to receive the delivery of policies. But the modern teak box was based on those developed for Cooper's grand 1928 Room, with diminutive stalls or "perches" for brokers (commensurate with their lower status), and lacking glass partitions due to better heating and the inclusion of rubber flooring to improve acoustics.[91] In the early stages, the architects explored the idea of retaining the existing boxes from the 1958 Room, a rich mix of Cooper-style originals, alongside varying adaptations and bespoke creations of the 1960s and 1970s. Due to the desire to preserve the original character of the room and the anxiety surrounding the loss of authenticity in a contemporary model, the Box Redesign Working Party drew up plans to modify the existing boxes by literally cutting them lengthways through the middle, in order to add a "technology slice" to accommodate computers and air-conditioning units, though this eventually proved to be unfeasible.[92] In short, the box came to be viewed as a mode of risk management for the institution, ensuring the continued relevance of its ritualistic behaviors in the face of a global culture of deregulation.

But beyond acting as a safe signifier of continuity, and thus negating any risks that come with the new, on a more profound level, the materiality of the boxes gestured toward a specific kind of organizational psychology at work in Lloyd's. Here, performative and patriarchal individualism was perceived to be in service of the greater collective, underpinning the stability of the whole. As a member-run market, the Lloyd's Redevelopment Committee comprised high-ranking members of not only Lloyd's Corporation, but also the Lloyd's Underwriters Association, the Non-marine Association, the Lloyd's Aviation Underwriters Association, the Lloyd's Motor Underwriters Association, and the Lloyd's Insurance Brokers Committee. As members of all these committees worked in the Room on a daily basis, Rogers + Partners' designs came under substantial scrutiny from these various interests. For

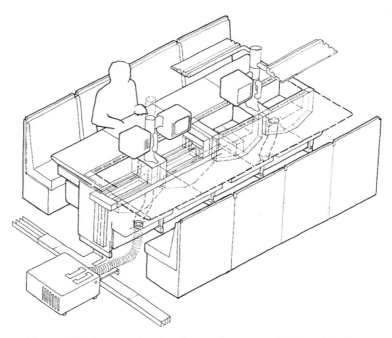

Initial proposal for the new underwriters' boxes, 1983. Courtesy of RHSP and Lloyd's of London.

the older generation, traditional form permitted the dignity of continuity, which had for so long protected Lloyd's against public criticism and promoted an inexplicably transcendent aura. As *The Times* insurance correspondent observed in 1977: "In a sense this reverential treatment of Lloyd's is a curious phenomenon. It funds no political lobby, and would be acutely embarrassed by the blatant corporate image boosting campaigns its fellows in the international insurance world find necessary. Yet, when a cartoonist pokes fun at capitalism he characterizes the public impression of a pinstriped, multi-chinned, cigar-smoking banker, stockbroker or property developer. The 'man from the pru' may be a cartoon character, but never the Lloyd's member."[93]

Internally, its mythical status was promoted by the elitism of private membership and the requisite moral vetting undergone by all accredited Lloyd's brokers and underwriters to uphold the integrity of the institution. Prior to the acceptance of corporate names in 1994, Lloyd's was dubbed "a market of unlimited liability for hazards unlimited" as it accepted only private investors who could offer unlimited liability, rather than corporations that would be entitled to offer limited liability on account of their sharehold-ers. One of the most prominent arguments against designing a new box was the fear that each box would look the same, and thereby homogenize the diverse "society of individuals" that com-prised the Lloyd's market. After a number of complaints, the archi-tects commissioned a photographic survey of the 1958 Room in February 1982, to investigate the individualities of each box. This survey, comprising hundreds of photographs, captured a range of box types, including low-backed "open top" boxes, some with indi-vidual chairs; oddly shaped boxes surrounding centralized shelv-ing; and a cacophony of storage types, technology choices, and improvised wiring.[94] In a subsequent report, it was calculated that only 20 percent of syndicates were using bespoke boxes. However, the belief that these pieces of furniture represented the individ-ual characters of Lloyd's members was deeply ingrained into the structure of the Room.[95]

Boxes were immovable in the Room. Fixed to the floor, they represented a kind of stability in a market that was changing all the time, and thus reinforced Lloyd's brand on the world stage at a moment when its status was under threat. In doing so, the objects managed both the internal and external perception of the Room. They were, in some sense then, performative objects, through which a collective identity was forged. One instance where this was most literally displayed was through the experiments in dura-bility in the design process. The final prototype, designed by the Milan-based manufacturer Tecno, was based on a modular "kit of parts" to cater for the varying sizes and preferences of each syndicate, and constructed in a thick teak veneer reinforced by a solid metal frame.[96] In addition to enabling the easy installation and servicing of technology and ventilation, the frame intended to provide a sturdy surface to cope with heavy ledgers and—in more extreme circumstances—to take the weight of underwrit-ers. As Jiřičná explained: "The boxes had to be extremely heavy because when a contract was won or a ship lost, [the underwrit-ers] jumped on the desks ... making loud noises to celebrate or mourn. It was absolutely incredible how they abused the desks! That is why the structure of each box is massive, because we had to test it with the load of four heavy men jumping on the top of it."[97] In its brief to Tecno, the working party stipulated that the box "must be as strong as a workbench and finished as a piece of furniture."[98]

Despite the highly physical, chest-beating display of macho-masculinity described by Jiřičná, Lloyd's of the 1970s was still the domain of the gentlemanly patriarch. McDowell and Court note that members of this tribe of City workers "quite self-consciously referred to their work as a performance," whereby selling one-self, paying great attention to dress codes and formalities, was considered to be part of the job.[99] Wood and marble were logical extensions to the sartorial expression of formal masculinity, whereas steel and concrete offered the architectural equivalent of the much-ridiculed brown shoes. It is perhaps unsurprising that in the rooms of the highest status in the Rogers building, the high-tech aesthetic was overruled. Despite Jiřičná's attempts to offer a softer alternative for the executive suites, Lloyd's gave the commission to French interior decorator Jacques Grange, known for his lavish neoclassically inspired modern interiors. Wooden furniture, plush carpet, and regally upholstered sofas produced a jarring counterpoint to Rogers + Partners' modern exoskeleton, and muddied the impact of the famous eighteenth-century board room designed by Robert Adam (1763) on the eleventh floor, reconstructed and transplanted from its original location as the dining room at Bowood House in Wiltshire. Grange's interior continued the long-standing tradition of the luxurious and domestic executive office, which evoked status and power through its connection to the stately home.

In its final iteration, the new Lloyd's Room attempted to balance the high tech with the old guard. Criss-crossing banks of escalators, soaring concrete columns, and a profusion of steel and glass was tempered by heritage; its lofty eighty-meter-high nave-like interior, surrounded by twelve open floors, gave the Room an ecclesiastical air, anchored by the wooden boxes and centered round the ceremonial heart of the Rostrum. Yet despite the lengthy consultations and research carried out in an attempt to replicate and reproduce the character of the old Room in the new, Rogers + Partners received intense criticism from the Lloyd's community about the new building after its opening in 1986. According to one survey of underwriters and brokers carried out in 1987, roughly 75 percent considered the building to be "not as good" as the old building, and only 15 percent believed it to be an improvement. Most of the complaints involved the inability to navigate through the giant atrium easily due to the scale and the placement of the lifts on the exterior and—ironically—the inflexibility of the

Adam Room, Lloyd's Boardroom, originally in Bowood House Wiltshire (1763) by Robert Adam. Copyright Brian Harris / Alamy.

Room, as the cabling and ventilation made the boxes difficult to manipulate and move.

Perhaps unsurprisingly, the survey indicated that interior design was held in higher esteem than the exterior, with around 50 percent of brokers and 30 percent of underwriters liking the interior—although lamenting the "basic" feel of the restaurant and main entrance, two traditionally lavish spaces. Conversely, only 30 percent of brokers and 20 percent of underwriters liked the high-tech exterior.[100] As one underwriter put it: "I loathe the place ... it's too hi-tech and gloomy."[101] The implication was that Lloyd's did not perceive itself as a brand synonymous with high technology—in fact, quite the opposite. The typical way of working was on paper: brokers brought great long "slips" of paper to be signed by the underwriter, setting out in abbreviated form the risk that needed to be covered, which was later drawn up in a much lengthier document, the policy, by the broker.[102] While brokers were keen to see the adoption of computers to reduce queuing time, underwriters were reluctant to lose the traditional face-to-face approach to doing business and convinced the committee that computers would not be a necessary addition to the building. Consequently, Rogers + Partners' initial design lacked any IT infrastructure. Only in 1981 did the increased prominence of the microcomputer in financial services trigger Lloyd's to make a reassessment of its technology policies.[103] Fortunately, due to the in-built flexibility of the floorplan, the "servant" spaces on the exterior were expanded to accommodate ducts and cables for air-conditioning and electricity, and the plant houses on the roof of the building were increased in size to take greater loads.[104] Internally, underwriters refused to fully commit to technology and demanded that the new boxes had enough shelving and stability to carry stacks of slip books, while also having the capacity and accessibility to accommodate microcomputers and personal air-conditioning units—all the while retaining a traditional look. The Box Redesign Team designed cavities for wiring and cooling into the boxes and raised the entire Room up onto a plenum floor to allow space beneath for air-conditioning ducts.

Computer technology was slow to be accepted in the new Room because it dissipated the physical and ritualistic behaviors that were essential to the old style of risk management. These sensorial expressions of camaraderie and kinship were perceived to be at the core of the market's identity. Preserving such ideals was essential at a moment when the expansion and diversification of risk and the digitalization of procedures threatened the extinction of the Room's singular community. As Hobsbawm wrote: "When the system is at risk of being removed it becomes all the more important to reinforce community, legitimize the traditional course of action, and reinforce the belief systems therein."[105] In the early 1980s, Lloyd's had received an unprecedented amount of bad press thanks to scandals surrounding tax evasion and off-shoring, which had grown with the reinsurance market (a method of further distributing risk on a secondary financial market). Furthermore, Lloyd's was also facing competition from a new US-based competitor, the New York Insurance Exchange. Much like the Stock Exchange, during this period the Lloyd's Corporation had been required to make several reforms to improve its self-regulation and to modernize as an organization.[106] Thus the reestablishment of specific rituals was all the more important, as the informal systems that required their presence in the first place were gradually disappearing.

It wasn't only the Lloyd's community that had misgivings about the building. After its opening in 1986, Rogers + Partners received a slew of attacks ranging from Prince Charles sympathizers condemning its lack of "sensitivity" to the historic environment to sociologists critiquing its "inhumane" form—or as Sheena Wilson of Building Use Studies put it, a "design approach … guaranteed to induce a condition of mild clinical psychosis."[107] Despite the fact that Big Bang occurred in the same year of its opening, the financial district was still associated with the architectural and sartorial trappings of tradition. Journalist Brian Appleyard summarized the sentiment appositely in *The Times* in 1988, when he wrote, "Exactly 10 years ago a large number of men in perfectly boring suits embarked upon one of the most unexpected pieces of artistic patronage this country has seen. The committee of Lloyd's of London … might just as well have passed the port to the right or smoked before the Loyal Toast, so completely did this decision reverse normal City practice."[108]

When the new Lloyd's building project began, the business of risk management was intrinsically connected to the performativity and aesthetics associated the old Room. The Lloyd's Redevelopment Committee's challenge was, in a sense, to create space for a new conceptualization of insurance to grow. Here the Room became the heuristic device through which the new landscape of risk and the old social system of Lloyd's could be brought into contact.

Traditional furniture, hierarchical spatial organization, and symbolic set pieces, like the Grand Rostrum taken from Cooper's 1928 building and the Lutine bell, served to reinforce a singular ideal of the Lloyd's underwriter in the new Room. In doing so, it underscored the continued relevance of a very specific approach to handling risk—the gentleman's agreement. The new Room continued to be a stage set for a patriarchal and paternalistic form of capitalism, in which history was used to legitimize the continuation and existence of this community.

But deregulation was not the only threat to this scenography. The 1980s introduced another competitor into the City: women. Hidden within offices and back offices, women had formed an important part of the workforce since World War I, yet their visibility had been limited by restrictive male-only membership policies and other forms of structural and cultural discrimination. At Lloyd's, for example, women were excluded from working within the Room until 1973, yet the market employed hundreds of female clerical workers and machine operators in the Lloyd's intelligence offices scattered throughout the world and in the data processing facility at Chatham. Women's presence in the ceremonial spaces in the City was prohibited, but they underpinned the functioning of the financial district. Historically women in the City were considered as bodies, not minds. As secretaries, not executives. Their environmental remit was limited to the desk. But as women ascended the metaphorical ladder, the culture of the City's organizations began to be reformulated. And with it, their offices.

Defying Mahogany Gravity

> *The male is the name on the door, the hat on the coat rack, and the smoke in the corner room. But the male is not the office. The office is the competent woman at the other end of his buzzer, the two young ladies chanting his name monotonously into the mouthpieces of a kind of gutta-percha halter, the four girls in the glass coop pecking out his initials with pink fingernails on the keyboards of four voluble machines, the half dozen assorted skirts whisking through the filing cases of his correspondence, and the elegant miss in the reception room recognizing his friends and disposing of his antipathies with the pleased voice and impersonal eye of a presidential consort.*
>
> Excerpt from *Fortune* magazine editorial,
> quoted by C. Wright Mills in *White Collar*, 1951[109]

When sociologist C. Wright Mills quoted this *Fortune* editorial in his now famous examination of the postwar American white-collar worker, he was not equating the female body with the corporate body—this emblematic incarnation took the form of the male executive—but rather identifying a social phenomenon: the simultaneous standardization and feminization of office work. "It is as a secretary or clerk, a business woman or career girl, that the white-collar girl dominates our idea of the office," explained Mills, concluding, "she is the office." But for Mills, the office represented something sinister: disguised in shimmering glass and plush carpets, the office was simply the modern factory, alienating and homogenizing rising middle classes through means of a highly controlled, repeatable environment. As he wrote, "The office is the Unseen Hand become visible as a row of clerks and a set of IBM equipment, a pool of dictaphone transcribers, and sixty receptionists confronting the elevators, one above the other, on each floor."[110] Writing at the moment of radical innovations in office design, whereby modularity and standardization in both architecture and management enabled the potentially limitless expansion of American corporations, Mills recognized that the work environment meant more than the space in which people worked. Rather, it was a system that conditioned bodies—and in particular, female bodies.

Mills's modern description seems a far cry from the classic enfilade corporatism of the old City office, whereby rank was represented by proximity to the director's office—what Dickens so beautifully described in his novel *Dombey and Son* as "degrees of descent"—and tyrannical adherence to a tiered system of space standards.[111] But due to the postwar building boom, the open-plan office and its politics were commonplace in the Square Mile, despite the lack of a gridiron framework. Likewise, women's bodies dominated these spaces as clerical workers. Just as in America, where a combination of a growing crop of educated women and increasing demand for clerical work with the expansion of businesses triggered the fastest feminization of any occupation in history, in Britain, the absence of male clerks during World War I contributed to a comparable influx of women.[112] Following the war, many of these women were kept in employment due to increased labor demands in the banking and insurance sectors. Mergers in the early part of the century provoked expansion of business and turnover in individual firms, leading to the uptake of more staff.[113] At the same time, banks in particular took steps toward mechanizing office work, introducing adding and ledger-posting machines, which required an army of low-skilled operators. Young women were viewed as ideal candidates for such routine clerical labor as they offered lower salaries, minimal pension provision, little to no likelihood of promotion to the "appointed staff," and were consequently retained by many firms in the interwar period. It was felt by banks that the employment of women in the lowest clerical positions would also enable male staff to be promoted to higher ranks, thereby increasing job satisfaction and incentivizing young men to join the firm.[114]

By the time equal opportunities legislation was enacted in the 1970s, the role of women as clerical and process workers was so firmly entrenched in City culture that it was incredibly difficult for women to move beyond such roles into positions of management, both culturally and contractually. This was largely because gender was inscribed into the dominant management practices.

Photograph of the Dickensian City clerk's office at 33 Mark Lane, 1909. London Metropolitan Archives (City of London). London Picture Archive, ref 49343.

The expansion of staff and financial activities in the early part of the century had required firms to adopt rationalized techniques of management, actuating a new division of labor that placed women at the bottom of the organizational pyramid. The introduction of accounting machinery, followed by the arrival of computers and their concomitant labor requirements after World War II, prompted employers to reorganize clerical labor to keep costs down. Clerical labor was renamed *secretarial work*, created to perform the routine tasks of the executive, thereby saving him time and the firm money.[115] Employers also transformed their recruitment techniques and began to actively seek out young female workers and build in training provisions and salary scales to make the positions more attractive.[116] However, such employers also developed strategies to keep women from escalating through the ranks, the most common of which was the argument that women were unpredictable and likely to be lost to marriage and therefore, as "high turnover" staff, should not be invested in. Ironically, the imposition of a "marriage bar," requiring women to leave six months after marriage, ensured that this was a fait accompli.[117]

Thanks to their physical dominance in process-oriented roles, the female, secretarial body was not overlooked in the design of workplaces but rather became the subject of ergonomic experiments and standardization throughout the twentieth century in the name of productivity.[118] Designed for rather than with, the design and arrangement of office furniture reinforced their low status by reproducing the gender roles set out for women at the beginning of the century, rather than offering opportunities for growth. Lined up, row by row, with desks minimal and evenly spaced, the female clerical worker became associated with the aesthetic and functional precision of scientific management. Emanating from America, where practices of modularity linked the architectural and managerial design of the office environment, the universal space afforded by the modular steel frame office building provided a worksheet on which operational efficiency and profitability could be mapped out in spatial terms. Mimicking the efficiency of the gridded building structure, organizational structure adopted an orthogonal factory-like layout with rows of desks in a single space, according to the principals of the dominant management theory, scientific management. Introduced by Frederick Taylor in his *Principles of Scientific Management* in 1911, and translated for the office by William Leffingwell in 1927, the theory applied an

Women in the typing pool, Unilever House, City of London, 1930s. Reproduced by permission of Historic England / Heritage Images.

assembly-line approach to production. Where previously clerks acted as craftsman, overseeing many aspects of work, under scientific management the clerk was limited to one activity, repeated ad infinitum. In addition, the work environment—here limited to the worker's desk and chair—was standardized to reduce wastage in movement and time. Clerks should stay at their desks at all times, with messengers moving between them.[119]

This managerial kit of parts—which spread to Britain and Europe via trade journals and exhibitions, and courses on office management, although in a diluted, smaller, and less tyrannical form—rendered the office a spatialization of organizational hierarchies and thus of gender roles.[120] While the universal open plan in theory offered the possibility of collapsing hierarchies demonstrated in the space standards of older cellular workspaces, it in fact served to emphasize them. This went beyond the simple allocation of square feet according to status, which, as the British Civil Service demonstrated, was a long-standing marker of seniority.[121] The grid provided the perfect geometry for the gendered division of the wide open secretarial pool and the managerial offices at the perimeter. As sociologist Daphne Spain observed, this open-floor versus closed-door arrangement not only visualized women's lower status in the corporation, but reinforced it by prohibiting them from observing and participating in decision-making processes, while also removing their privacy. As Spain writes, "The lack of privacy, repeated interruptions, and potential for surveillance contribute to an inability to turn valuable knowledge into human capital that might advance careers or improve women's salaries relative to men's."[122]

Women's prospects were highly limited under scientific management, in part through a process known as the *standardization of personnel*, in which specific ideal characteristics were given to each job role and used in the hiring process. For Leffingwell, whereas executives should demonstrate "judgement," "aggressiveness," "tact," "diplomacy," "culture," and "knowledge," the clerk should have "skill in their specific lines" and show "thoroughness," but "initiative" should only be used to a "limited degree" and "its development ... strictly controlled." Executives and managers needed to exercise these mental faculties in enclosed spaces, whereas clerks required supervision and worked most efficiently in uniformity and a "straight-line flow of work."[123]

In design terms, loss of control brought with it a loss of individuality. Standardization became the order of the day, with homogenous designs for office equipment and furniture that aimed to increase efficiency through a strict material choreography of movements. Desks were the equivalent of flat-topped workbenches, stripped of any cluttering storage space, calculated to be the correct scale and shape so as to enable the fastest process. Swivel chairs on wheels were introduced to enable typists to access adjacent work surfaces for the input and output of documents, designed to improved posture and consequently limit fatigue.[124] The aim was to avoid the wasted time caused by extraneous movement and tiredness, thereby restricting the worker within the optimum circumference of productivity. As the Marxist political economist Harry Braverman noted in his famous examination of clerical work, "The care with which arrangements are made to avoid this 'waste' gives birth to the sedentary tradition which shackles the clerical worker as the factory worker is shackled—by placing everything within easy reach so that the clerk not only need not, but dare not, be too long away from the desk."[125]

As the main subject of office planners, the desk became a highly gendered object in the City, bound up with material signifiers of status and hierarchy. For City men, the typical freestanding mahogany desk was a luxurious rest stop in the busy movement of

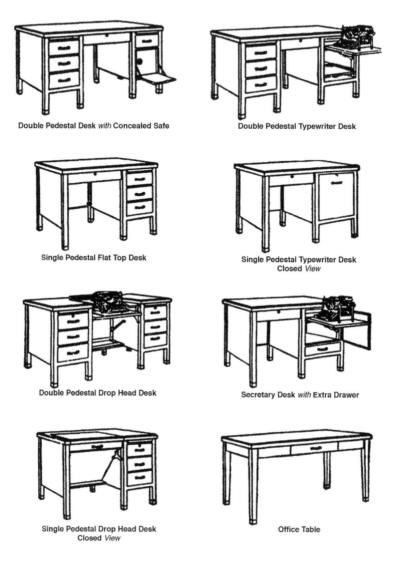

Double Pedestal Desk *with* Concealed Safe

Double Pedestal Typewriter Desk

Single Pedestal Flat Top Desk

Single Pedestal Typewriter Desk
Closed *View*

Double Pedestal Drop Head Desk

Secretary Desk *with* Extra Drawer

Single Pedestal Drop Head Desk
Closed *View*

Office Table

Desk variations from William Leffingwell and Edwin M. Robinson's *Textbook of Office Management*, 3rd ed. (New York: McGraw-Hill, 1960).

the day and part of a grand assemblage of domesticity in managerial offices. Even in the most modern of office buildings, such as the much-lauded interiors of the new offices of the National Mutual Life Assurance Society (NMLAS) at 5 Bow Churchyard (Ley Colbeck & Partners, 1960), which implemented a scientific managerial approach to the interior fit-out of its offices under the consultation of Leabank Office Planning service, executive spaces emulated the design language of the country manor.[126] As if to point to the landed heritage of most City men, the interior architecture of "executive" spaces was inscribed with signs of comfort, with soft furnishings and functionless apparel such as sofas and curtains, to denote rank and sophistication. Ironically, despite representing the spaces least available to women, these were the most "feminine" rooms in the office. As Katherine Shonfield writes: "This romanticized version of a home appears in the places where women's power is completely excluded. The interior architecture of the Executive Reception and Boardroom becomes inscribed with the signs of comfort—visibly supporting the executives 'in their illusions' while they are still at work."[127] In City offices, such spaces served to reinforce the domestic gender hierarchies and power structures at work, which were subsequently replayed through the relationship between a man and his secretary, or "office wife."

Typists, on the other hand, were provided with the smallest desks, suited to their single-task role, while machine operators worked on moveable trolleys mounted on rollers, which simultaneously doubled up as storage for the oversized policy slips still used by the firm. Others used large modular desks with storage on the other side, to be used by the worker in front. Their desks indicated the nature of the work: it was measurable, quantifiable, and infinitely repetitive. For the thousands of women employed as clerical workers, desks were little more than equipment—an efficient extension of the typewriter, which they operated for eight hours per day. Women were judged not by their social skills or by their reputations, as men were, but rather by their productivity and efficiency.

The distinction between thinking and doing was embedded in the office environment, thus casting the female as a manual rather than cerebral worker. As Elizabeth Grosz writes, the man/woman dichotomy has historically been closely aligned with the mind/body distinction. Women's sexualized reproductive associations, what Grosz calls women's *corporeal specificity*, has historically been

Fourth-floor room in Midland Bank, Poultry, 1975. London Metropolitan Archives (City of London). London Picture Archive, ref 48840.

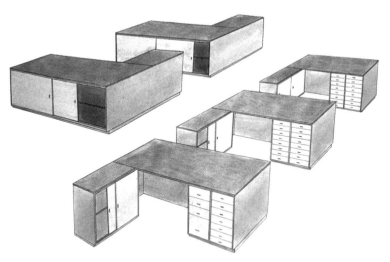

Desk design for the NMLAS offices, 5 Bow Churchyard. Use-area calculations were used to ensure labor efficiency and economy. Courtesy of London Metropolitan Archives, National Mutual Assurance Collection.

NMLAS offices, 5 Bow Churchyard, 1960, by Ley Colbeck and Partners. Courtesy of London Metropolitan Archives, National Mutual Assurance Collection.

mobilized to "explain and justify the different ... social positions and cognitive abilities of the two sexes. By implication, women's bodies are presumed to be incapable of men's achievements, being weaker, more prone to ... irregularities, intrusions and unpre-dictabilities."[128] In the workplace, the reproductive specificity of a woman's body enabled a secondary opposition to emerge, between work and home. As Dolores Hayden argued so compel-lingly in 1980, the success of the suburbs in postwar America was predicated on the gendered division of labor between these two sites; the home was "a spur for male paid labor, and a container for unpaid female labor," taking on a complimentary role in work-ing men's lives and a problematic relationship in working wom-en's lives.[129] The corollary was that the white-collar workplace only made room for a highly limited definition of a female office worker: a single woman, someone not yet married, spinster, or widow. She should be productive, not reproductive. Of course, the female office worker was further discerned by both race and class. Although offering comparable wages to factory work, the attractive office environment was an aspirational space for white working-class women and one of the few socially acceptable career choices for white middle-class women. Conversely, thanks to discriminatory

Interior   277

hiring policy, it was inaccessible for women of color and differently abled women.[130] The success of the "new office" was predicated on a universal system of norms that carried through from building to desk to worker.

As with all highly regulated systems, embedded within the theory of scientific management was the kernel of its potential undoing. Taylor and Leffingwell recognized that work was in part a psychological endeavor. This was arguably the main cause of workplace inefficiency—as overcrowding or bad task allocation could lead to unruliness or, worse, showing too much initiative. What scientific management achieved was the conscious elimination of emotions in the workplace. Such displays of personality were reserved for home and could defeat the object of the organization as "a collection of persons working together for a common end."[131] But by the 1950s, several studies of industrial work in the US and UK found such assumptions to be wrong, showing that the mind/body split inherent within scientific management led to negative attitudes and poor health in workers.[132]

While scientific management recognized that the environment had a psychological impact on its workers, the definition of the term *environment* was highly limited. The experiments led by Elton Mayo and the Harvard Fatigue lab in 1927 and 1932 at the Hawthorne Works of Western Electric Co., which tried to assess if productivity could be increased through environmental changes, had already challenged such a definition. Whatever changes took place to the six female clerical workers, be it lighting, rest periods, or furniture, their productivity increased. Mayo concluded that it was the act of being observed, of receiving attention and guessing what the researchers were looking for, that improved productivity. In other words, as Barling and Griffiths put it, "it became apparent that the workers perceptions of, and feelings about, what was happening to them, were important."[133] The so-called Hawthorne effect led to the birth of human relations, a school of management that recognized a more holistic work environment, which included the psychological, cultural, and social dimensions of work.

These transformations opened the way for new design theories that had the potential to destabilize women's fixity within the organization. If women had previously been conceived as mere bodies in the "straight-line flow," the emphasis on a nurturing psychosocial environment theoretically meant that women might also be encouraged to break free of their restrictive workplace identities.

Hawthorne experiments by the Harvard Fatigue Laboratory. Women in the Relay Assembly Test Room, ca. 1930. Western Electric Company Hawthorne Studies Collection. Baker Library, Harvard Business School. Courtesy of AT&T Archives and History Center.

In Europe, the emergence of *Bürolandschaft* (office landscaping), devised by the Quickborner Team (established by Eberhard and Wolfgang Schnelle in Germany in the late 1950s), gave rise to a workplace model that, on the surface, seemed to do away the stringent hierarchies and oppressive layouts of scientific management. Using communication as a guiding principle, Quickborner organized desks in working groups divided by plants and furniture, placing all workers—including managers—in a large open space. It encouraged the mixing of managers with all strata of the organization, as well as the personalization of workplaces and general softening of the workplace environment (anathema to efficiency theorists). Yet despite relinquishing the orthogonal and, initially, all visible signs of status, *Bürolandschaft* used the organizing potential of the universal open plan in much the same top-down way that scientific management had. As the Quickborner Team itself commented, "we realized that the office building is, in effect, management's most important tool. ... The effective functioning of the organization is decisively determined by the type of office building and/or office layout used."[134] Drawing on cybernetic systems analysis, the goal of Burolandschaft was to maximize productivity through spatial arrangement; working groups were modules in a wider system. Despite its friendly, domestic aesthetic, the approach had very little to do with the psychological freedom of its employees.

For women, such transformations had little impact on their status in the workplace or the distinction of gender roles and workplace stereotypes, not least because most organizations later added screened-off areas or offices for managers, reinstating the visible signs of hierarchy. In fact, the inherent flexibility of such systems meant they could be molded to existing management practices, rather than encouraging new, egalitarian approaches, as evidenced in America by the misuse of Herman Miller's Action Office screen-mounted furniture as a closed cubicle, rather than its intended form as an open-ended system to catalyze movement and interaction.[135] Although not popular, screens did enter into some City offices as a way of demarcating rank.

In the City, the visual presence of hierarchy and tradition was still extremely important, despite the transition to an increasingly informal business culture in the 1960s. During this period, the boom in the service economy and the expansion of the financial district opened up clerical vacancies for young, unmarried women. Temping agencies emerged all over London, providing secretaries for junior, middle, and senior management for the first time. As Steve Humphries and John Taylor note, "The dolly-bird secretary was, at once and the same time, the latest male executive toy—an office wife to tend to business and personal needs, and the greatest office status symbol that a man could possess."[136] With this, office culture became increasingly sexualized. Where previously women had been more conservative, wearing plain suits and at times overalls, female attire became increasingly attuned with the London as a cosmopolitan city and "style capital of the world," epitomized by heavy makeup and the miniskirt. The predominance of the latter even demanded changes to the office desk, as women requested "modesty boards" to conceal their legs and thus prevent men from staring in excitement or blushing in embarrassment. "It became one of the perks of a job," as one female office worker wrote. "You not only asked for rather a good salary and an electric typewriter, but also modesty boards."[137]

As Shonfield argues in her analysis of the films *The Apartment* (1960) and *Darling* (1961), the preponderance of the male gaze rendered the office eroticized territory, the space of the lover, while the home remained the site of the wife. At the office, the young

Cubicles installed in 24–28 Lombard Street, 1974. London Metropolitan Archives (City of London). London Picture Archive, ref 55052.

secretary "embodied a portable interior phantasmagoria, a new design furnishing that was commonly referred to as 'brightening the place up.'"[138] Such transformations were in part a product of the transference of American office culture with the arrival of US corporations into London. As Murray Fraser writes, "For many British citizens, the chance to work in a post-war office block offered them an intense and prolonged experience of Americanized spaces of modernity. These workers found themselves inhabiting the value systems of attitudes to the workplace created on the other side of the Atlantic."[139] While the City remained a world apart from the cut-and-thrust management techniques of American firms like McKinsey & Co., which had recently opened an overseas office in London, the informalization of the open-plan office and the transformation of gender relationships repositioned the office within British society.

The improved aesthetic quality—what Forty has called *domestication*—of the new office seemed to reinforce the gender roles associated with the work/home division, through the emphasis on the mind/body opposition. Burolandschaft and the Action Office fed into the new psychologically oriented management strategies that focused on cultivating the knowledge worker in the new service economy. Theorists like Peter Drucker emphasized the importance of the executive and manager as creative individuals and problem-solvers, rather than agents of the organization.[140] In this context, women as clerical workers were even further estranged from their male counterparts. As the work of men became specific and intellectualized through management literature, so the work of women became perceived as more generic. This dichotomy continued to be represented spatially and materially in the office through standardized secretarial equipment, designed to ergonomically fit a woman's, rather than a man's, body, and through unsubtle hierarchies of materials and scale.[141] Furthermore, the language surrounding the marketing of office furniture—influenced by popular films about the workplace—eroticized the role of the secretary relative to the seriousness of the male executive, thus fetishizing the sexual harassment experienced by women due to these inherent power imbalances.

To some extent, women's inequality at work was linked to the general powerlessness of the employee over their work environment in large bureaucratic organizations. In Europe during the 1970s, the situation changed as labor movements gave workers rights in organizational decision-making. With these rights, employees lobbied against the office landscape, on the basis that noise levels, temperature changes, and the lack of space, natural light, air, and access to a view was harming their health. In response, some countries developed detailed regulations in workplace design, leading to an increase in space standards per employee.[142] Burolandschaft died out as a leading model for workplace design, and in its place grew an egalitarian cellular plan along a corridor spine, offering offices for each worker or small group.

In Britain, however, the hierarchies embedded within British culture and the growing dominance of shareholder capitalism meant that workers continued to have little say in the design of their workplaces. Furthermore, the persistence of traditional modes of working in the City of London leading up to the 1980s ensured that developments in office planning occurring elsewhere in the country escaped the attention of most City firms, with the exception of newer international banks arriving in the 1970s, such as American Express on Cannon Street designed by DEGW. With an office economy based on speculative rental properties, rather than the owner-occupied model in northern Europe, the open-plan office ringed by managerial office cells prevailed in the City. All this was exacerbated by deregulation, and its technological and organizational demands, with the foregrounding of the American-style deep plan.[143] Where previously the desire for economy and scarcity of land had led to the predominance of the fourteen-meter-wide building with two rows of cellular offices, medium to large City office developments during the 1980s ranged from 2,000 m^2 to 4,000 m^2, a vast increase from the 400 m^2 average of the previous decade.[144]

Rather than the factory-style rows of former clerical offices, or the closed-door domesticity of merchant houses, both of which were commonplace in previous decades, open-plan layouts now positioned desks in working groups, using furniture, rather than walls, to divide the space. Such spaces worsened working conditions for women. As Michelle Murphy has shown, the connection between the deep plan and poor health in women became a prominent subject of debate in America during the 1970s. The women workers' movement exposed the hermetically sealed, deep-plan office as harmful to women physically, psychologically, and socially.[145] In addition to scrutinizing everyday materials and technologies used by women in the office for potentially harmful toxins, the movement critiqued issues of lighting, lack of access to windows, air quality, furniture, and noise as hazards in the workplace putting women in danger.[146] In particular, there were concerns about the video display terminals (VDTs) emitting radiation, causing miscarriages and impairing reproductive abilities.[147]

Although the women workers' movement did not gain such visibility in the UK, in Britain and Europe there was much concern about the impact of automation and computer usage on women's physical and psychological health, leading to studies and campaigns to understand both long- and short-term impacts.[148] In the City, by the mid-1960s, all of the Big Five banks had adopted computers into their day-to-day operations.[149] Although the initial aim of automation was to reduce workloads (and thus potentially reduce the number of paid clerical staff), the earliest computers required intense supporting manual labor for dealing with the volume of paper produced and subsequently for punched-card data entry. The excess labor was considered to be an extension of existing mechanical data processing work, and thus female employees were transferred from clerical positions to assist in the operations of the new computers.[150] As computing technology developed and became more widely used, in order to avoid the ever-increasing premium on London property, it was common for banks and insurance companies to decentralize back-office activities even more widely, to the outer edges of London and beyond to the suburbs.[151] In addition to the geographical alienation, work in these centers grew increasingly monotonous and divorced from the visible operations of the company. Whereas secretarial work enabled elements of human interaction, preparation of papers, and organization, working in a computer center was very close to factory work in character. Other firms, like the stockbroking firm Phillips & Drew, had dedicated floors. Located in a basement room in their new premises in Lee House on London Wall in 1965, the punch girls working in the computer room were subject to unfavorable working conditions due to the heat generated by the computer equipment and the increasingly heavy operating load of the computer, leading to regular weekend, evening, and all-night sessions.[152]

By distancing women from the opportunities for interaction with other levels of staff occurring in head offices and branches, there was little scope for growth and promotion; such exclusionary practices ensured that the Equal Pay legislation of the early 1970s

Woman operating the Orion Computer at the National Provincial Bank Computer Centre, St Swithin's House, 1965. Reproduced by kind permission of NatWest Group © 2023.

remained not only ineffectual, but also irrelevant.[153] By the 1980s, the emergence of mainframe technology and microcomputers led to the increased use of computers in everyday activities in the office, which transformed the structure of organizations. For secretarial labor, the most important development was the word processor, adopted by firms in an attempt to cut down on rapidly spiraling labor costs. The traditional model of each executive and manager having access to his own personal secretary was increasingly seen as "wasteful, inefficient and impossible to monitor," and thus, early on, many firms made the decision to centralize such functions in word processing centers, whereby small teams of secretaries would be assigned to entire departments.[154] Consisting of a keyboard and video display unit (VDU) linked to a computer, the benefit of the word processor to the employer was that it enabled increased managerial control through the division of secretarial tasks: "typing becomes the sole job of the word-processor 'operator,' whose activities are strictly dictated by the machine in front of her."[155]

As secretarial labor became a more sedentary and stationary activity requiring little movement out of the seat throughout

Photograph showing National Provincial staff using computers, 1969. The difference between female (manual) and male (cerebral) work is made explicit. Reproduced by kind permission of NatWest Group © 2023.

the day, complaints of backache, eyestrain, dizziness, distraction, and fatigue became commonplace.[156] Because offices were initially ill-equipped to adapt to the new technology, the working environment rapidly became hostile. Offices were cluttered with equipment, with departments using makeshift ancillary spaces as on-site computer rooms, which "were beginning to resemble factories rather than offices."[157] Sources of complaint involved the noise and heat generated by large-scale printers and cooling equipment, the glare and flicker on VDU screens, and the reflections from harsh fluorescent lighting overhead. By the beginning of the 1980s, office furniture manufacturers had gone some way to addressing these issues, "using ergonomics as a selling point for adjustable and supportive chairs, adjustable VDU tables, and glare free lighting such as uplighting."[158] In many ways, the recommendations for healthy user environments resembled the earlier "scientific" advice given to factory owners, with precise diagrams suggesting optimum ergonomic angles of elbows, knees, and forearms, screen-to-eye distances, and desk space measurements for lecterns. Furniture manufacturers, such as American company Steelcase Inc., argued that such furniture was not only necessary for the physical health of the worker, but would also "improve efficiency, morale ... and productivity."[159]

When compared to industrial workplaces, offices were presumed to be very comfortable, with no specific "disease" associated with them.[160] But as IT use increased and workers' movements placed more emphasis on the impact of the environment on physical and mental well-being, the office was revealed to be the site of a pervasive complaint: stress. Research into work stress became a highly potent and influential topic in social psychology and sociology, and even made its way into social epidemiology during the 1980s in Britain and Europe as it began to be considered a significant risk to public health.[161] The epidemiological view was critical in terms of the design of the workplace, as it said that stress was not simply a psychological problem, but a social issue, caused by "environmental factors," with real physiological impacts, like heart attacks. Women, thought to be more prone to stress-related illnesses, were central to such discussions.[162]

It was within this context of an expanded definition of occupational health, through psychology, that women's personal experiences of the physical workplace were elevated to the realm of scientific knowledge—but in doing so, they were depoliticized.

In occupational health literature, stress became a biological reaction to immediate environmental stressors, and the focus became much more on coping strategies than on political action and organizational change. With the move toward neoliberal economic models in the UK and in Europe, and the trend toward individualism in management literature, the political aspect of the conversation became downplayed: well-being was divided between the scientific (light, heat, sound, air nexus) and a focus on the subjective aspects of mental health, and specifically on coping strategies rather than the sociopolitical factors of work. Nowhere was this more apparent than in the phenomenon of sick building syndrome (SBS), which emerged in the 1980s. Described as a collection of nebulous symptoms caused by hermetically sealed air-conditioned buildings and the repetitive nature of office work, it seemed to repeat the concerns raised in the previous decade. But although women seemed to suffer from SBS more than men, it was not politicized as a women's issue.[163] Despite lacking serious evidence, SBS was mobilized as way to reconsider the "healthy workplace" without having to adjust the social and economic inequalities underpinning the office environment.[164]

Despite the neutralizing of work stress in relation to women's position in the organization, the emotional life of the worker took center stage in management literature at the end of the century. In parallel with the increase of women in management positions following the spread of equal opportunities legislation, softer, "feminized" approaches to management came to dominate. Where previously the office was predicated on the separation of thinking and planning (the job of the manager) from the actual doing of the work (the job of subordinates), in the knowledge economy, the manager's role became simply to coordinate, facilitate, coach, support, and nurture their employees, who were apparently now "self-managing." In the context of a global economy in which companies had to scale down to become agile and reactive to frequent market fluctuations, emphasis was placed on teamwork and communication rather than bureaucracy. Sometimes referred to as the *female advantage perspective* or *feminine management*, the new management theories grounded in the psychology of sex differences claimed that typically female traits like empathy, nurturance, and attention to goals like cohesiveness and stability were more effective tools than traditionally masculine traits like self-interest and control.[165] Ironically, such strategies went hand in hand with an explicit linguistic degendering of the workplace elsewhere, with the gradual scrapping of terms like *secretaries* in favor of *clerical workers* or *management assistants*.

Concepts like facilitation and responsiveness entered into the design of workplaces in the 1980s and 1990s as these theories came to dominate corporate culture. Figures like Duffy, and Franklin Becker in the US, promoted responsive and responsible workplaces to enable new collaborative and human-centered ways of working. By the 1990s, the ideal British office was conceived as a combination of social work spaces and more generic open-plan arrangements of "hot" desks, to cultivate more collaborative work cultures. At the core of all these strategies was observation-based design, building offices that were responsive, rather than prescriptive at their core, with the idea that they would create more dynamic organizations. In the City, the increased prominence of the building in management theory brought with it a general improvement in architectural standards from the 1960s onward, and between 1965 and 1986 the average percentage of commercial building costs spent on office interiors and services in Britain increased from 30 percent to 60 percent.[166] Lightweight, mobile, fashionable furniture, alongside improved lighting, acoustic insulation, and the inclusion of softer decorative elements with domestic overtones, such as plants and artwork, were introduced to make office work more appealing.[167]

As the finance industry grew in scale and value, offices were not simply an attractor of new talent, but continued to be used as an indicator of social values. While in theory a flexible building offered the infrastructure to do away with social hierarchies, by the 1980s, firms such as DEGW were questioning the wisdom of the status-less office on the grounds that hierarchy was an essential aspect of corporate life and therefore ought to be reiterated spatially. As Duffy and Colin Cave wrote, "It is now clear in both organisations which intercommunicate massively and those which intercommunicate less that status is very important and to neglect it is foolish," reasoning that "status makes communication within an organisation authentic and intelligible."[168] In the new City office, status was usually retained through the provision of cellular office space for senior level staff, with all other staff existing within landscaped open-plan layouts or densely packed dealing floors. In many companies, there was still a huge differential in both the salary and space allocation between those high on the payroll and those at the bottom, thereby implying "that space and salary were comparable measures of worth." As Joanne Eley and Alexi Marmot point out, in such instances space was calculated "on a cost-per-square-metre basis, so the most highly paid people were ... making personal use of a much larger share of the accommodation cost."[169]

At the same time, managerial and clerical staff underwent a radical process of sociospatial integration via an open-plan layout and the overall assimilation of so-called space standards for the majority of the workforce.[170] With this came a change in attitude toward furniture design in the office. In the tradition of the American Action Office, most firms in the City adopted systems furniture, offering a modular solution to accommodate different levels of staff in the same office while also offering the flexibility to manage churn. U- and L-shaped desks were very popular, as they offered large and efficient working surfaces that could be grouped together. For nonclerical staff, aural and visual privacy could be provided by low screens inserted between the desks, thereby enabling subtle hierarchies to be made visible even within the generic modular framework.[171]

Despite the gradual overhaul of the informal fraternal networks in the City with deregulation and the rise of job opportunities for women in the City (where employment grew eight times faster than anywhere else in the UK), the social barriers that had perpetuated its patriarchal structure continued to undermine policy-level changes.[172] By 1993, women held places on the board of directors of only three banks, nearly twenty years after the first women had been allowed onto the Stock Exchange floor.[173] In the new fast-paced City, the exploitation of the time zone advantage between New York and Tokyo meant longer working hours for employees, and by the 1990s individuals in professional classes worked on average between ten and twelve hours per day, arriving by 8:00 a.m. and staying late in the evening (occasionally overnight when workloads were high). This timetable was difficult for women with families, and in these years there were few schemes to help women with childcare, further stifling the attempts of women to break through the (albeit higher) glass ceiling.[174] The obstructions facing women were linked to the cultural practices of both old and new institutions in the City.

Although most of the newly merged banks in the City were attempting to modernize their image, many relied on the semblance of tradition as part of their trademark. Central to the idea of tradition was the reinforcement of existing hierarchies, recruitment practices, and social behavior that perpetuated the exclusion of women in the centuries before. While many more women were arriving at in the City as graduates from the "right" schools and universities, and therefore were armed with the correct social class attributes required to be accepted, "the very top jobs in the City remained the preserve of the traditional ruling class" and thus typical prejudices prevailed.[175] Such practices were translated into the spatial and stylistic choices made by some of the more established merchant-cum-investment-banks, in which a selective collage of cut-and-thrust capitalism and gentlemanly behavior was used to display wealth and power. Hambros Bank's new headquarters building in Tower Hill was an example of such rhetoric. Housed in an old speculative Seifert building, redeveloped by Fitzroy Robinson, the more rudimentary spaces and noisy dealing floors were concealed behind a careful blend of modern design and heritage materials. The use of stone, wood, and brass differentiated the bank in class terms from the ungentlemanly boisterousness of the new investment banks. As Anthony Sampson wrote in his 1983 edition of *The Changing Anatomy of Britain*, "Most of the merchant banks are at least a century old, and they deliberately cultivate a mahogany gravity; but those with the gravest expressions may be taking the most daring risks."[176] This architectural reinforcement of provenance set the more traditional merchant banks apart from the larger, international investment banks that were dominating the City.

Yet even among these stalwarts of tradition, the flexible deep-plan office became the dominant form of office building in the City in the 1990s, not simply because it enabled organizational change, but also because it made visible to the employee core elements of a human relations–based management strategy: open circulation paths and working clusters articulated ideas like collaboration, connectivity, and choice. The latter was particularly significant as it reaffirmed the central differentiator between the knowledge worker and the old assembly-line worker: the privilege of agency. The freedom for the individual worker to self-manage and self-improve (itself a mode of investment in human capital) was a core principle of a market-driven economy, as self-interest was the mechanism behind competition. As such, the architectural expression of freedom and choice in the workplace was not merely in the interest of the worker, but an investment in the capital assets of the firm. The responsive office was required due to the

The Boardroom at the old offices of Hambros in the early 1980s. Printed in Jacques Lowe and Sandy McLachlan, *The City: The Traditions and Powerful Personalities of the World's Greatest Financial Centre* (London: Quartet Books, 1983). Courtesy of Quartet Books.

Coopers & Lybrand offices, Plumtree Court, City of London: an open-plan office, 1986. Martin Charles / RIBA Collections.

increase in personnel churn experienced by organizations, exacerbated by just-in-time management approaches. In the following decades, the continued language of these design approaches—via hot desking, coworking spaces, and distributed and hybrid working—embodied the heightened precariousness of work in the global financialized economy.

"Head into the Goldman Sachs building on London's Fleet Street and you're greeted by wall to wall marble, a bank of receptionists and a water feature. So far, so City," began a 2017 article on the BBC News website. "But wind your way past the lifts through an anonymous fire door," it went on, "and you enter a world that couldn't be less corporate. The sounds, colours and laughter of a nursery." Claiming that the center at Goldman Sachs was "both incongruous" and "an anomaly" as the City's only onsite childcare facility, the article revealed that some thirty years after women's access into the higher echelons began, the design of the City still adhered to a traditional patriarchal worldview: the division of work and home, men and women, mind and body.[177]

Despite the fact that there are more women in high-ranking positions than ever before in the City's history, the continued absence of adequate facilities for childcare and breast pumping, well-designed toilets, and appropriate furniture, and the perpetuation of poor leave structures and precarious contracts, show how the design of the financial center continues to privilege the male working body over the female working body. On the face of it, the design distinctions between job role and gender are almost obliterated. But the new office continues to force women to perform the unreproductive, defeminized versions of themselves (Duffy's "sets" have an unexpected resonance here): timing menstruation to begin at weekends, concealing pregnancies, egg freezing, and stopping breastfeeding. Such a performance is simply a continuation of the ways that women's bodies, despite being the clerical "standard," have always been understood as abnormal in the City. Emotional displays and bodily processes associated with womanhood belong at home, not at work.[178]

Empty Desks

Peering through the window into the City's interior worlds, we see a distorted impression of the new sociology of finance. When compared with the lofty trading halls and cramped, ledger-lined offices of 1945, the picture is a vision of global modernity. The old symbols and distinctions of class, gender, and rank have been destroyed, and now egalitarian open-plan spaces are all pervasive. Surfaces are seamless; all infrastructure is within, between, and below. Technology has always been there. Time is endless; working days blur into nights. Materials are brilliant, glossy, and smooth. But this snapshot denies the mess of history and the inconsistencies of the present. The process of deregulation and going global was violent and destructive, fast and slow. The Stock Exchange was emptied within a matter of weeks, yet the mahogany desk and its attendant meanings persisted for decades. Old conversational ways of working were obliterated with new technology, but new, equally exclusive practices emerged. The old boys' network was moved out of the exchange floor and into the luxurious new interiors of bars and hotels. The financial crash of 2008 exposed a crisis of masculinity that had been building for decades in the City's new high-intensity dealing rooms. Dubbed by the Fawcett Society a *lap-dance ethos*, and later by Linda McDowell *testosterone capitalism*, the connection between the financial crash and male overconfidence became a well-known narrative, no doubt fueling the republication of Wolfe's *Bonfire of the Vanities* and the release of the film *The Wolf of Wall Street* in 2013.[179] So although so much had changed, the City remained an isolated place, with its own culture, its own rituals, and its own materiality.

In 2020, the City's desks sat empty as the COVID-19 pandemic forced its employees to work from home. Just as the postwar planners were forced to reassess the meaning of the financial district in public and economic life, so the pandemic has forced the City to question its own sense of worth. On one hand, it exposed the absurdity of the financial district as a space built almost exclusively for work in an age where this work can be done anywhere. The sheer cost and architectural exuberance of its interiors appeared ridiculous as the City popped up on people's kitchen tables, sofas, and gardens. But the pandemic also destroyed the City's raison d'être. By collapsing the final frontier between work and life, it revealed the stark artificiality of the distinction between home and the office. In doing so, it also brought to the surface the long-standing gendered distinctions between these spaces. Working from home increased the already unequal burden of care shouldered by women, causing more women to leave the labor market than men.[180] Remote working reinforced the systems of exclusion and gendered networks underpinning the City, just as hybrid working threatens to enhance the problem of presenteeism facing women, who constitute most part-time workers.[181]

Yet on the other hand, the pandemic rendered the City a momentary archaeological site in which the historical anthropology of work could be seen, assessed, and uncovered. The material culture of its vacant corner offices, dealing rooms, cafes, and pubs showed the importance of the City as a place in the formation of the finance industry; its community and way of working has been formed through its physicality. So as real estate strategists and their clients begin to decrease their real estate holdings, and as desks disappear from offices and resurface in coworking hubs, cafes, snugs, and sitting rooms, the question is: What value does the City have in a digital, postpandemic (not to mention post-Brexit) world? As the scenography of trade is taken away, perhaps its ungodly roar will be silenced and London's dark center will be reduced to a sea of distributed dark screens. Just numbers, skidding across.

On April 24, 1993, a bomb planted by the Provisional Irish Republican Army in an IVECO tipper truck exploded on Bishopsgate. It killed one person, injured ninety-four, and caused considerable damage to nearby buildings. Intended to put pressure on the British government to withdraw troops from Northern Ireland, the bomb was the fifth attack on the City in three years. Beginning with an explosion in the Stock Exchange visitor gallery in July 1990, devices of varying severity were subsequently detonated on Furnival Street (February 1992), outside the Baltic Exchange (April 1992), and on Coleman Street (June 1992). These incidents triggered the comprehensive fortification of the City's streets and buildings in the months and years to come.[1]

Six years later, on June 18, 1999, between six thousand and ten thousand protestors descended upon the Square Mile in a "Carnival against Capitalism." What started as a peaceful process swiftly became a riot. Protestors forced their way into key institutions, including Lloyds Bank in Cheapside and NatWest, chaining themselves to the interiors. Others attempted to climb Tower Bridge, while one protester was said to have superglued his head to the front door of the Bank of England. Cyclists from the Reclaim the Streets movement also brought traffic to a halt at the Bank intersection, the Chartered Institute of Bankers, and Liverpool Street station.[2]

Attacks, protests, destruction, and reconstruction. This is a familiar cycle in the City. From the devastation wrought by the Luftwaffe *Blitzkrieg* to IRA aggression, the financial center has been habitually stricken by its opponents, leading to new strategies to further harden its surroundings. Following the Bishopsgate bomb of 1993, for example, the City implemented war zone security tactics in consultation with the Royal Ulster Constabulary. Based on Belfast's security cordon, the so-called ring of steel comprised CCTV cameras (later including vehicle number plate detection and face-recognition software) and a security cordon blocking off all major entry/exit points to the Square Mile.[3] After the protest riot of 1999, these measures were further reinforced.[4] Like some kind of Schumpeterian idyll, destruction gave rise to new innovations in surveillance and secured-by-design strategies, which subsequently became the industry standard.

But these literal assaults were more than just creative destruction. They were eruptions of discontent, presenting an equal and opposite reaction to the financial system's own violent cycles of boom and bust. Responding to the crash of the early 1990s, the Carnival against Capitalism sought to disrupt an impenetrable symbol of capitalist greed and power by misappropriating its architecture and infrastructure. Likewise, the Occupy Movement in 2011 was an enactment of claiming space for the 99 percent in a territory that had caused the 2008 financial crisis. The Bishopsgate bomb detonated on the day that the European Bank of Reconstruction and Development met in the City. Aiming to cause disruption to the symbolic heart of Britain's economic and political elite, it may well have thwarted London's bid as the location for the European Central Bank (it was subsequently located in Frankfurt).[5] The City was a target because it was a symbol. Of wealth, of power, and of influence.

And the imagery was spectacular. Windows blown out with blinds fluttering in the wind. Paper, debris everywhere. Streets desolate. Crumbling facades. The detritus of trade spilling out onto every pavement. Like the artist J. M. Gandy's unforgettable translation of the Bank of England as a future ruin, the photography of the Bishopsgate bombing seemed to project the City of London as the wreckage of a great empire. It was the logical conclusion to the greed of Thatcher's political regime. An inflated, unstoppable force destroyed through its own magnitude. Yet just as Gandy's representation implied historical permanence, so the tragic shells of Bishopsgate implied a state of continuity. Buildings would be reconstructed. Streets would be pedestrianized. Defenses would be mounted. The City would become a citadel once again.

Such allegory has become all the more potent with the globalization of finance. Between 1990 and 1995, terror attacks took place in the central business districts of Manhattan, Tokyo, Madrid, Paris, and other cities across the world.[6] Following the deregulatory policies in the 1970s and 1980s, the ever more visible skylines of financial centers were increasingly regarded as the source of inequality and economic instability. In the City, developments in trading and communications and the opening of new markets rendered it an increasingly attractive site for international firms. Land values rose in the Square Mile and throughout the capital. Yet simultaneously, the absence of adequate regulation following the Big Bang and growing market volatility resulted in the collapse of several prominent British banks. These included the dramatic loss of Baring Brothers in 1995 and the demise of Warburg, one of the most successful merchant banks. These problems, in tandem with renewed calls to abolish the City of London Corporation's protectorate of the "rotten borough," provoked a period of fear for the City's future.[7]

Yet it was perhaps the indestructible nature of the City that rendered it all the more problematic to its critics. For the first time ever, the City's fate depended more on its global relationships than on its national standing, meaning that it emerged into the 2000s relatively unscathed in economic terms. Critics termed this situation the *Wimbledon effect*: just as Britain hosted the world's biggest tennis tournament but had not then produced a British champion since the 1930s, so the City was the world's most prominent financial center but lacked strong British financial institutions.[8] Its strength as a global financial hub ensured its continued growth throughout the next decade, spreading beyond its boundaries to Mayfair and Canary Wharf. The latter, following a spell of bankruptcy in the early 1990s, became a successful adjunct to the Square Mile. Barclays's move to Canary Wharf from its two-hundred-year-old site on Lombard Street in 2005, and the Financial Services Authority in 2010, confirmed the locational acceptability of Docklands for the City's revered institutions. As one of its developers, Edward Reichmann, observed, "Canary Wharf is part of the City now; it is not a rival."[9]

Paradoxically, the City's hyperconnectedness as a global city made it seem all the more isolated from the local context. Increasingly, parts of the City fell into foreign hands. The City's transition to global capital markets made land and buildings highly desirable for international investment. Whereas only 10 percent of its office space was held in foreign ownership in 1980, the financialization of the property market saw this figure grow to 21 percent in 1990, 35 percent in 2000, and 50 percent in 2010.[10] Offshore currency markets and the growing complexity of digital trading further contributed to the growing deterritorialization of the City. Surrounded by the so-called ring of steel, this global space was locked down, seemingly inaccessible to London's local residents. The City of London became what Graham and Marvin described as "a paradigm example of splintering urbanism."[11] Its status as an *elsewhere* was taken to absurd extremes.

In the last three decades, the Square Mile's symbolism has become all the more prominent. Nowhere is this more visible

Joseph Michael Gandy, *A Bird's-Eye View of the Bank of England*, 1830. Copyright Sir John Soane's Museum, London.

Photograph of Wormwood Street following the Bishopsgate bombing of 1993. Courtesy Andre Camara.

than its ever-growing skyline. As the Corporation promotes every new silhouette—each with a catchy nickname like the Gherkin, the Cheesegrater, or the Walkie-Talkie—so the City is reduced to a two-dimensional mnemonic. Similarly, the emphasis on its built and cultural heritage as a selling tool seems designed to convince a critical audience of its historical significance and benign character. As one journalist put it in 1999, such developments are "a clever distraction, a theme-park of Britishness to lure foreign corporations and domestic politicians alike." This imagery paints the picture as a world apart from its surroundings. It diverts attention from the City's lack of involvement with the impoverished neighboring boroughs of Hackney and Tower Hamlets, which "have gained little from their neighbours' frequent boomtimes, except a view of cranes and new plate glass."[12]

But the City is a place within a place. Architectural icons act like masks, propagating its mystique, reinforcing its myths. As the City's long-standing *Dictum meum pactum* culture has shown, myths serve specific communities while disadvantaging others. The idea that the City is separate from the city, from the rest of British society, is perhaps the most damaging of such folklores. Abercrombie and Forshaw's 1943 map seemed to preempt the power that such an image could have. As the financial system has become more technologically complex, the idea that the City is a black box has only become more potent. This fantasy removes accountability from the government and regulatory bodies that oversee the financial center. As the events since the 1990s have shown, its flourishing as a global city could not have occurred without ideological sympathy from those at the heart of British politics. Deregulation under the Conservatives, followed by New Labour's vigorous support after 1997, protected and promoted the City's independence. In fact, this interconnectedness with government interests has arguably made the City of London more powerful today than it was at the height of empire.

Such fables also distract from the embeddedness of the City in the British economic landscape. In a postindustrial society, dependent on the service sector, the City of London has become an important source of income for the nation. In 2020, the financial services industry generated 8.6 percent of GDP, despite only employing 3.3 percent of workers. Half of this output was produced in London.[13] In this context, Greater London has provided an important support system for the Square Mile. Major infrastructural developments in transport/communications have been implemented to service the central business district. The City's spread into Spitalfields, Southwark, and Docklands has caused the selective partial transformation of neighboring areas, either through large office developments or gated luxury apartments. Much of this been to the detriment of London's inhabitants, worsening inequality and creating a spatialized class divide between core and periphery. Infrastructure has also tended to bypass poorer areas, as demonstrated by the initial plans for the Docklands Light Railway, and subsequently with the Crossrail scheme. These schemes impact the allocation of government spending, which more often than not is skewed to facilitate the City's growth at the expense of the rest of London. Nowhere was this more starkly realized than George Osborne's 2010 spending review, which announced that millions would be invested into Crossrail to better connect the City to London's largest international airport at Heathrow, while simultaneously cutting the social housing budget by half.[14] The financial center is deeply rooted within the capital and the nation; the epithet *global* does nothing to disturb this fact.

So while the LCC's opaque cartography lives on in the popular psyche, it remains an illusion. Only by casting a historical light on this small patch of London is it possible to see past the political mythologies and the fog of financial jargon. In the form of a kind of Summersonian time-lapse through the life of the City since World War II, this book has endeavored to illuminate the dark spot. It reveals the biography of a place caught among parliamentary policies, invented traditions, technological innovations, and real estate fluctuations. It shows a site formed by big ideas like deregulation, which are enacted through slow and often small-scale interventions in its built fabric.

Yet just as Summerson's air-view provided merely a starting point for his grand analysis of Georgian London, this story has focused in on the territory below, moving beyond that "startling impression of automatic movement, of mindless growth."[15] The transformation to a modern global financial center was not frictionless, and was anything but automatic. Shifting through the scales, from city to desk, what emerges is a narrative of conflict, of unsatisfactory compromises. As an urban entity, its postwar development was fraught. Subject to the demands of the LCC, the government and City businesses, and the unstable identity of City

Carl Laubin, *The Square Mile*, 1997. Oil on canvas. Courtesy Carl Laubin.

of London Corporation, it emerged as entirely incoherent. Heavy regulations on building paradoxically produced bursts of unregulated construction, leading to unlikely and perhaps undesirable partnerships among architects, developers, municipal authorities, and investors. These relationships flourished as the City's financial markets grew increasingly deregulated, but remained contentious despite being highly productive.

In the same vein, a journey through the Square Mile's streets paints a contradictory picture of continuity and rupture. On the surface, the architecture of the short view prevails as alleyways and small squares provide stage sets upon which the *Dictum meum pactum* myth has been played and replayed. Yet take a cross section and this artifice is quickly exposed. Layers of urban theories intersect and collide with the relentless march of technology. Cutting a slice through the City's crust, one finds the dead ends of pedways, two-dimensional retained facades, and the miles of subterranean cable tunnels servicing screens and surveillance above.

But the City's stage sets provide more than scenography. These facades embody the tension between the shifting desires of occupiers and the demands of real estate developers. A tension expressed in the gradual dissolving of the facade into the mechanism of the building-as-investment. As the City deregulated, office buildings became a technology of flexibility. With this, the facade became a contractual layer in the financial agreements among an ever-growing number of building specialists.

Inside these buildings, a traumatic eviction was taking place. From World War II, a slow but violent overhaul of the club-like fraternities in the City ensued. Digitalization, internationalization, and feminization of the office after the Big Bang provoked a shift in the layout and material trappings in the workplace. Yet mahogany gravity was difficult to defy. Heavy desks in the corner office remained obstinately, while lightweight, flexible alternatives proliferated. Old versions of patriarchal behavior were supplemented with alternative, though no less toxic, definitions of masculinity. And as technological innovations transformed the psychology and sociology of financial transactions, new meanings of exchange, risk, and speculation were configured, in turn introducing new patterns of sociability. Rather than existing in simultaneous yet separate realms, the digital and the physical existed as interwoven phenomena. Modernization processes were sticky and accidental at times; if old power structures and rituals were removed, new types were added. Indeed, as the "freedoms" of the club-like City disintegrated, they were replaced by liberties afforded by the free market, generating permissive environments that enabled new social codes to exist.

Moving beyond the air-view, it becomes apparent that the built environment is not merely diagrammatic of the complex processes that produce global markets and regulatory regimes: visualization is not tantamount to simplification. Architecture, urban design, and infrastructure are fundamental material components within such processes; the form of the City's streets, facades, trading floors, and offices are active agents, and even catalysts, in shaping financial practice as much as they are products of it. In the City of London, it becomes evident that architectural and infrastructural developments went hand in hand with the broader regulatory developments in Britain's financial system; in the switch from a Keynesian to a monetarist model, the City's built environment at times assisted and at times restricted innovation. It was a nonlinear and often awkward process, whereby the push of modernization and the pull of tradition were in a continual dialogue throughout the entire postwar period.

So, as Summerson writes, the narrative of the City's postwar development is "made up of topography, biography, and architecture." But we can also add to that economy. At each scale, the influence of money, finance, and politics has revealed itself in different ways, from the changing urban morphology to the architectural trappings of a handshake. In the Square Mile, the base and the superstructure are inextricably intertwined. Only by shedding light on these processes is the fantasy of the black spot exposed as a concrete reality.

Acknowledgments

This book has developed with me. We have both been transformed by two transatlantic moves, a marriage, two children, and some astute editorial and collegial guidance. The book began its life as a PhD thesis written at the Bartlett School of Architecture, University College London. Here there are too many people to thank. My supervisor, Murray Fraser, was incredibly generous with his time and support, and had unfailing confidence in me and the project even when I didn't. Iain Borden, my second supervisor, had faith in the topic when it was just a kernel of an idea. If not for his encouragement during my master's degree, I might never have embarked upon the PhD in the first place. I was also fortunate to have two very attentive examiners, Daniel Abramson and Michael Hebbert, whose judicious critique has stayed with me throughout the rewriting process. The Bartlett was a special place to begin my career, and I continue to feel its influence. Adrian Forty taught me that we can learn the most about societies by looking at the things we take most for granted. Barbara Penner taught me to (try to) love writing. Peg Rawes, Penelope Haralambidou, Jonathan Hill, and Jane Rendell created a nurturing yet critical research environment. I was also lucky enough to be part of an amazing cohort of PhD scholars who have become lifelong friends, including Danielle Willkens, David Roberts, Berni Devilat, Felipe Lanuza, Sabina Andron, Sophie Read, Anne Ulrike Andersen, and Stelios Giamarelos, to name just a few.

Researching the City of London was not always a straightforward process thanks to its esoteric forms and systems. A vast number of people helped me to understand and discover it. I am indebted to Peter Rees, Alexi Marmot, Michael Hebbert, Francis Duffy, John Worthington, Eva Jiřičná, David Needham, Harry Dawe-Lane, Donald MacKenzie, and Brian Winterflood for sharing their specialist knowledge with me. There are also many institutions without which this research would have been impossible. In particular, I am indebted to the librarians and archivists of the London Metropolitan Archives (LMA) and Guildhall Library for their vast expertise and patience, with special thanks to Jeremy Smith and Wendy Hawke, who have been so helpful with navigating the LMA's vast image collection. I would like to thank all the staff at the British Library and UCL libraries, where I spent too many hours to count, as well as those from the archives and collections of the Bank of England, DEGW, GMW, Royal Institute of British Architects, Royal Bank of Scotland Group, Lloyd's of London, and RHSP.

The metamorphosis from thesis to book brought me into the orbit of more brilliant people. My editor, Thomas Weaver, has patiently guided me through the writing process, helping me know when to take care and slow down, and when to get on with it. Our many long conversations were made all the more fruitful due to his extensive knowledge of British architectural history and all the more enjoyable thanks to his good humor. Thank you also to Kathleen Caruso and Melinda Rankin for their meticulous copyediting. All outstanding errors are my own. I have been fortunate to get feedback on parts of this book from many people who have made the writing infinitely better, including Abi Palmer, Charles Rice, Barbara Penner, Kenny Cupers, Catharina Gabrielsson, Helena Mattsson, Reinhold Martin, Claire Zimmerman, Daniel Abramson, Adrian Forty, Mathew Aitchison, Nick Beech, and some anonymous reviewers. I must also thank several people for the care and attention paid to the aesthetic aspect of the book, including: Zuzanna Śliwińska for her superlative ability to traverse the complex terrain of image permissions and copyright; Thomas Weaver for his insistence on an elegant template and advice on image selection; Ollie Palmer, my all-around graphics guru; and Brian Griffin and Carl Laubin for so kindly agreeing to let me include their artwork in the book.

The research and production of this book were enabled through the generous funding of numerous organizations: the Schools Competition Act Settlement Trust (SCAST) Postgraduate Bursary funded the initial PhD research; the Paul Mellon Centre for Studies in British Art Publication Fund contributed to publication costs; the Dutch Research Council (NWO) enabled parts of the research on gender and office design to be completed through the VENI Talent Programme; and TU Delft Department of Architecture kindly supported the acquisition of image reproduction rights.

There are many close friends, colleagues, and family who, in different ways, have offered support during the writing process, including Alice Ladenburg, Anderson Ferreira, Danielle Willkens, David Roberts, María Novas Ferradás, Rachel Lee, Angeliki Sioli, Toby Parker, Tatsiana Zhurauliova, Katherine Fischer Taylor, and Salomon Frausto. I am very grateful to Daniel Rosbottom, Mark Pimlott, and my colleagues in the Interiors Buildings Cities group for generously giving me the space and time to finish the manuscript. Sarah Withers, Richard Withers, Stephen Thomas, Julie Thomas, Freddy Thomas, Harri Withers, Angharad Withers, and Alfie Withers, thank you all for your unfailing love and support, as always.

My greatest debt is to my husband, Ollie Palmer, who has endured the ebbs and flows of this project with me since the beginning, and to my girls, Ada and Orla, who always bring me back into the moment.

Notes

Prologue

1. This is not the case in the general sense as the nonbuilt history of the City has been addressed extensively by economic and business historians. See, for example, David Kynaston, *The City of London Vol 4, A Club No More, 1945–2000* (London: Chatto & Windus, 2000); Ranald Michie, *The Development of London as a Financial Centre* (London: I. B. Tauris, 1998).

2. There are a number of architectural surveys of the City's buildings. Simon Bradley and Nikolaus Pevsner, *London 1: The City of London* (London: Penguin, 1997); Nikolaus Pevsner and Simon Bradley, *London: The City Churches* (New Haven, CT: Yale University Press, 1998); Ken Allinson and Victoria Thornton, *London's Contemporary Architecture: An Explorer's Guide* (London: Routledge, 2014); Alec Forshaw, *New City: Contemporary Architecture in the City of London* (London: Merrell, 2013); Sally Jeffery, *The Mansion House* (Chichester: Phillimore, 1993); Nicholas Kenyon, *The City of London: Architectural Tradition & Innovation in the Square Mile* (London: Thames & Hudson, 2011); Nicholas Kenyon, ed., *The City of London: A Companion Guide* (London: Thames & Hudson, 2012); Stephen Millar, *London's City Churches* (London: Metro, 2011).

3. Some important works have addressed the interconnectedness of real estate and architecture in the City, including Murray Fraser, *Architecture and the 'Special Relationship': The American Influence on Post-War British Architecture* (Abingdon: Routledge, 2007); Susan S. Fainstein, *The City Builders: Property, Politics, and Planning in London and New York* (Oxford: Blackwell, 1994); Nicholas Bullock, *Building the Post-War World* (London: Routledge, 2002); Barnabas Calder, *Raw Concrete: The Beauty of Brutalism* (London: William Heinemann, 2016); Elain Harwood and Alan Powers, eds., *The Sixties: Life, Style, Architecture* (London: Twentieth Century Society, 2002); Alan Powers, *Britain* (London: Reaktion, 2007).

4. Christine Stevenson, *The City and the King: Architecture and Politics in Restoration London* (New Haven, CT: Yale University Press, 2013).

5. City of London Corporation, "The City's Government," City of London, July 19, 2022, https://www.cityoflondon.gov.uk/about-us/law-historic-governance/the-citys-government.

6. Nick Mathiason and Melanie Newman, "City of London Corporation: A Lesson in Lobbying," *The Guardian*, July 9, 2012, http://www.theguardian.com/business/2012/jul/09/city-london-corporation-lesson-lobbying; John McDonnell, "Time to Abolish the UK's Last 'Rotten Borough'—the City of London Corporation," *New Statesman*, October 15, 2012, http://www.newstatesman.com/politics/2012/10/time-abolish-uks-last-rotten-borough-city-london-corporation; Andy Beckett, "Lord of the Ring of Steel," *The Guardian*, November 25, 1999, http://www.theguardian.com/politics/1999/nov/25/londonmayor.uk; Nick Cohen, "Without Prejudice: Last Rotten Borough," *Observer*, June 27, 1999; George Clark, David Blake, and Philip Howard, "Labour Group Seeks Abolition of City Corporation," *The Times*, August 19, 1975, The Times Digital Archive; George Monbiot, "The Medieval, Unaccountable Corporation of London Is Ripe for Protest," *The Guardian*, October 31, 2010, http://www.theguardian.com/commentisfree/2011/oct/31/corporation-london-city-medieval.

7. Critics have attributed the prominent role that the City has in the offshore financial system to this relationship. See Gary Burn, "The State, the City and the Euromarkets," *Review of International Political Economy* 6, no. 2 (July 1, 1999): 225–261; Gary Burn, *The Re-Emergence of Global Finance* (Basingstoke: Palgrave Macmillan, 2006); Nicholas Shaxson, *Treasure Islands: Tax Havens and the Men Who Stole the World* (London: Bodley Head, 2011); Ronen Palan, Christian Chavagneux, and Richard Murphy, *Tax Havens: How Globalization Really Works* (Ithaca: Cornell University Press, 2010); Ronen Palan, "Tax Havens and the Commercialization of State Sovereignty," *International Organization* 56, no. 1 (2002): 151–176; Ronen Palan, *The Offshore World: Sovereign Markets, Virtual Places, and Nomad Millionaires* (Ithaca; London: Cornell University Press, 2003); Susan Roberts, "Fictitious Capital, Fictitious Spaces:

The Geography of Offshore
Financial Flows," in *Money,
Power and Space*, ed. Stuart
Corbridge, Nigel Thrift, and
Ron Martin (Oxford: Black-
well, 1994).

8. City of London Corporation, "Ward Elections," City
of London, accessed July 19,
2022, https://www.cityof
london.gov.uk/about-us
/voting-elections/ward
-elections.

9. Peter Wynne Rees, *Core
Strategy Development Plan Doc-
ument: Delivering a World Class
City*, City of London Local
Development Framework
(London: City of London
Department of Planning and
Transportation, 2011), 16.

10. Bradley and Pevsner,
London 1: The City of London,
26.

11. Economists Advisory
Group, *An Economic Study of
the City of London* (London:
Allen and Unwin, 1971), 33.
For a compelling account
of the legacies of the City's
imperial past on architecture
today, see Jane M. Jacobs, *Edge
of Empire: Postcolonialism and
the City* (London: Routledge,
1996).

12. Economists Advisory
Group, *Economic Study of the
City of London*, 34.

13. Economists Advisory
Group, 36.

14. In 2022, the daytime
population was 513,000, with
approximately 8,000 resi-
dents. City of London Corporation, "Our Role in London,"
City of London, July 19, 2022,
https://www.cityoflondon
.gov.uk/about-us/about-the-
city-of-london-corporation/
our-role-in-london.

15. Bradley and Pevsner,
London 1: The City of London,
95.

16. D. Kynaston, "A Changing Workscape: The City of
London since the 1840s," *London Journal* 13, no. 2 (1987): 103.

17. Ranald Michie, "The
Emergence and Survival of
a Financial Cluster in Brit-
ain," in *Learning from Some of
Britain's Successful Sectors: An
Historical Analysis of the Role of
Government*, Bank for Interna-
tional Settlements Economics
Paper 6 (BIS Department for
Business Innovation & Skills,
2010), 98.

18. John Summerson, *Georgian London* (London: Barrie
& Jenkins, 1988), 2.

Chapter 1

1. Harvey was born in
Newfoundland before com-
ing to Britain, where he
trained as an architect at
the Bartlett School. Peter J.
Larkham, "Selling the Future
City: Images in UK Post-War
Reconstruction Plans," in
*Man-Made Future: Planning,
Education and Design in Mid-
20th Century Britain*, ed. Iain
Boyd Whyte (London: Rout-
ledge, 2006), 102.

2. Corporation of London
Improvements and Town
Planning Committee, *Report
of the Improvements and Town
Planning Committee on the Pre-
liminary Draft Proposals for Post-
War Reconstruction in the City of
London* (London: Corporation
of London, 1944), b.

3. Corporation of London
Improvements and Town
Planning Committee, *Report of
Improvements*, 2.

4. Peter Larkham J. and
David Adams, "The Post-War
Reconstruction Planning of
London: A Wider Perspective"
(Birmingham City University
Centre for Environment and
Society Research: Working

Paper Series No. 8, 2011),
19–20.

5. Corporation of London
Improvements and Town
Planning Committee, *Report of
Improvements*, 2.

6. The 1932 Town and
Country Planning Act gave
the Corporation the power to
act as the planning authority
for the Square Mile (giving it
the status of a local author-
ity). Richard Theodore Beck,
"The Development of the
Post of City Architect and
Planning Officer, 1478–1965,"
Guildhall Historical Association
6 (1991): 1–7; Corporation of
London Improvements and
Town Planning Committee,
Report of Improvements, 1.

7. Betty R. Masters, "The
City Surveyor, the City Engineer, and the City Archi-
tect and Planning Officer,"
Guildhall Miscellany 4, no. 4
(April 1973): 237; Larkham and
Adams, "Post-War Recon-
struction Planning of London," 18.

8. Larkham and Adams,
"Post-War Reconstruction
Planning of London," 7.

9. Larkham and Adams,
19–20.

10. Sir Patrick Abercrom-
bie, Edward J. Carter, and
Erno Goldfinger, *The County
of London Plan, Explained by
E. J. Carter and Erno Goldfinger* (London: Penguin Books,
1945), 10.

11. Abercrombie, Carter,
and Goldfinger, *County of London Plan*, 13.

12. Charles Holden
and William Holford, *The
City of London: A Record of
Destruction and Survival; The
Proposals for Reconstruction as
Presented, in 1947, to the Court
of Common Council* (London:
Architectural Press for the

Corporation of London, 1951), 42; letter from S. L. G. Beaufoy, Assistant Secretary to the Ministry of Works, to George Pepler, Chief Technical Advisor to the Ministry of Works, September 16, 1943, quoted in Larkham and Adams, "Post-War Reconstruction Planning of London," 18.

13. Corporation of London Improvements and Town Planning Committee, *Report of Improvements*, 2.

14. Larkham and Adams, "Post-War Reconstruction Planning of London," 15.

15. Ashley Maher, *Reconstructing Modernism: British Literature, Modern Architecture, and the State* (Oxford: Oxford University Press, 2020), 178.

16. Carter quoted in Maher, *Reconstructing Modernism*, 178.

17. Gordon Cherry and L. Penny, *Holford: A Study in Architecture, Planning and Civic Design* (London: Routledge, 2005), 128.

18. Larkham and Adams, "Post-War Reconstruction Planning of London," 20, 27n.

19. Larkham and Adams, 22. The 1951 development plan (approved in 1955) incorporated most of Holden and Holford's proposals, except its designation as a single use "commercial" zone and the plot ratios, which were reduced to 3.5:1 at the City fringes to reduce the City's impact on neighboring boroughs.

20. Cherry and Penny, *Holford*, 129.

21. Holden and Holford, *City of London*, 231–264.

22. Holden and Holford, 90.

23. Holden and Holford, 301.

24. Nikolaus Pevsner, "Visual Planning and the City of London," in *Visual Planning and the Picturesque*, ed. Mathew Aitchison (Los Angeles: Getty Research Institute, 2010), 187–192. Under the leadership of Arthur Ling (a modernist who had worked with Walter Gropius and Maxwell Fry before the war and headed the town planning division of the LCC Architects' Department), MARS—an affiliate of the Congrès internationaux d'architecture moderne—had produced a radical modernist grid plan for the City in response to the uninspiring initial plan put forward by the Corporation's engineer. Lionel Esher, *A Broken Wave: The Rebuilding of England 1940–1980* (London: Allen Lane, 1981).

25. Mira Engler, *Cut and Paste Urban Landscape: The Work of Gordon Cullen* (London; New York: Routledge, 2015), 26.

26. Richard Barras, *The Development Cycle in the City of London* (London: Centre for Environmental Studies, 1979), 26.

27. "Background of City Planning Policies," in City of London Department of Architecture and Planning, *City of London Development Plan: Background Study Summary: Economic Activity* (London: Corporation of London, 1976).

28. Economists Advisory Group, *Economic Study of the City of London*, 46.

29. Nicholas Bullock, "The Revival of Private and Commercial Practice," in *Building the Post-War World: Modern Architecture and Reconstruction in Britain* (London: Routledge, 2002), 245–276.

30. Peter Scott, *The Property Masters: A History of the British Commercial Property Sector* (London: E & FN Spon, 1996), 119; Oliver Marriott, *The Property Boom* (London: Hamilton, 1967), 2.

31. Regulations included a 100 percent development charge on new schemes and building license enforcement. Barras, *Development Cycle*, 26.

32. Barras, 58; Amy Thomas, "'Mart of the World': An Architectural and Geographical History of the London Stock Exchange," *The Journal of Architecture* 17, no. 6 (December 1, 2012): 1009–1048, https://doi.org/10.1080/13602365.2012.746020.

33. For example, after buying the leasehold for the site of Lee House, an office block on London Wall, developer Joe Gold sublet the land for £67,538 a year more than he was paying the Corporation, making a profit of approximately £1 million for almost no expenditure. Marriott, *Property Boom*, 70.

34. Scott, *Property Masters*, 119.

35. Marriott, *Property Boom*, 38.

36. Economists Advisory Group, *Economic Study of the City of London*, 31.

37. Barras, *Development Cycle*, 34.

38. Barras, 59.

39. Bradley and Pevsner, *London 1: The City of London*, 131.

40. Jack Rose, *The Dynamics of Urban Property Development* (London: Spon, 1985), 153.

41. Marriott, *Property Boom*, 29.

42. Introduction to the 1957 edition, in Nikolaus Pevsner and Bridget Cherry, *London 1:*

The Cities of London and Westminster (London: Penguin, 1978), 109.

43. Lionel Brett, "The Developers," *Architectural Review* 140, no. 823 (September 1965): 165.

44. Information from my unpublished inventory of architectural developments between 1945 and 1993 in the City. This is the only comprehensive postwar register, taken from the Corporation's development schedules, which themselves were filed in various committee archives under multiple (inconsistent) titles. The inventory details around 840 projects with architects and floor space figures for most of the buildings. Despite searching through archives, contacting planners, and seeking advice from LMA archivists, the district surveyor, and the Survey of London team, I have been unable to locate all data for the years 1963–1973 (inclusive). As such, this remains an incomplete project.

45. Marriott, *Property Boom*, 27–28.

46. Marriott, 29.

47. Marriott, 46.

48. Bullock, "Revival of Private and Commercial Practice," 247–251.

49. Nick Beech, "Humdrum Tasks of the Salaried Men: Edwin Williams, a London County Council Architect at War," *Footprint* 9, no. 2 (December 20, 2015): 9–26, https://doi.org/10.7480/footprint.9.2.864.

50. Daniel M. Abramson, *Obsolescence: An Architectural History* (Chicago: University of Chicago Press, 2016), 67–78.

51. These constructed intellectual distinctions had historically emerged from class-based antagonisms between the landed gentry and the new industrialists. See Stefan Collini, *Public Moralists: Political Thought and Intellectual Life in Britain* (Oxford: Clarendon Press, 1993); Eric Hobsbawm and Terence O. Ranger, *The Invention of Tradition* (Cambridge: Cambridge University Press, 2007). This hostility to entrepreneurship would have been far more present among the postwar British architectural avant-garde than it is today, as most prominent architects were privately educated members of the liberal elite. I owe this observation to Adrian Forty, who has also written extensively on the relationship between class construction and design in Adrian Forty, *Objects of Desire: Design and Society, 1750–1980* (London: Thames and Hudson, 1986).

52. Scott, *Property Masters*, 118. Calder points out that this was also made apparent in John Betjeman's reference to Richard Seifert as "the Colonel" (a jibe at Seifert for using his wartime rank in civilian life) in his satirical column in *Private Eye*. Seifert also changed his name from Rubin to Richard. Barnabas Calder, *Raw Concrete: The Beauty of Brutalism* (London: William Heinemann, 2016), 229.

53. Alan Powers, *Britain, Modern Architectures in History* (London: Reaktion, 2007), 145.

54. Richard Seifert, "An Architect's Approach to Architecture: Richard Seifert," *RIBA Transactions* 4, no. 1 (1985): 55.

55. Mary Haddock, "Architects and Their Offices: Influence of the Management Handbook Surveyed: R. Seifert & Partners," *Building*, February 10, 1967, 94.

56. Marriott, *Property Boom*, 45.

57. Bradley and Pevsner, *London 1: The City of London*, 127.

58. Ranald Michie, "The City of London in Literature: Place, People and Pursuits" (transcript, Gresham College, May 16, 2013), https://www.gresham.ac.uk/watch-now/city-london-literature-place-people-and-pursuits.

59. Pevsner and Cherry, *London 1: The Cities of London and Westminster*, 111.

60. It was agreed that a blanket "general zone" ought to be applied to the Square Mile, permitting commercial architecture of any sort—offices, warehouses, exchanges, hotels, some residential buildings—to be built anywhere, with other types of building (including public, industrial, and transport structures) requiring special permission and subject to more stringent geographical restrictions. Holden and Holford, *City of London*, 291–292.

61. Holden and Holford, 292. Although not yet nationalized, the Bank of England often acted as an intermediary between City and government interests. See Burn, "State, the City and the Euromarkets," 225–261.

62. "City of London Reconstruction Advisory Council: Formation of. Secretary's Files: City Representative Bodies. Minutes and Papers"

(London, April 23, 1942), G15/508, Bank of England.

63. Letter from Sir Wilfred Eady to Austen Hall, June 13, 1942, Chairman of Customs and Excise. "City of London Reconstruction Advisory Council: Formation of. Secretary's Files: City Representative Bodies. Minutes and Papers."

64. "City Planning," September 4, 1942. "City of London Reconstruction Advisory Council: Formation of. Secretary's Files: City Representative Bodies. Minutes and Papers."

65. "City of London Reconstruction Advisory Council: Formation of. Secretary's Files: City Representative Bodies. Minutes and Papers."

66. One reason given for this was the passing of the 1947 Town and Country Planning Act, which gave ultimate planning authority to the LCC as the designated "local planning authority" for the administrative County of London. Thus the council agreed that it would remain dormant until the time that a change in government policy occurred. "City of London Reconstruction Advisory Council—Winding up of. Secretary's Files: City Representative Bodies. Minutes and Papers. 6 Jan 1950–23 Jan 1968" (London, January 6, 1950), G15/509, Bank of England.

67. "City of London Reconstruction Advisory Council: Formation of. Secretarys Files: City Representative Bodies. Minutes and Papers"; Corporation of London Improvements and Town Planning Committee, *Report of Improvements*, 6; Holden

and Holford, *City of London*, 291.

68. Peter J. Cain and Antony G. Hopkins, *British Imperialism: 1688–2000* (Harlow: Longman, 2001), 31.

69. Cain and Hopkins, *British Imperialism*, 69, 73.

70. Michael Moran, *The British Regulatory State: High Modernism and Hyper-Innovation* (Oxford: Oxford University Press, 2003), 2.

71. Nigel Thrift, "On the Social and Cultural Determinants of International Financial Centres: The Case of the City of London," in *Money, Power and Space*, ed. Stuart Corbridge, Ron Martin, and Nigel Thrift (Oxford: Blackwell, 1994), 343.

72. M. J. Hailey and J. Wanley, *Report to the Working Group on the Automation of Money Transfer and Settlement Procedures between Financial Institutions in the City: The "CHAPS" Working Group* (London: Interbank Research Organisation, October 1973), 1A18, Bank of England.

73. Michael Pryke, "An International City Going 'Global': Spatial Change in the City of London," *Environment and Planning D: Society and Space* 9, no. 2 (1991): 204.

74. The plan reasoned that the area "has a great number of important commercial buildings, many of them head offices, for which proximity to one another is of great consequence." Holden and Holford, *City of London*, 302.

75. Great Britain Town and Country Planning Association, *The Paper Metropolis: The Report of a Study of the Growth of Office Employment in London and a Survey of Decentralised

Offices* (London: Town and Country Planning Association, 1962).

76. See "Sterling and the City-Bank-Treasury Nexus," in *The Re-Emergence of Global Finance*, ed. Gary Burn (London: Palgrave Macmillan UK, 2006), 42–62, https://doi.org/10.1057/9780230501591_3; Burn, "State, the City and the Euromarkets," 241.

77. David Kynaston, *The City of London: The History* (London: Chatto & Windus, 2011), 424.

78. Burn, "State, the City and the Euromarkets," 228.

79. Daniel M. Abramson, *Building the Bank of England: Money, Architecture, Society, 1694–1942* (New Haven, CT: Yale University Press, 2005), 223.

80. Pryke, "International City Going 'Global,'" 204.

81. London Representative Offices of Foreign Banks, "Banks and Bankers: Representative Offices. Minutes and Papers. 15 Sep 1975–1 Oct 1976" (London, September 15, 1975), 7A150/1, Bank of England.

82. London Representative Offices of Foreign Banks, "Banks and Bankers: Representative Offices. Minutes and Papers. 15 Sep 1975–1 Oct 1976."

83. London Representative Offices of Foreign Banks.

84. See also Pryke, "International City Going 'Global,'" 206.

85. Pryke, 200.

86. Between 1968 and 1971, the number of people employed in branch and representative offices of foreign banks increased from 8,120 to 10,777. City of London Department of Architecture

and Planning, *City of London Development Plan: Background Study Summary: Economic Activity*, 4.23.

87. Aled Davies, *The City of London and Social Democracy: The Political Economy of Finance in Britain, 1959—1979* (Oxford: Oxford University Press, 2017), 146.

88. Burn, "State, the City and the Euromarkets," 246.

89. Burn, 236–237.

90. Cain and Hopkins, *British Imperialism*, 666–678.

91. Cain and Hopkins, 672.

92. The governor of the Bank "was keen that the relatively flexible legal and tax framework for foreign banks in London should in no way be jeopardised." Kynaston, *City of London*, 474, 501.

93. Nicholas Shaxson, *Treasure Islands: Tax Havens and the Men Who Stole the World* (London: Bodley Head, 2011), 92.

94. This is a process that Palan has called "sovereign bifurcation"—namely, the division of "sovereign space into heavy and lightly regulated realms." Ronen Palan, *The Offshore World: Sovereign Markets, Virtual Places, and Nomad Millionaires* (Ithaca, NY: Cornell University Press, 2003), 8.

95. Kynaston, *City of London*, 501.

96. See Andrew Leyshon, "The Transformation of Regulatory Order: Regulating the Global Economy and Environment," *Geoforum* 23, no. 3 (1992): 249–267.

97. Michael D. Bordo, Owen F. Humpage, and Anna J. Schwartz, "Bretton Woods and the U.S. Decision to Intervene in the Foreign-Exchange Market, 1957–1962" (Federal Reserve Bank of Cleveland: Working Paper 06–09, August 2006), 5–6; Susan Roberts, "Fictitious Capital, Fictitious Spaces: The Geography of Offshore Financial Flows," in *Money, Power and Space*, ed. Stuart Corbridge, Nigel Thrift, and Ron Martin (Oxford: Blackwell, 1994), 94.

98. Kynaston, *City of London*, 502.

99. D. Kynaston, "A Changing Workspace: The City of London since the 1840s," *London Journal* 13, no. 2 (1987): 104.

100. See Maps 3 and 4 in Holden and Holford, *City of London*.

101. Kynaston, *City of London*, 404.

102. Pryke, "International City Going 'Global,'" 204–209.

103. Holden and Holford, *City of London*, 81–82.

104. David Kynaston, *The City of London: Vol. 4, A Club No More, 1945–2000* (London: Chatto & Windus, 2000), 324.

105. Steve Humphries and John Taylor, *The Making of Modern London, 1945–1985* (London: Sidgwick & Jackson, 1986), 59.

106. Davies, *City of London and Social Democracy*, 14.

107. Corporation of London Special Committee, "Special Committee Report: Transportable City of London Pavilion for Display at British Weeks Abroad," Report to the Common Council (Corporation of London, October 8, 1964), London Metropolitan Archives.

108. Corporation of London, *Photographs of the City of London Pavilion at Brussels Universal and International Exhibition, 1958*, COL/SP/07/042, City of London Corporation, London Metropolitan Archives.

109. Ministry of Health, "Circular 197/45. Notes of the Special Committee" (London, November 14, 1945), COL/CC/SPC/03, London Metropolitan Archives.

110. Ministry of Health, "Publicity for Government," HMSO, 1947; Corporation of London Special Committee, "Publicity for the Corporation" (papers, London, 1947–50), COL/CC/SPC/03/017, London Metropolitan Archives.

111. Corporation of London Special Committee, "Publicity for the Corporation."

112. Corporation of London Special Committee, "Special Committee Report: 'Information Centre,'" Report to the Common Council (Corporation of London, July 29, 1950), COL/CC/SPC/04/001, London Metropolitan Archives.

113. Corporation of London Special Committee, "Special Committee Report: Public Relations. Services of Outside Consultants," Report to the Common Council (Corporation of London, June 20, 1963), COL/CC/SPC/04/001, London Metropolitan Archives.

114. Corporation of London Improvements and Town Planning Committee, "Annual Reports of the Improvements and Town Planning Committee," Report to the Common Council, 1958–1961, London Metropolitan Archives.

115. Corporation of London Special Committee, "Services of Outside Consultants."

116. Corporation of London Special Committee, "'Information Centre.'"

117. Corporation of London, "Minutes of the Proceedings of the Court of Common Council," London, 1963, 175, London Metropolitan Archives.

118. These began in the mid-1950s. See, for example, Corporation of London, *The City of London Official Guide* (Cheltenham: Burrow, 1956).

119. Corporation of London Special Committee, "Special Committee Report: 'City of London' Film," Report to the Common Council, November 22, 1951, London Metropolitan Archives.

120. "Outline of the Proposed Film on the City of London," appendix to Corporation of London Special Committee, "'City of London Film."

121. Corporation of London Special Committee, "'City of London Film.'"

122. As with most of the Corporation's commissioned documentaries, the films were circulated to theaters and schools throughout the country to be used as educational tools—and, if they were good enough, entered into documentary film festivals.

123. Report of the Royal Commission on Local Government in Greater London, quoted in Robert Bellinger, "The Civic and Financial City," Guildhall Historical Association, September 30, 1975, 165.

124. Corporation of London Special Committee, "Services of Outside Consultants."

125. Mathers Public Relations Ltd., "Corporation of London: Proposals for Public Relations Services for 1964–65"; Corporation of London Special Committee, "Special

Committee Report: Public Relations Services," Report to the Common Council (Corporation of London, 1964), London Metropolitan Archives.

126. John R. Haughton, *Walk a Modern City: A Look at the City of London* (London: Corporation of London, 1967), 1–2.

127. Corporation of London Policy and Parliamentary Committee, "Policy and Parliamentary Committee Report: Public Relations Activities 1967–68" (Corporation of London, February 6, 1969), London Metropolitan Archives.

128. Corporation of London Policy and Parliamentary Committee, "Public Relations Activities"; "Festival '66," *Guildhall*, July 1966, London Metropolitan Archives.

129. Barras, *Development Cycle*, 21.

130. Corporation of London Policy and Parliamentary Committee, "Policy and Parliamentary Committee Report: Public Relations Activities 1967–68."

131. Davies, *City of London and Social Democracy*, 88.

132. Davies, 89.

133. See David Edgerton, *The Rise and Fall of the British Nation: A Twentieth-Century History* (London: Penguin Books, 2018).

134. Davies, *City of London and Social Democracy*, 10.

135. Edgerton, *Rise and Fall of the British Nation*, 132.

136. Davies, *City of London and Social Democracy*, 13–14, 155.

137. For an extensive analysis of the Campaign for Invisible Earnings, see Davies, 140–180.

138. Davies, 35.

139. Foreword by Peter Studd, Lord Mayor 1970–1971, to Economists Advisory Group, *Economic Study of the City of London*.

140. Davies, *City of London and Social Democracy*, 167.

141. Humphries and Taylor, *Making of Modern London, 1945–1985*, 14.

142. A. Abel Smith, "British Weeks," *Stock Exchange Journal*, September 1965, 8.

143. Abel Smith, "British Weeks," 9–10.

144. Ronald Dickens, "Project for a Transportable Pavilion," appendix to the Report of the Special Committee, October 8, 1964

145. Ronald Dickens, "Project for a Transportable Pavilion."

146. Corporation of London Special Committee, "Special Committee Report: Transportable City of London Pavilion for Display at British Weeks Abroad."

147. "Man Charged with Oslo Fire," *The Times*, April 28, 1966, London Metropolitan Archives.

148. "Mobile City of London Pavilion; Designers: R. Dickens and A. E. Smith," *Wood*, December 1966, 24–26.

149. Corporation of London Policy and Parliamentary Committee, "Policy and Parliamentary Committee Report: Public Relations Activities 1967–68."

150. City of London Department of Architecture and Planning, *City of London Development Plan: Background Study Summary: Economic Activity*, 4.24; Anthony D. King, *Global Cities: Post-Imperialism and the Internationalization of London* (London: Routledge, 1990), 90.

151. City of London Department of Architecture and Planning, *City of London Development Plan: Background Study Summary: Economic Activity*, 4.24.

152. Corporation of London Policy and Parliamentary Committee, "Policy and Parliamentary Committee Report: Public Relations Activities 1970–71" (Corporation of London, March 23, 1972), London Metropolitan Archives.

153. Corporation of London Policy and Parliamentary Committee, "Public Relations Activities 1970–71."

154. Corporation of London Policy and Parliamentary Committee, "Policy and Parliamentary Committee Report: Public Relations Activities 1969–70" (Corporation of London, April 15, 1971), London Metropolitan Archives.

155. Economists Advisory Group, *Economic Study of the City of London*.

156. Barras, *Development Cycle in the City of London*, 25.

157. Corporation of London Policy and Parliamentary Committee, "Policy and Parliamentary Committee Report: Public Relations Activities 1970–71."

158. Peter Cowan and Daniel Fine, *The Office: A Facet of Urban Growth*, Report of the Joint Unit for Planning Research, University College London and the London School of Economics (London: Heinemann Educational, 1969), 148–149.

159. Corporation of London Policy and Parliamentary Committee, "Policy and Parliamentary Committee

Report: Public Relations Activities 1971–72" (Corporation of London, 8 March 1973), London Metropolitan Archives.

160. Corporation of London Policy and Parliamentary Committee, "Public Relations Activities 1969–70."

161. Corporation of London Policy and Parliamentary Committee.

162. Publications included an illustrated publication on the Barbican, and numerous guides to the City with titles such as "Places of Interest," "A Young Visitors Guide to the City," and "Open Spaces." Corporation of London, "Minutes of the Proceedings of the Court of Common Council" (1973); Corporation of London, "Minutes of the Proceedings of the Court of Common Council" (1974).

163. Corporation of London Policy and Parliamentary Committee, "Policy and Parliamentary Committee Report: Public Relations Activities 1973" (Corporation of London, 21 March 1974), London Metropolitan Archives. See also John Campbell, *Edward Heath: A Biography* (New York: Random House, 2013), 317–322.

164. George Clark, "Labour Group Seeks Abolition of City Corporation," *The Times*, August 19, 1975.

165. Corporation of London Policy and Parliamentary Committee, "Public Relations Activities 1973."

166. Corporation of London Policy and Parliamentary Committee.

167. Nicolas Adam, "Epitaph for the City," *Illustrated London News* 262 (September 1974): 39–43. See Colin Amery

and Dan Cruickshank, *The Rape of Britain* (London: Elek, 1975); Christopher Booker and Candida Lycett Green, *Goodbye London: An Illustrated Guide to Threatened Buildings* (London: Collins, 1973); SAVE Britain's Heritage, *Save the City: A Conservation Study of the City of London* (London: Society for the Protection of Ancient Buildings, 1976); Save Britain's Heritage Association, *The Concrete Jerusalem: The Failure of the Clean Sweep: (A Special Report on Urban Development and Conservation in Britain)* (London: New Society, 1976).

168. Jane Jacobs, "The Battle of Bank Junction: The Contested Iconography of Capital," in *Money, Power and Space*, ed. M. Corbridge, N. Thrift, and M. Martin (Oxford: Blackwell, 1994), 365.

169. Barras, *Development Cycle in the City of London*, 34.

170. Corporation of London Policy and Parliamentary Committee, "Public Relations Activities 1971–72."

171. Michael J. Cassidy, "A Decade of Commercial Property Development," Guildhall Historical Association, May 29, 1990, 2.

172. Centre for Policy Studies, *Comments on 'the City of London Draft Local Plan' of November 1984* (London: Centre for Policy Studies, 1985).

173. Centre for Policy Studies, "Comments," 33–36.

174. Kynaston, *City of London*.

175. Corporation of London Policy and Resources Committee, *Policy and Resources Committee Report: Public Relations—Committee Control* (London: Corporation of London, April 3, 1986), London

Metropolitan Archives; City of London Department of Architecture and Planning, *Draft Local Plan: Analysis of Comments Received between November 1984 and August 1985* (London: Corporation of London, 1985).

176. Centre for Policy Studies, *Comments*, 33, 35–36.

177. Brian Griffin, "Photography Projects: The Big Tie Series," 2022, http://www.briangriffin.co.uk/photography/projects/the-big-tie/image~612.

178. David Kynaston, *The City of London Vol. 4, A Club No More, 1945–2000* (London: Chatto & Windus, 2000), 631.

179. Philip Augar, *The Death of Gentlemanly Capitalism: The Rise and Fall of London's Investment Banks* (London: Penguin, 2008), 52.

180. Eric K. Clemons and Bruce W. Weber, "London's Big Bang: A Case Study of Information Technology, Competitive Impact, and Organizational Change," *Journal of Management Information Systems* 6, no. 4 (April 1, 1990): 55.

181. Augar, *Death of Gentlemanly Capitalism*, 61.

182. Clemons and Weber, "London's Big Bang," 43.

183. Francis Duffy, *The Changing Workplace* (London: Phaidon Press, 1992), 218.

184. Avigail Sachs, "Architects, Users and the Social Sciences in Postwar America," in *Use Matters: An Alternative History of Architecture*, ed. Kenny Cupers (London: Routledge, 2013), 77–78.

185. DEGW and Eosys Ltd., *The ORBIT Study: Information Technology and Office Design* (London: DEGW and Eosys, 1983), 2.

186. For the specific transformations in financial services and their relation to built change, see Francis Duffy, *The Changing City* (London: Bulstrode Press, 1989).

187. See Linda McDowell, *Capital Culture: Gender at Work in the City* (Oxford: Blackwell, 1997).

188. Francis Duffy, "A Case for More Collaboration (1986)," in Francis Duffy and Les Hutton, *Architectural Knowledge: The Idea of a Profession* (London: E & FN Spon, 1998), 96–101.

189. City of London Department of Architecture and Planning, *Draft Local Plan*.

190. City of London Department of Architecture and Planning, 33.

191. Pryke, "International City Going 'Global,'" 209–210; Alexi Ferster Marmot and John Worthington, "Great Fire to Big Bang: Private and Public Designs on the City of London," *Built Environment (1978–)* 12, no. 4 (January 1, 1986): 219.

192. City of London Department of Architecture and Planning, *Draft Local Plan*, 34.

193. Pryke, "International City Going 'Global,'" 216.

194. Kevin Morgan, "Digital Highways: The New Telecommunications Era," *Geoforum* 23, no. 3 (1992): 319.

195. Barney Warf, "Telecommunications and the Globalization of Financial Services," *Professional Geographer* 41, no. 3 (1989): 259; Morgan, "Digital Highways," 320.

196. London Business School, *The Competitive Position of London's Financial Services: Final Report*, City Research Project (London: Corporation of London, 1995), sec. 6; Morgan, "Digital Highways," 320.

197. Morgan, "Digital Highways," 320. For an in-depth account of the logistics of installing the new telecommunications infrastructure and its politics, see Stephen Graham and Simon Marvin, *Splintering Urbanism: Networked Infrastructures, Technological Mobilities and the Urban Condition* (London: Routledge, 2001), 318–323.

198. See Sara Stevens, "'Visually Stunning' While Financially Safe: Neoliberalism and Financialization at Canary Wharf," *Ardeth: A Magazine on the Power of the Project*, no. 6 (September 1, 2020): 79–99.

199. Sam Wetherell, "Freedom Planned: Enterprise Zones and Urban Non-Planning in Post-War Britain," *Twentieth Century British History* 27, no. 2 (June 1, 2016): 276–277, https://doi.org/10.1093/tcbh/hww004.

200. Wetherell, "Freedom Planned," 276.

201. Quoted in Wetherell, 278.

202. City of London Planning and Communications Committee, *City of London Local Plan: Modifications to the Revised Plan* (London: Corporation of London, December 4, 1986).

203. Cassidy, "Decade of Commercial Property Development," 3.

204. Martin Spring, "Twin Tower Bridge," *Building*, June 19, 1992, 37–43.

205. King, *Global Cities*, 91, 98.

206. Clemons and Weber, "London's Big Bang," 55.

207. City of London Department of Planning, *City of London Monitoring Report, 1986–1993: An Analysis of the Policies and Context of the City of London Local Plans* (London: Corporation of London, 1995), 1.

208. Bradley and Pevsner, *London 1: The City of London*, 142.

209. City of London Department of Planning, *City of London Monitoring Report, 1986–1993*, 1.

210. Peter Rees, interview with the author, July 10, 2013.

211. Rees, interview with author.

212. Peter Wynne Rees, interview with Chris Ingram, recorded October 8, 2012. Published with kind permission of the interviewer.

213. Rees, interview with Ingram.

214. In the City today, there are thirty-four members in the Planning and Transport Committee, compared to ten to fifteen in most other London councils. "Committee Details—Planning and Transportation Committee," August 28, 2019, http://democracy.cityoflondon.gov.uk/mgCommitteeDetails.aspx?ID=143.

215. Rees, interview with the author.

216. Rees, interview.

217. Fainstein, *City Builders*, 108; David Harvey, "From Managerialism to Entrepreneurialism: The Transformation in Urban Governance in Late Capitalism," *Geografiska Annaler. Series B, Human Geography* 71, no. 1 (1989): 4, https://doi.org/10.2307/490503.

218. Andy Thornley, "The Ghost of Thatcherism," in *Urban Planning and the British New Right*, ed. Philip Allmendinger and Huw Thomas (London: Routledge, 1998), 220.

219. Fainstein, *City Builders*, 107.

220. Alan Prior, "UK Planning Reform: A Regulationist Interpretation," *Planning Theory & Practice* 6, no. 4 (December 1, 2005): 475, https://doi.org/10.1080/14649350500349631.

221. The GLC's abolition ought to have been profitable for the Corporation; in theory, the City would no longer be required to pay rates for services it didn't use on account of its proportionately miniscule residential population of around five thousand. But the government introduced an extended London rate equalization scheme, into which the City, Westminster, and Camden paid contributions, which were then redistributed throughout the other boroughs. The consequence was that the Corporation paid around £56 million per year for services it claimed not to use. In addition, the Corporation was handed responsibility for a number of services formerly devolved to the GLC, including waste management, highway and traffic management, and building control. Geoffrey Rowley, "The Abolition of the GLC and Its Effects on the City," Guildhall Historical Association, July 29, 1986, 6.

222. Prior, "UK Planning Reform," 475; Scott, *Property Masters*, 219.

223. Scott, *Property Masters*, 223.

224. Fainstein, *City Builders*, 198; Mark Harvey, "The United Kingdom: Privatization, Fragmentation and Inflexible Flexibilization in the UK Construction Industry," in *Building Chaos: An International Comparison of Deregulation in the Construction Industry*, ed. Gerhard Bosch and Peter Philips (London: Routledge, 2003), 201.

225. Maxwell Hutchinson, "Stuart Lipton Interviewed by Maxwell Hutchinson," in *Paternoster Square and the New Classical Tradition*, ed. Andreas C. Papadakis (London: Academy, 1992), viii–xvii; Alastair Ross Goobey, *Bricks and Mortals: Dream of the 80s and the Nightmare of the 90s: The Inside Story of the Property World*, 2nd edition (London: Random House Business Books, 1993), 65–84.

226. Brett, "Developers," 165.

227. DEGW and Eosys Ltd., *Orbit Study*, 2; Duffy, *Changing Workplace*, 227.

228. Duffy, "Case for More Collaboration (1986)," 113.

229. Duffy, 113.

230. See Graham Ive, "Commercial Architecture," in *Architecture and the Sites of History: Interpretations of Buildings and Cities*, ed. Iain Borden and David Dunster (New York: Whitney Library of Design, 1996), 375–382.

231. Tim Brindley, Yvonne Rydin, and Gerry Stoker, "Popular Planning: Coin Street, London," in *Remaking Planning: The Politics of Urban Change* (London: Routledge, 2005), 60–76.

232. Goobey, *Bricks and Mortals*, 71.

233. Despina Katsikakis, interview with the author via Skype, February 2, 2018.

234. City of London Department of Planning, "City of London Monitoring Report, 1986–1993: An Analysis of the Policies and Context of the City of London Local Plans," 12, 17.

235. The complex originally extended into the neighboring borough of Hackney. In 1993, the local authority boundaries were redrawn to incorporate Broadgate within the City boundary.

236. Rees, interview with the author.

237. P. W. Daniels and J. M. Bobe, "Extending the Boundary of the City of London? The Development of Canary Wharf," *Environment and Planning A* 25 (1993): 540.

238. From 1969 to 1984, the number of foreign banks with offices in the Square Mile increased from 135 to 470. City of London Department of Planning, "City of London Monitoring Report, 1986–1993: An Analysis of the Policies and Context of the City of London Local Plans," 1.

239. Maria Kaika, "Architecture and Crisis: Re-inventing the Icon, Re-imag(in)ing London and Re-branding the City," *Transactions of the Institute of British Geographers* 35, no. 4 (2010): 459.

240. Clemons and Weber, "London's Big Bang," 48.

241. Duffy, "Case for More Collaboration (1986)," 97.

242. This is not true of the insurance sector, which was still heavily clustered around Lloyd's of London.

243. P. W. Daniels and J. M. Bobe, "Office Building in the City of London: A Decade of Change," *Area* 24, no. 3 (1992): 255–256.

Chapter 2

1. Walter Bagehot, *Lombard Street: A Description of the Money Market* (London: Henry S. King, 1873), 4, available at https://www.gutenberg.org /ebooks/4359, 2003, 4.

2. Quoted in Derek Keene, "The Setting of the Royal Exchange: Continuity and Change in the Financial District of the City of London 1300–1871," in *The Royal Exchange*, by Ann Saunders (London: London Topographical Society, 1997), 310.

3. F. M. Locker, "The Evolution of Victorian and Early Twentieth Century Office Buildings in Britain" (PhD diss., University of Edinburgh, 1984), vol. 1, 41–42, http://ethos.bl.uk /OrderDetails.do?uin=uk.bl .ethos.348537.

4. Holden and Holford, *City of London*, 22–23.

5. Holden and Holford, 231.

6. Holden and Holford, 72.

7. Holden and Holford, 232.

8. Bryant Lillywhite, *London Coffee Houses: A Reference Book of Coffee Houses of the Seventeenth, Eighteenth, and Nineteenth Centuries* (London: Allen and Unwin, 1963), 27.

9. C. F. Smith, "The Early History of the London Stock Exchange," *American Economic Review* 19, no. 2 (1929): 208.

10. D. M. Evans, *The City: Or, the Physiology of London Business; with Sketches on Change, and at the Coffee Houses* (London: Groombridge & Sons, 1852), 150.

11. Bradley and Pevsner, *London 1: The City of London*, 472.

12. Nick Durlacher, quoted in Cathy Courtney and Paul Thompson, *City Lives: The Changing Voice of British Finance* (London: Methuen, 1996), 205.

13. Economists Advisory Group, *Economic Study of the City of London*, 282.

14. There was a subset of town clearing that dealt with settlements for nonclearing banks and businesses located outside of the town clearing area, known as walks clearing. The latter was carried out by special messengers using carts. M. J. Hailey and J. Wanley, *Report to the Working Group on the Automation of Money Transfer and Settlement Procedures between Financial Institutions in the City. The "CHAPS" Working Group* (London: Interbank Research Organisation, October 1973), 1A18, Bank of England.

15. Economists Advisory Group, *Economic Study of the City of London*, 280.

16. Roy Battersby, dir., "The Stockbroker's World," *Men and Money*, BBC 2, 1964, http://www.bbc.co.uk /archive/menandmoney/6802 .shtml.

17. Hobsbawm and Ranger, *Invention of Tradition*, 1.

18. Brian Winterflood, interview with author, voice recording, March 26, 2013.

19. Michael Pryke, "International City Going 'Global,'" 204.

20. Paul Ferris, *The City* (Letchworth: Victor Gollancz, 1960), 72.

21. Ferris, *The City*, 62.

22. Ferris, 63.

23. Ferris, 62–63.

24. Ferris, 63.

25. Ferris, 72.

26. David Kynaston, *The City of London Vol 4, A Club No More, 1945–2000* (London: Chatto & Windus, 2000), 54.

27. Ferris, *The City*, 69.

28. Holden and Holford, *City of London*, 240.

29. Mathew Aitchison, "Townscape: Scope, Scale and Extent," *Journal of Architecture* 17, no. 5 (October 1, 2012): 629.

30. Aitchison, "Townscape," 627.

31. Anthony Raynsford, "Urban Contrast and Neo-Toryism: On the Social and Political Symbolism of *The Architectural Review*'s Townscape Campaign," *Planning Perspectives* 30, no. 1 (January 2, 2015): 105, https://doi.org/10.1080/02665433.2014.918861.

32. Raynsford, "Urban Contrast and Neo-Toryism," 98.

33. Hubert de Cronin Hastings, "A Programme for the City of London," *Architectural Review* 97 (June 1945): 170.

34. Hastings, 171.

35. Kynaston, *The City of London Vol 4, A Club No More, 1945–2000*, 129.

36. Winterflood, interview.

37. The original calculation would have totaled 296, "but it was considered that because the state of development was then such as virtually to preclude any increase on those already planned, and also for economic reasons that a total of 260 was more realistic." Bernard J. Brown, "The Post-War Planning of Public Houses with Particular Reference to the City of London," Guildhall Historical Association, March 30, 1982, 3.

38. Brown, "Post-War Planning," 3.

39. Holden and Holford, *City of London*, 231–264.

40. Holden and Holford, 289.

41. Holden and Holford, 301.

42. Holden and Holford, 72.

43. Holden and Holford, 42.

44. Holden and Holford, 46.

45. Nick Durlacher quoted in Courtney and Thompson, *City Lives*, 205.

46. Kynaston, *City of London: The History*, 404.

47. Economists Advisory Group, *Economic Study of the City of London*, 297. For example, in May 1968, the Bank of England allowed the discount houses to deal as principles in bills of exchange in foreign currencies, and just two years later, the members of the Union Discount Company were carrying walkie-talkies around with them on their daily visits. Kynaston, *City of London*, 504.

48. Richard B. Smith, "A Piece of Paper," *Business Lawyer* 25, no. 3 (April 1, 1970): 926.

49. Smith, "Piece of Paper," 927.

50. Economists Advisory Group, *Economic Study of the City of London*, 278.

51. Economists Advisory Group, 239.

52. "Progress and Tradition: Electronic Robots," *The Times*, October 24, 1960.

53. Bernardo Batiz-Lazo and Douglas Wood, "An Historical Appraisal of Information Technology in Commercial Banking," *Electronic Markets* 12, no. 3 (2002): 9.

54. For example, in 1964, the Stock Exchange purchased the IBM 360, permitting labor cost savings of around £42,600 per year. Economists Advisory Group, *Economic Study of the City of London*, 276; Elizabeth Hennessy, *Coffee House to Cyber Market: The London Stock Exchange 1801–2001* (London: Ebury, 2000), 248.

55. Economists Advisory Group, *Economic Study of the City of London*, 161–168.

56. Economists Advisory Group, 9.

57. Economists Advisory Group, 168–169.

58. Economists Advisory Group, 171; Sidney M. Robbins and Nestor E. Terleckyj, *Money Metropolis: A Locational Study of the Financial Activities in the New York Region* (Cambridge, MA: Harvard University Press, 1960), 33.

59. Robbins and Terleckyj, *Money Metropolis*, 34.

60. City of London Department of Architecture and Planning, *City of London Development Plan: Background Study Summary: Walkways & Pedestrians* (London: Corporation of London, 1978), 21–24.

61. City of London Improvements and Town Planning Committee and R. B. Stucke, *Greater London Development Plan Preliminary Report 19th January 1967* (London: Corporation of London, 1967), 3.

62. City of London Improvements and Town Planning Committee and Stucke, *Greater London Development*, 3.

63. City of London Improvements and Town Planning Committee and Stucke, 3.

64. See Colin Buchanan and Sir Geoffrey Crowther, *Traffic in Towns: A Study of the Long Term Problems of Traffic in Urban Areas: Reports of the Steering Group and Working Group Appointed by the Minister of Transport* (London: HMSO, 1963).

65. Michael Hebbert, "The City of London Walkway Experiment," *Journal of the*

American Planning Association 59, no. 4 (1993): 435–443.

66. Bradley and Pevsner, *London 1: The City of London*, 131.

67. See the 1976 pedway map in City of London Department of Architecture and Planning, *Walkways & Pedestrians*.

68. Great Britain, "City of London (Various Powers) Bill with Respect to City Walkways" (1967).

69. Jim Antoniou, *Environmental Management: Planning for Traffic* (London: McGraw-Hill, 1971), 56.

70. City of London Department of Architecture and Planning, *Walkways & Pedestrians*, 29.

71. Peter Revell-Smith, "The Changing City," Guildhall Historical Association, April 29, 1968, 191.

72. Antoniou, *Environmental Management*, 16–17.

73. E. G. Chandler, "A Working Walking City, RIBA Conference Feature," *Building*, July 25, 1975, 91.

74. City of London Department of Architecture and Planning, *Walkways & Pedestrians*, 31; SAVE Britain's Heritage, *Save the City*.

75. City of London Department of Architecture and Planning, *Walkways & Pedestrians*; Jim Antoniou, "Access Networks: Basic Requirements in Planning for Pedestrians," *Official Architecture and Planning*, June 1970, 510–526.

76. Chandler, "Working Walking City," 91.

77. City of London Department of Architecture and Planning, *Walkways & Pedestrians*, 30.

78. David Smith, *The Rise and Fall of Monetarism* (London: Penguin, 1991), 81.

79. Michael Moran, *The British Regulatory State: High Modernism and Hyper-Innovation* (Oxford: Oxford University Press, 2003), 75.

80. Moran, *British Regulatory State*, 75.

81. Economists Advisory Group, *Economic Study of the City of London*, 295. The report quips, "like the traditional top hat, [it] is little more than a gesture. Firms admit (a little shamefacedly) that they get the news quicker by closed-circuit television."

82. Nick Durlacher, quoted in Courtney and Thompson, *City Lives*, 205.

83. Economists Advisory Group, *Economic Study of the City of London*, 296.

84. Edward Nevin, *The London Clearing Banks* (London: Elek Books, 1970), 209.

85. Batiz-Lazo and Wood, "Historical Appraisal," 11; Nigel Thrift, "New Urban Eras and Old Technological Fears: Reconfiguring the Goodwill of Electronic Things," *Urban Studies* 33, no. 8 (October 1996): 1480.

86. Batiz-Lazo and Wood, "Historical Appraisal," 11.

87. Clearing banks became known as retail banks in 1973. Nonclearing banks were able to use the system, but only through using a clearing bank as an intermediary. Batiz-Lazo and Wood, 11.

88. Inter-Bank Research Organisation, "Clearing House Automated Payments System (CHAPS) Minutes and Papers," London, March 1972, 1A18, Bank of England.

89. Inter-Bank Research Organisation, "Minutes and Papers."

90. Inter-Bank Research Organisation.

91. Inter-Bank Research Organisation.

92. "Bank of England, Sterling Operations: Market Operations Timeline," accessed December 11, 2013, http://www.bankofengland.co.uk/markets/Pages/sterlingoperations/timeline/default.aspx.

93. R.T. Clark, "Electronic Funds Transfer: The Creeping Revolution," *Telecommunications Policy* 8, no. 1 (March 1984): 36–37.

94. Jon Dennis, "Britain's Biggest Robberies," *The Guardian*, February 18, 2002, http://www.theguardian.com/uk/2002/feb/18/dome.ukcrime; "Bank of England, Sterling Operations."

95. George Simmel, *The Philosophy of Money*, trans. David Frisby and Tom Bottomore (London: Routledge, 1990), 172.

96. Pryke, "International City Going 'Global,'" 203.

97. HRH the Prince of Wales, "A Speech by HRH The Prince of Wales at the Corporation of London Planning and Communication Committees Annual Dinner, Mansion House, London," December 1, 1987, https://www.princeofwales.gov.uk/speech/speech-hrh-prince-wales-corporation-london-planning-and-communication-committees-annual.

98. Bradley and Pevsner, *London 1: The City of London*, 595.

99. "An Interview with Carl Laubin," Plus One Gallery, November 30, 2016, https://www.plusonegallery.com/blog/79/.

100. City of London Department of Architecture

and Planning, *Draft Local Plan: Written Statement and Proposals Map* (London: Corporation of London, 1984), 139–174.

101. City of London Department of Architecture and Planning, *City of London Development Plan: Background Study Summary: Environmental Quality* (London: Corporation of London, 1979), 11.

102. City of London Department of Architecture and Planning, *Environmental Quality*, 43.

103. City of London Department of Architecture and Planning, *Written Statement and Proposals Map*, 146.

104. Antoniou, *Environmental Management*, 26.

105. Antoniou, 43.

106. City of London Department of Architecture and Planning, *Walkways & Pedestrians*, 31.

107. City of London Department of Architecture and Planning, 31, 4.

108. David Crawford and Commercial Union Assurance Company, *The City of London: Its Architectural Heritage* (Cambridge: Woodhead-Faulkner, 1976).

109. City of London Department of Architecture and Planning, *Draft Local Plan: Analysis of Comments Received between November 1984 and August 1985* (London: Corporation of London, 1985), 207–208.

110. City of London Department of Architecture and Planning, *Environmental Quality*, 21.

111. City of London Department of Architecture and Planning, *City of London Development Plan: Background Study: Recreation & Leisure* (London:

Corporation of London, 1978), 28.

112. See, for example, Centre for Policy Studies, *Comments on 'the City of London Draft Local Plan' of November 1984* (London: Centre for Policy Studies, 1985).

113. Charles McVeigh III, quoted in Courtney and Thompson, *City Lives*, 198.

114. Winterflood, interview.

115. Ferris, *The City*, 66.

116. Steve Humphries and John Taylor, *The Making of Modern London, 1945–1985* (London: Sidgwick & Jackson, 1986), 71.

117. City of London Department of Architecture and Planning, *City of London Local Plan: Written Statement and Proposals Map* (London: City of London Corporation, 1986), 57.

118. Peter F. Drucker, "Knowledge-Worker Productivity: The Biggest Challenge," *California Management Review* 41, no. 2 (Winter 1999): 87.

119. Drucker, 87.

120. Bryan Appleyard, "Architecture at the Barricades," *The Times*, April 30, 1984.

121. Jane Jacobs, "The Battle of Bank Junction: The Contested Iconography of Capital," in *Money, Power and Space*, ed. M. Corbridge, N. Thrift, and M. Martin (Oxford: Blackwell, 1994), 369.

122. City of London Department of Architecture and Planning, *City of London Local Plan: Written Statement and Proposals Map*, 59.

123. Bill Hillier, Tadeusz Grajewski, Liz Jones, Xu Jianming, and Marguerita Greene, *Broadgate Spaces: Life in Public Places. Report of Research into the Use of the Public Spaces in the*

Broadgate Development (London: Unit for Architectural Studies, Bartlett School of Architecture and Planning, University College London, January 1990), 1.

124. Hillier et al., *Broadgate Spaces*, 2.

125. Oscar Newman, *Defensible Space: Crime Prevention through Urban Design* (New York: Macmillan, 1972).

126. Jon Coaffee, *Terrorism, Risk and the Global City: Towards Urban Resilience* (London: Ashgate, 2009), 118.

127. Coaffee, 118–119.

128. Peter Rees, interview with author via email, July 30, 2015.

129. Peter Rees, interview with author, "Email Interview: Ring of Steel, Part 2," July 31, 2015.

130. Rees, interview, July 30, 2015.

131. City of London Department of Planning, *City of London Monitoring Report, 1986–1993: An Analysis of the Policies and Context of the City of London Local Plans* (London: Corporation of London, 1995), 86.

132. City of London Department of Planning, *Monitoring Report, 1986–1993*, 81.

133. Duncan Campbell, "A Christmas Party for the Moles," *New Statesman*, December 19, 1980.

134. Campbell.

135. Philip Kelly, "The First Transatlantic Telephone Cable System—Linking the Old and New Worlds," in *Institution of Engineering and Technology Seminar on the Story of Transatlantic Communications 2008* (Stevenage, Hertfordshire, UK: Institution of Engineering and Technology,

2008), 73–83, https://doi
.org/10.1049/ic:20080671.

136. Duncan Campbell,
*Phone Tappers and the Security
State: Big Brother Is Listening*,
rev. ed. (London: New Statesman, 1981).

137. Bradley L. Garrett,
"Underground London:
Adventures in the Secret
City beneath Our Feet," *The
Guardian*, November 11, 2014,
http://www.theguardian
.com/cities/2014/nov/11/-sp
-underground-london-secret
-city-ghost-tube-stations.

138. Thrift, "New Urban
Eras and Old Technological
Fears," 1480.

139. Barney Warf, "Tele-
communications and the
Globalization of Financial
Services," *Professional Geographer* 41, no. 3 (1989): 263.

140. Kevin Morgan, "Digital
Highways: The New Telecommunications Era," *Geoforum*
23, no. 3 (1992): 319.

141. Warf, "Telecommuni-
cations and the Globalization
of Financial Services," 259.

142. Morgan, "Digital Highways," 320.

143. London Business
School, *The Competitive Posi-
tion of London's Financial
Services: Final Report*, City
Research Project (London:
Corporation of London, 1995),
section 6.

144. Warf, "Telecommuni-
cations and the Globalization
of Financial Services," 259.

145. Stephen Graham and
Simon Marvin, *Splintering
Urbanism: Networked Infrastructures, Technological Mobilities
and the Urban Condition* (London: Routledge, 2001), 316.

146. London Business
School, "Competitive Posi-
tion of London's Financial
Services," section 6.

147. For example, as Gra-
ham pointed out in 1998,
"With only 180km of fibre
constructed within the City,
the London WorldCom net-
work has already secured fully
20% of the whole of the UK's
international telecommunications traffic." "Global Grids of
Glass: On Global Cities, Telecommunications, and Plane-
tary Urban Networks," *Urban
Studies*, May 1999, 19.

148. Graham and Marvin,
Splintering Urbanism, 318.

149. David Harvey, *Con-
sciousness and the Urban Experience* (London: Blackwell,
1985), 27.

150. Inter-Bank Research
Organisation, "Minutes and
Papers."

151. Graham and Marvin,
Splintering Urbanism, 318.

152. Jenny Ireland, "The
Importance of Telecommunications to London as an International Financial Centre,"
City Research Project (London Business School; Corporation of London, 1994), 41.

153. Clark, "Electronic
Funds Transfer," 40.

154. Clark, 40.

155. City of London Depart-
ment of Architecture and
Planning, *Draft Local Plan:
Written Statement and Proposals
Map*.

156. Jonathan Rutherford, *A
Tale of Two Global Cities: Comparing the Territorialities of Telecommunications Developments
in Paris and London* (London:
Ashgate, 2004), 123.

157. Rutherford, *Tale of Two
Global Cities*, 123.

158. URS Corporation, *City
of London Decentralised Energy
& Pipe Subways Study: Baseline
Report* (London: City of London Corporation, December
2009), 14.

159. City of London Depart-
ment of Architecture and
Planning, *Draft Local Plan*;
City of London Planning and
Communications Commit-
tee, *City of London Local Plan:
Modifications to the Revised Plan*
(London: Corporation of Lon-
don, December 4, 1986).

160. City of London
Department of Architecture
and Planning, *Draft Local
Plan*, 33.

161. City of London Department of Planning, "City of
London Monitoring Report,
1986–1993: An Analysis of the
Policies and Context of the
City of London Local Plans,"
21.

162. City of London Department of Planning, "Monitoring Report, 1986–1993," 21.

163. Graham and Marvin,
Splintering Urbanism, 321.

164. Alan Jenkins, *The
Stock Exchange Story* (London:
Heinemann, 1973), 103.

165. Jenkins, *Stock Exchange
Story*, 103.

166. Winterflood,
interview.

167. London Business
School, "The Competitive
Position of Londons Finan-
cial Services," section 5.

168. "City trading desk
transactions with the London Stock Exchange serv-
ers located in the City was
achieved in 0.1µs, while connection to the NYSE Euronext
site in Basildon took 0.43µs,
and connection with the
Chi X server in Slough took
0.47µs. These time advan-
tages, however small, are
important." Simon Mollan
and Ranald Michie, "The City
of London as an International
Commercial and Financial
Center since 1900," *Enterprise
and Society* 13, no. 3 (2012): 36.

169. Mollan and Michie, "City of London," 38–39.

170. Walter Bagehot, *Lombard Street: A Description of the Money Market* (Westport, CT: Hyperion Press, 1979), 6.

Chapter 3

1. Roy Battersby, dir., "A Question of Confidence," *Men and Money*, BBC 2, 1964.

2. The 1918 mergers included National Provincial, Union of London, and Smith's; London, City and Midland with London Joint Stock Bank; Lloyds with Capital and Counties; Barclays with London, Provincial, and South Western; and London, County, and Westminster, with Parr's. John Booker, *Temples of Mammon: The Architecture of Banking* (Edinburgh: Edinburgh University Press, 1990), 220.

3. Ian Nairn, *Nairn's London* (Middlesex: Penguin, 1967), 3.

4. Pevsner and Cherry, *London 1: The Cities of London and Westminster* (London: Penguin, 1978), 225.

5. Gavin Stamp, "Anti-Ugly Action: An Episode in the History of British Modernism," *AA Files*, no. 70 (n.d.): 76–88.

6. Steve Parnell, "Ian Nairn: The Pioneer of Outrage," *Architectural Review* (blog), May 27, 2014, https://www.architectural-review.com/essays/outrage/ian-nairn-the-pioneer-of-outrage.

7. See Hélène Lipstadt, "Polemic and Parody in the Battle for British Modernism," *Oxford Art Journal* 5, no. 2 (1983): 22–30.

8. Gillian Darley, "Ian Nairn and Jane Jacobs, the Lessons from Britain and America," *Journal of Architecture* 17, no. 5

(October 1, 2012): 734, https://doi.org/10.1080/13602365.2012.724856.

9. Nairn, *Nairn's London*, 16.

10. Charles Holden and William Holford, *The City of London: A Record of Destruction and Survival; the Proposals for Reconstruction as Presented, in 1947, to the Court of Common Council* (London: Architectural Press for the Corporation of London, 1951), 24–27.

11. John Summerson, *Georgian London* (London: Barrie & Jenkins, 1988), 292.

12. Nairn, *Nairn's London*, 17.

13. Summerson, *Georgian London*, 292.

14. Bradley and Pevsner, *London 1: The City of London*, 136, 87.

15. Nairn, *Nairn's London*, 16.

16. See Edward Denison, "Crime against Architecture," *AA Files* 68 (2014): 61–68.

17. Anthony Vidler, "Losing Face: Notes on the Modern Museum," *Assemblage*, no. 9 (June 1989): 46.

18. Richard Barras, *The Development Cycle in the City of London* (London: Centre for Environmental Studies, 1979), 68.

19. Barras, 68; Booker, *Temples of Mammon*, 236.

20. Booker, *Temples of Mammon*, 251.

21. Robert Byron, cited in Gavin Stamp, "Our Love Affair with Georgian Architecture," *Country Life*, 29 March 2014, https://www.countrylife.co.uk/out-and-about/theatre-film-music/our-love-affair-with-georgian-architecture-1799. The debate was broadcast at 8:30 p.m. on January 4, 1938.

22. Gavin Stamp, *Anti-Ugly: Excursions in English Architecture*

and *Design* (London: Aurum Press, 2013), 210.

23. Elizabeth Hennessy, *A Domestic History of the Bank of England, 1930–1960* (Cambridge: Cambridge University Press, 1992), 72.

24. Barclays Bank Group, *A Story of a Site* (London: Barclays Bank, 1959), 21.

25. Oliver Marriott, *The Property Boom* (London: Hamilton, 1967), 92.

26. Marriott, *Property Boom*, 92.

27. Bradley and Pevsner, *London 1: The City of London*, 134.

28. Bradley and Pevsner, 135.

29. Pevsner and Cherry, *London 1: The Cities of London and Westminster*, 1:219; 248.

30. Paul Ferris, *The City* (Letchworth: Victor Gollancz, 1960), 80.

31. Booker, *Temples of Mammon*, 236.

32. Ferris, *The City*, 80.

33. George Cleaver and Union Discount Company of London, *The Union Discount: A Centenary Album* (London: Union Discount Company of London, 1985), 103.

34. G. A. Fletcher, *The Discount Houses in London: Principles, Operations and Change* (London: Macmillan, 1976), xii.

35. Iain S. Black, "Spaces of Capital: Bank Office Building in the City of London, 1830–1870," *Journal of Historical Geography* 26, no. 3 (2000): 357.

36. See Booker, *Temples of Mammon*; Iain S. Black, "Rebuilding 'the Heart of the Empire': Bank Headquarters in the City of London, 1919–1939," *Art History* 22, no. 4 (1999): 593–618; Black, "Spaces of Capital."

37. Black, "Spaces of Capital," 365.

38. Booker, *Temples of Mammon*, 234.

39. Black, "Spaces of Capital," 367; Barclays Bank Group, *Story of a Site*, 14.

40. Booker, *Temples of Mammon*, 236.

41. Pevsner and Cherry, *London 1: The Cities of London and Westminster*, 1:346; Murray Fraser, *Architecture and the "Special Relationship": The American Influence on Post-War British Architecture* (Abingdon: Routledge, 2007), 93–96.

42. Booker, *Temples of Mammon*, 226.

43. Quoted in Nikolaus Pevsner, *A History of Building Types* (London: Thames and Hudson, 1976), 210.

44. John Ruskin, *The Stones of Venice: The Foundations* (Cosimo, Inc., 2013), 35.

45. "'Pneumonia Corridor' at N.P. Bank Headquarters," *Financial Times*, February 26, 1964, NAT/348, Royal Bank of Scotland Group.

46. "National Provincial Bank Ltd Press Release Prior to the Public Inquiry (to Be Held at the Guildhall at 10.00am on February the 18th 1964) into the Bishopsgate Redevelopment Scheme" (papers, London, February 1964), NAT/348, Royal Bank of Scotland Group.

47. Barras, *Development Cycle in the City of London*, 68.

48. Despite merging in 1968, the two banks didn't begin trading as a single entity until 1970.

49. David Kynaston, *The City of London Vol 4, A Club No More, 1945–2000* (London: Chatto & Windus, 2000), 379–380.

50. "National Provincial Bank Ltd Press Release."

51. Ten years later, Powell and Moya built a sixth tower for the Corporation on the Museum of London site.

52. Nairn, *Nairn's London*, 40; Pevsner and Cherry, *London 1: The Cities of London and Westminster*, 1:111.

53. Alan Powers, *Britain: Modern Architectures in History* (London: Reaktion, 2007), 127; City of London Planning and Communications Committee, *1962 High Buildings Policy: Appendix to Report of the Planning and Communications Committee Relative to Mansion House Square, Presented to Common Council* (London: Corporation of London, May 22, 1969), London Metropolitan Archives.

54. For a close reading of the Mies saga, see Jane Jacobs, "Battle of Bank Junction."

55. Rodney Gordon, "Modern Architecture for the Masses: The Owen Luder Partnership 1960–67," in *The Sixties: Life, Style, Architecture*, ed. Elain Harwood and Alan Powers (London: Twentieth Century Society, 2002), 74–75.

56. Reinhold Martin, *The Organizational Complex: Architecture, Media, and Corporate Space* (Cambridge, MA: MIT Press, 2003), 82.

57. "National Provincial Bank Ltd Press Release."

58. Booker, *Temples of Mammon*, 259.

59. Ann-Christine Frandsen, Tammy Bunn Hiller, Janice Traflet, and Elton G. McGoun, "From Money Storage to Money Store: Openness and Transparency in Bank Architecture," *Business History* 55, no. 5 (2013): 701–704.

60. "Sir Keith Saves City Banking Hall," *Evening Standard*, August 7, 1964, NAT/348, Royal Bank of Scotland Group.

61. Stephen Wood, "The NatWest Tower Went up ... and Up," *Sunday Times*, color supplement, March 17, 1980.

62. "Bank Architect Cramped by Ministers Decision," *City Press*, August 14, 1964.

63. National Provincial Bank Ltd., *A New London Landmark: Illustrated Brochure Produced to Mark the Opening of Drapers Gardens* (London: National Provincial Bank Ltd., 1967), 8.

64. Barras, *Development Cycle in the City of London*, 70.

65. "Drapers Gardens, London, EC2," *Building*, August 16, 1968, 67–74.

66. "National Provincial Headquarters," *Stock Exchange Gazette*, March 25, 1965, NAT/348, Royal Bank of Scotland Group.

67. Booker, *Temples of Mammon*, 259.

68. National Provincial Bank Ltd., *A New London Landmark*, 10.

69. "Corporation of London: Information Sheet and Comment Form for the General Public on Proposals for the National Westminster Bank Scheme, 1968–1969" (document, London, 1969 1968), NAT/348, Royal Bank of Scotland Group.

70. Richard Seifert, interview with Louise Brodie for *Architects' Lives*, British Library National Life Stories Collection, 1996, British Library Sound Archive.

71. "Architect, Businessman, Accountant ... ," *Building*, October 17, 1969, 42.

72. Lionel Brett, "The Developers," *Architectural Review* 140, no. 823 (September 1965): 167.

73. Godfrey Golzen, *How Architects Get Work: Interviews with Architects, Clients and Intermediaries* (London: Architecture and Building Practice Guides, 1984), 142.

74. Seifert, "Architect's Approach to Architecture," 58, 57.

75. Brian Burns, Chief Architect of National Westminster, quoted in Wood, "NatWest Tower Went up … and Up"; Richard Seifert, interview for *Architects' Lives*.

76. Adrian Forty, *Concrete and Culture: A Material History* (London: Reaktion Books, 2013), 113.

77. Ada Louise Huxtable, "Londons New Buildings Are Closer to Miami," *New York Times*, June 12, 1971, 31.

78. Wood, "NatWest Tower"; Seifert, interview for *Architects' Lives*.

79. Wood, "NatWest Tower."

80. "Corporation of London: Information Sheet and Comment Form for the General Public on Proposals for the National Westminster Bank Scheme, 1968–1969."

81. Wood, "NatWest Tower."

82. "Letter from the General Manager of National Westminster Premises Division, to the Deputy Chief Executive of National Westminster Bank Ltd. Discussing the Visit of the Bishopsgate Working Party to the US" (London, May 1970), NWB 552/5/4, Royal Bank of Scotland Group.

83. Dennis Sharp, Martin Spring, and Brian Waters, "National West Tower: A Review," *Building* 240, no. 7174 (January 23, 1981); "Note for Chairman: Bishopsgate Development, 3 August 1972" (London, August 3, 1972), NWB/806/5, Royal Bank of Scotland Group.

84. "Note for Deputy Chairman from Chairman, 6th December 1974" (London, December 6, 1974), NWB 552/5/4, Royal Bank of Scotland Group.

85. "Note for Deputy Chairman from Chairman, 6th December 1974."

86. "Note for Deputy Chairman from Chairman, 6th December 1974"; "Memorandum for the Chairmans Committee from the Premises Division: Bishopsgate Redevelopment Complex, 14th February 1977" (London, February 14, 1977), NWB/805/5/2, Royal Bank of Scotland Group.

87. "National Westminster Tower," *Daily Telegraph*, July 22, 1975, NWB 552/5/4, Royal Bank of Scotland Group.

88. Discussions concerning the rehousing of the international and overseas arm had been in progress since 1974, on account of its rapid growth and increasingly scattered presence throughout the City on Lothbury, Moorgate, and Threadneedle Street. Projected expansion of these departments outstripped any other sector of the bank by a considerable margin, with estimated space needs increasing from sixty-six thousand square feet to one hundred thousand square feet between 1976 and 1984. "Memorandum for the Board from the General Manager of the Business Development Division: Occupational Strategy, 8 June 1976" (London, June 8, 1976), appendix 2, 7, NWB/552/5/6, Royal Bank of Scotland Group.

89. National Westminster Bank Ltd., "Press Release Concerning the Completion of the First Phases of the National Westminster Tower" (October 1980), NWB/904, Royal Bank of Scotland Group; National Westminster Bank Ltd., *National Westminster Tower: Brochure Produced for the Opening of the Tower* (London, 1981); *Tower over London*, DVD (National Westminster Bank, 1982).

90. Michael Lafferty, *Financial Times*, May 3, 1980, quoted in Kynaston, *The City of London Vol 4, A Club No More, 1945–2000*, 600.

91. Francis Duffy, *The Changing Workplace* (London: Phaidon Press, 1992), 232.

92. Peter Wynne Rees, interview with Chris Ingram, recording, October 8, 2012, published with kind permission of the interviewer.

93. Rees, interview.

94. Fraser, *Architecture and the "Special Relationship*," 195.

95. See Francis Duffy, *The Changing City* (London: Bulstrode Press, 1989); Duffy, *Changing Workplace*.

96. Adrian Forty, *Words and Buildings: A Vocabulary of Modern Architecture* (London: Thames & Hudson, 2000), 143.

97. Herman Hertzberger and John Kirkpatrick, *Architecture and Structuralism: The Ordering of Space* (Rotterdam: Nai010 Publishers, 2015), 133.

98. Daniel M. Abramson, *Obsolescence: An Architectural*

History (Chicago: University of Chicago Press, 2016).

99. Richard Llewelyn-Davies, "Endless Architecture," *Architectural Association Journal*, July 1951, 106–112.

100. Duffy, *Changing City*, 95. The 1987 crash of the stock market in particular took its toll on a number of investment banks, leading to a bout of large-scale redundancies, retrenchment in certain markets, and subsequent transformations in the internal organization of departments.

101. Duffy, 106.

102. Duffy goes on, "The costs of 'churn' combined with the costs of accommodating IT are very high in unsuitable buildings. For example, one bank found that the cost of moving a particular department had been about £200,000 and took six weeks when it was in an old building. The cost reduced to £10,000 and took only two weekends in a new building which had been designed to allow ease of movement." Duffy, 40.

103. Duffy, 23.

104. Duffy, 61.

105. Duffy, *Changing Workplace*, 218.

106. Duffy, quoted in Stewart Brand, *How Buildings Learn: What Happens after They're Built* (New York: Penguin, 1995), 12.

107. Duffy, quoted in Brand, *How Buildings Learn*, 12.

108. Douglas Spencer, *The Architecture of Neoliberalism: How Contemporary Architecture Became an Instrument of Control and Compliance* (London: Bloomsbury Academic, 2016), 18.

109. Francis Duffy, "Architects and the Social Sciences (Originally Published 1968),"

in Duffy and Hutton, *Architectural Knowledge*, 9.

110. Francis Duffy, "Petrified Typologies (Originally Published 1969)," in Duffy and Hutton, *Architectural Knowledge*, 22.

111. Duffy quoted in Brand, *How Buildings Learn*, 12.

112. Francis Duffy, "The Changing Role of the Architect (Originally Published 1984)," in Duffy and Hutton, *Architectural Knowledge*, 100.

113. Powers, *Britain*, 197.

114. Les Hutton, "The Profession in the Marketplace," in Duffy and Hutton, *Architectural Knowledge*, 75.

115. Godfrey Golzen, *How Architects Get Work: Interviews with Architects, Clients and Intermediaries* (London: Architecture and Building Practice Guides, 1984), 76, 151, 73, 134.

116. See Golzen, *How Architects Get Work*.

117. Duffy, *Changing Workplace*, 232.

118. Duffy, 232.

119. Kenneth Powell, *Design for Change: The Architecture of DEGW* (Basel: Birkhäuser, 1998), 47.

120. Duffy, "The Changing Role of the Architect (Originally Published 1984)," 100.

121. Peter Buchanan, "High-Tech: Another British Thoroughbred," *Architectural Review: High Tech Special Issue*, July 1983, https://www.archi tectural-review.com/rethink /viewpoints/high-tech -another-british-thorough bred/8604479.article.

122. Peter Scott, *The Property Masters: A History of the British Commercial Property Sector* (London: E & FN Spon, 1996), 214.

123. Scott, *Property Masters*, 214.

124. Scott, 214.

125. See Graham Ive, "Commercial Architecture," in *Architecture and the Sites of History: Interpretations of Buildings and Cities*, ed. Iain Borden and David Dunster (New York: Whitney Library of Design, 1996), 375–82.

126. Rees, interview.

127. Francis Duffy, "Systems Thinking (First Published 1991)," in Duffy and Hutton, *Architectural Knowledge*, 54–55.

128. SAVE Britain's Heritage, *Save the City: A Conservation Study of the City of London* (London: Society for the Protection of Ancient Buildings, 1976), 181.

129. Bradley and Pevsner, *London 1: The City of London*, 147.

130. Peter Rees, interview with the author, July 10, 2013.

131. Scott, *Property Masters*, 226.

132. Scott, 221, 225.

133. Fredric Jameson, "The Brick and the Balloon: Architecture, Idealism and Land Speculation," *New Left Review*, no. 228 (April 1998): 43.

Chapter 4

1. "Midas" of the *Financial News* (1933), quoted in Elizabeth Hennessy, *Coffee House to Cyber Market: The London Stock Exchange 1801–2001* (London: Ebury, 2000), 122.

2. Juan Pablo Pardo-Guerra, *Automating Finance: Infrastructures, Engineers, and the Making of Electronic Markets* (Cambridge: Cambridge University Press, 2019), 66.

3. F. R. Althaus, "Is Our Face Red," *Stock Exchange Journal*, September 1965, 4.

4. Brian Winterflood, interview with author, voice recording, March 26,

2013; Alan Jenkins, *The Stock Exchange Story* (London: Heinemann, 1973), 97.

5. Winterflood, interview.

6. Ranald Michie, *The London Stock Exchange: A History* (Oxford: Oxford University Press, 1999), 480.

7. Hennessy, *Coffee House to Cyber Market*, 141.

8. "Dictum Meum Pactum: The New Stock Exchange Building," *Architects' Journal* 156, no. 45 (November 8, 1972): 1041–1042.

9. Hennessy, *Coffee House to Cyber Market*, 144.

10. Charles Duguid, *The Story of the Stock Exchange* (London: Grant Richards, 1901), 177.

11. Juan Pablo Pardo-Guerra, "The Automated House: The Digitalization of the London Stock Exchange, 1955–1990," in *Technological Innovation in Retail Finance: International Historical Perspectives*, ed. Bernardo Batiz-Lazo, J. Carles Maixé-Altés, and Paul Thomes (London: Routledge, 2010), 200.

12. Quoted in Michie, *London Stock Exchange*, 485.

13. Michie, 472; Hennessy, *Coffee House to Cyber Market*, 157.

14. Peter J. Cain and Antony G. Hopkins, *British Imperialism: 1688–2000* (Harlow: Longman, 2001), 642.

15. Anthony D. King, *Global Cities: Post-Imperialism and the Internationalization of London* (London: Routledge, 1990), 94.

16. Quoted in David Kynaston, *The City of London Vol 4, A Club No More, 1945–2000* (London: Chatto & Windus, 2000), 652.

17. Ranald Michie, "Friend or Foe? Information Technology and the London Stock Exchange since 1700," *Journal of Historical Geography* 23, no. 3 (1997): 319.

18. Eric K. Clemons and Bruce W. Weber, "London's Big Bang: A Case Study of Information Technology, Competitive Impact, and Organizational Change," *Journal of Management Information Systems* 6, no. 4 (April 1, 1990): 48.

19. Clemons and Weber, "London's Big Bang," 43.

20. See Andrew Leyshon and Nigel Thrift, *Money/Space: Geographies of Monetary Transformation* (London: Routledge, 1996).

21. Francis Duffy, *The Changing City* (London: Bulstrode Press, 1989), 23.

22. Philip Augar, *The Death of Gentlemanly Capitalism: The Rise and Fall of London's Investment Banks* (London: Penguin, 2008), 90.

23. Duffy, *Changing City*, 23.

24. Jacques Lowe and Sandy McLachlan, *The City: The Traditions and Powerful Personalities of the World's Greatest Financial Centre* (London: Quartet Books, 1983), 104; Cathy Courtney and Paul Thompson, *City Lives: The Changing Voice of British Finance* (London: Methuen, 1996), 206.

25. Lowe and McLachlan, *The City*, 123.

26. DEGW, *Trading in Two Cities: Design Guidelines for Trading Floors: A Report for Rosehaugh Stanhope Developments Plc* (London: DEGW, March 1986), 2.

27. Annabel Olivier-Wright, *Big Bang* (Central Office of Information, 1987).

28. Augar, *Death of Gentlemanly Capitalism*, 90.

29. DEGW, *Trading in Two Cities*, 2.

30. DEGW, *Comparing the Design of Five Trading Floors in New York and London for Citicorp Investment Bank Ltd* (London: DEGW, January 29, 1986), 1. The studies of other trading floors were collated by DEGW in DEGW, *Trading in Two Cities*.

31. Donald MacKenzie, "What's in a Number?," *London Review of Books*, September 25, 2008.

32. Daniel Benuza and David Stark, "Seeing through the Eyes of Others: Dissonance within and across Trading Rooms," in *The Oxford Handbook of the Sociology of Finance*, ed. Karin Knorr Cetina and Alex Preda (Oxford: Oxford University Press, 2012), 206.

33. Francis Duffy and Brian Waters, "Squaring up for the Big Bang: Redesign the Office," *Building* 250, no. 13 (March 28, 1986): 30–32.

34. DEGW, *Broadgate, Phase 6: Fit-out Analysis. A Report for Rosehaugh Stanhope Developments Plc* (London: DEGW, May 1990).

35. Leyshon and Thrift, *Money/Space*, 169.

36. Linda McDowell, *Capital Culture: Gender at Work in the City* (Oxford: Blackwell, 1997), 121.

37. Leyshon and Thrift, *Money/Space*, 146–147.

38. Linda McDowell and Gillian Court, "Missing Subjects: Gender, Power, and Sexuality in Merchant Banking," *Economic Geography* 70, no. 3 (July 1, 1994): 241.

39. Michael Lewis, *Liar's Poker: Rising though the Wreckage on Wall Street* (New York: W. W. Norton & Company, 2010), 51.

40. DEGW, *Trading in Two Cities*, 19.

41. McDowell, *Capital Culture*, 169–170.

42. Max Haiven, *Cultures of Financialization: Fictitious Capital in Popular Culture and Everyday Life* (Basingstoke: Palgrave Macmillan, 2014), 32.

43. David Kynaston, *LIFFE: A Market and Its Makers* (Cambridge: Granta, 1997), 2–4.

44. Caitlin Zaloom, "Markets and Machines: Work in the Technological Sensoryscapes of Finance," *American Quarterly* 58, no. 3 (September 1, 2006): 818.

45. Kynaston, *The City of London Vol 4, A Club No More, 1945–2000*, 608.

46. Kynaston, *LIFFE*, 17.

47. Kynaston, 55.

48. Zaloom, "Markets and Machines," 828.

49. Zaloom, 819.

50. Kynaston, *The City of London Vol 4, A Club No More, 1945–2000*, 610.

51. Kynaston, *LIFFE*, 60.

52. Brian Waters, "Made for LIFFE," *Building* 243, no. 7254 (August 13, 1982): 30.

53. Kynaston, *LIFFE*, 60; Waters, "Made for LIFFE," 30.

54. Kynaston, 65.

55. Waters, "Made for LIFFE," 30.

56. Caitlin Zaloom, "The Productive Life of Risk," *Cultural Anthropology* 19, no. 3 (2004): 371, https://doi.org/10.1525/can.2004.19.3.365.

57. Zaloom, "Productive Life of Risk," 368.

58. Courtney and Thompson, *City Lives*, 193.

59. Courtney and Thompson, 193.

60. Ruti Ahronee, "LIFFE Open Outcry Trading in '80s in The Royal Exchange, Ruti Ahronee," video, 9:32, posted May 9, 2012, https://www.youtube.com/watch?v=QRi9k2SpyO0.

61. Kynaston, *The City of London Vol 4, A Club No More, 1945–2000*, 707.

62. Quoted in Kynaston, 705.

63. Kynaston, *LIFFE*, 741.

64. Denise Chevin, "LIFFE Must Go On," *Building*, November 2, 1990, 46–50.

65. Kynaston, *LIFFE*, 239–240.

66. Tony Whitehead, "A New Lease of LIFFE; Architects: Whinney Mackay-Lewis Partnership," *Building*, August 30, 1991, 50.

67. Thanks to the Lloyd's archivist Victoria Lane for this information. Victoria Lane, email to the author, "Bateman Cartoons," January 11, 2021.

68. Bryan Appleyard, "Lloyds, the Decade of Controversy," *The Times*, December 16, 1988.

69. In 1981, the worldwide market premium income was £20,848 million. Of this, just £2,869 million related to Lloyd's, with £17,988 connected to the companies. Vanessa Harding and Priscilla Metcalf, *Lloyd's at Home* (London: Lloyd's of London, 1986), 52.

70. Harding and Metcalf, *Lloyd's at Home*, 102.

71. Harding and Metcalf, 119, 135.

72. David Needham and Harry Dawe-Lane, interview with author, voice recording, October 29, 2014.

73. Michael Moran, *The British Regulatory State: High Modernism and Hyper-Innovation* (Oxford: Oxford University Press, 2003), 69.

74. Jonathan Levy, *Freaks of Fortune: The Emerging World of Capitalism and Risk in America* (Cambridge, MA: Harvard University Press, 2012), 1–6, https://doi.org/10.4159/harvard.9780674067202.

75. William Clarke, *Inside the City: A Guide to London as a Financial Centre* (London: Routledge, 2018), 61–62.

76. Kynaston, *The City of London Vol 4, A Club No More, 1945–2000*, 354, 408.

77. John Brennan, "Lloyd's Outgrows Its Trading Floor," *The Times*, June 23, 1977.

78. Ulrich Beck, *Risk Society: Towards a New Modernity* (London: SAGE Publications, 1992), 22.

79. Wayne Asher and Patrick Harverson, "The Four Faces of Lloyd's," in *A New Look at Lloyd's*, ed. Barbara Hadley (London: ReActions Ltd., 1986), 34.

80. Anthony Giddens, "Risk and Responsibility," *Modern Law Review* 62, no. 1 (1999): 4.

81. Wayne Asher and Patrick Harverson, "The Tools of the Electronic Age," in Hadley, *A New Look at Lloyd's*, 15.

82. Asher and Harverson, "Four Faces of Lloyd's," 45–46.

83. Asher and Harverson, 41.

84. Assisted by the RIBA's president, Gordon Graham, Iain Findlay (deputy chairman of Lloyd's) selected "a list of 15 British firms to provide brochures and information on the basis of which a shortlist could be chosen." The final shortlist of architects came down to an international mix of practices: Norman Foster & Partners (UK), Rogers + Partners (UK), Arup Associates (UK), I M Pei (USA), Webb Zarafa Menkes Housden

Partnership (Canada), and Serete (France). According to Peter Murray, each of these remaining practices was paid £10,000 "to prepare proposals as to how they would deal with the problems posed by Lloyd's requirements over the next fifty years; they were not asked to produce designs for a building." Peter Murray, "The Frontiers of Patronage," *RIBA Journal* 86, no. 9 (September 1979): 406.

85. Eva Jiricna, interview with author, November 27, 2014; Ted Stevens, "Underwriting Architecture," *RIBA Journal* 88, no. 5 (May 1981): 42.

86. Richard Rogers + Partners, "Project Report: Outline Proposals Report" (London, June 1979), 24, ARC3389, Rogers Stirk Harbour + Partners.

87. Giddens, "Risk and Responsibility," 4.

88. Harding and Metcalf, *Lloyd's at Home*, 164.

89. Richard Rogers + Partners, "Box Redesign Core Group Study Report [DRAFT]" (London, May 1982), 8, ARC70791, Rogers Stirk Harbour + Partners.

90. Jiricna, interview.

91. Harding and Metcalf, *Lloyd's at Home*, 119, 135.

92. Richard Rogers + Partners, "Photographic Survey Contact Sheets and Modular Designs for Modifications of the Old Boxes. Lloyds Boxes Phase II" (London, 87 1982), ARC81894, Rogers Stirk Harbour + Partners.

93. John Brennan, "Lloyds," *The Times*, June 29, 1977.

94. Richard Rogers + Partners, "Lloyds Boxes Photographic Survey" (London, ca. 1978), ARC81895, Rogers Stirk Harbour + Partners.

95. Richard Rogers + Partners, "Box Redesign Core Group Study Report [DRAFT]," 14.

96. Robert Timosci, "Putting Together the Boxes," in *Serving the World: The New Lloyd's Building, a Lloyd's List Special Report* (Essex: Lloyd's List, Lloyd's of London Press, 1986), 17.

97. Jiricna, interview.

98. Timosci, "Putting Together the Boxes," 17.

99. McDowell and Court, "Missing Subjects," 243.

100. David Hamilton Eddy, "The Myth of the Mechanical," *World Architecture Journal* 1, no. 2 (1989): 78–83.

101. Mike Harris, quoted in Appleyard, "Lloyds, the Decade of Controversy."

102. British Pathé, "This Is Lloyds Aka All Risks—Reel 2," video, 12:25, recorded 1961, posted April 13, 2014, https://www.youtube.com/watch?v=qFxq5Y5wLpc&feature=youtube_gdata_player.

103. Richard Rogers + Partners, "Box Redesign Core Group Study Report [DRAFT]," 2.4.2

104. Roy Farndon, "Architect in Light and Shadow," in *Serving the World*, 14.

105. Eric Hobsbawm and Terence O. Ranger, *The Invention of Tradition* (Cambridge: Cambridge University Press, 2007), 9.

106. Wayne Asher and Patrick Harverson, "The Reinsurance Factor," in *A New Look at Lloyd's*, 23–24.

107. Sheena Wilson quoted in Appleyard, "Lloyds, the Decade of Controversy."

108. Appleyard.

109. C. Wright Mills, *White Collar: The American Middle Classes* (New York: Oxford University Press, 1951), 200.

110. Mills, *White Collar*, 189.

111. Charles Dickens, *Dombey and Son*, vol. 1 (London: Chapman and Hall, 1848), 207.

112. Ellen Lupton, *Mechanical Brides: Women and Machines from Home to Office* (New York: Princeton Architectural Press, 1997), 43.

113. Adrian Forty, *Objects of Desire: Design and Society, 1750–1980* (London: Thames and Hudson, 1986), 121.

114. Alan Booth, "Technological Change and Gender in the Labour Policies of British Retail Banks, 1945–1970," in *Managing the Modern Workplace: Productivity, Politics and Workplace Culture in Postwar Britain*, ed. Joseph Melling and Alan Booth (Aldershot: Ashgate, 2008), 103–104.

115. Forty, *Objects of Desire*, 140.

116. Booth, "Technological Change and Gender," 108.

117. Booth, 112; Gillian Wright, interview with Katherine Thompson for *City Lives*, British Library National Life Stories Collection, February 1992, British Library Sound Archive.

118. Forty, *Objects of Desire*; Jennifer Kaufmann-Buhler, "If the Chair Fits: Sexism in American Office Furniture Design," *Journal of Design History* 32, no. 4 (December 6, 2019): 376–391, https://doi.org/10.1093/jdh/epz022.

119. William Henry Leffingwell and Edward Marshall Robinson, *Textbook of Office Management*, 3rd ed. (New York: McGraw-Hill, 1960), 366.

120. Juriaan van Meel, *The European Office: Office Design and National Context*

(Rotterdam: 010 Publishers, 2000), 27.

121. M. H. Port, *Imperial London: Civil Government Building in London 1851–1915* (New Haven, CT: Paul Mellon Centre, 1995), 32.

122. Daphne Spain, *The Contemporary Workplace* (Chapel Hill: University of North Carolina Press, 1992), 212.

123. Leffingwell and Robinson, *Textbook of Office Management*, 393, 365.

124. Forty, *Objects of Desire*, 130–132.

125. Harry Braverman, *Labor and Monopoly Capital: The Degradation of Work in the Twentieth Century* (New York: Monthly Review Press, 1974), 310.

126. "Notes on Desks," in National Mutual Life Assurance Society, "Designs for Office Furniture and the Layout for the New Building at Bow Churchyard, Compiled by Lionel Shotlander" (London, 1961), CLC/B/166/MS34577, National Mutual Life Assurance Society Collection, London Metropolitan Archives.

127. Katherine Shonfield, *Walls Have Feelings: Architecture, Film and the City* (London: Routledge, 2000), 96.

128. Elizabeth Grosz, *Volatile Bodies: Toward a Corporeal Feminism* (Bloomington: Indiana University Press, 1994), 14.

129. Dolores Hayden, "What Would a Non-sexist City Be Like? Speculations on Housing, Urban Design, and Human Work," *Signs: Journal of Women in Culture and Society* 5, no. 3 (1980): 172.

130. Forty, *Objects of Desire*, xx; Michelle Murphy, *Sick*

Building Syndrome and the Problem of Uncertainty: Environmental Politics, Technoscience, and Women Workers (Durham, NC: Duke University Press, 2006), 40–41.

131. Leffingwell and Robinson, *Textbook of Office Management*, 386.

132. E. Trist and K. Bamforth, "Some Social and Psychological Consequences of the Longwall Method of Coal Getting. Human Relations," *Human Relations* 4, no. 3 (1951).

133. Julian Barling and Amanda Griffiths, "A History of Occupational Health Psychology," in *Handbook of Occupational Health Psychology* (Washington, DC: American Psychological Association, 2003), 23, https://doi.org/10.1037/10474-002.

134. Quickborner Team, quoted in Francis Duffy, Colin Cave, and John Worthington, *Planning Office Space* (London: Architectural Press, 1976), 62.

135. See Nikil Saval, *Cubed: A Secret History of the Workplace* (New York: Doubleday, 2014); Jennifer Kaufmann-Buhler, *Open Plan: A Design History of the American Office* (Bloomsbury Publishing, 2020).

136. Steve Humphries and John Taylor, *The Making of Modern London, 1945–1985* (London: Sidgwick & Jackson, 1986), 68–69.

137. Humphries and Taylor, *Making of Modern London*, 69.

138. Shonfield, *Walls Have Feelings*, 92.

139. Murray Fraser, *Architecture and the "Special Relationship": The American Influence on Post-War British Architecture* (Abingdon: Routledge, 2007), 197.

140. Peter F. Drucker, "Knowledge-Worker

Productivity: The Biggest Challenge," *California Management Review* 41, no. 2 (Winter 1999): 79–94.

141. Kaufmann-Buhler, "If the Chair Fits."

142. In the Netherlands, the space per worker increased from 17.5 m² in 1950 to 25.2 GEA m² in 1977. Meel, *European Office*, 38.

143. Duffy, *Changing City*, 22.

144. Duffy, 53, 56–57.

145. Murphy, *Sick Building Syndrome and the Problem of Uncertainty*.

146. Murphy, 66.

147. Murphy, 66.

148. Kea G. Tijdens, "Behind the Screens: The Foreseen and Unforeseen Impact of Computerization on Female Office Worker's Jobs," *Gender, Work & Organization* 6, no. 1 (1999): 47–57, https://doi.org/10.1111/1468-0432.00068; L. Stepulevage, "Computer-Based Office Work: Stories of Gender, Design, and Use," *IEEE Annals of the History of Computing* 25, no. 4 (October 2003): 67–72; Celia Stanworth, "Women and Work in the Information Age," *Gender, Work & Organization* 7, no. 1 (2000): 20–32, https://doi.org/10.1111/1468-0432.00090.

149. Ian Martin, "Britain's First Computer Centre for Banking: What Did This Building Do?," in *Technological Innovation in Retail Finance: International Historical Perspectives*, ed. Bernardo Batiz-Lazo, J. Carles Maixe-Altes, and Paul Thomas (London: Routledge, 2011), 64.

150. M. Hicks, "Only the Clothes Changed: Women Operators in British Computing and Advertising, 1950–1970," *IEEE Annals of the*

History of Computing 32, no. 4 (October 2010): 6.

151. Economists Advisory Group, *Economic Study of the City of London*, 324–334.

152. John Smith, programmer, cited in W. J. Reader, *Phillips & Drew: Professionals in the City* (London: Robert Hale, 1998), 159.

153. Booth, "Technological Change and Gender," 117.

154. Amy Wharton and Val Burris, "Office Automation and Its Impact on Women Workers," *Humboldt Journal of Social Relations* 10, no. 2 (April 1, 1983): 118–119.

155. Wharton and Burris, "Office Automation," 119.

156. DEGW and Eosys Ltd., "ORBIT Appendix 6: Information Technology and the Worker," in *ORBIT Study*, 6.

157. DEGW and Eosys Ltd., "ORBIT Appendix 2: The Organisational Case Studies," in *ORBIT Study*, 29.

158. DEGW and Eosys Ltd., "ORBIT Appendix 6: Information Technology and the Worker," 6.

159. John Richter, "Office Furniture: Making a Wise Selection," *Purchasing World* 34, no. 8 (August 1990): 59.

160. Murphy, *Sick Building Syndrome and the Problem of Uncertainty*, 59.

161. For example, see the Whitehall II study of the British Civil Service, also known as the Stress and Health Study, founded by Sir Michael Marmot in 1985, ongoing today. See also Cary L. Cooper and Philip Dewe, *Stress: A Brief History* (Malden, MA: Blackwell, 2004); International Labour Office and Labour Inspection and Occupational Safety and Health Branch Labour Administration,

Workplace Stress: A Collective Challenge (Geneva: ILO, 2016); David Wainwright and Michael Calnan, *Work Stress: The Making of a Modern Epidemic* (Buckingham: Open University Press, 2002.

162. Murphy, *Sick Building Syndrome and the Problem of Uncertainty*, 75.

163. L. Soine, "Sick Building Syndrome and Gender Bias: Imperiling Women's Health," *Social Work in Health Care* 20, no. 3 (1995): 51–65, https://doi.org/10.1300/J010v20n03_04; Berndt Stenberg and Stig Wall, "Why Do Women Report 'Sick Building Symptoms' More Often than Men?," *Social Science & Medicine* 40, no. 4 (February 1, 1995): 491–502, https://doi.org/10.1016/0277-9536(94)E0104-Z; Great Britain Health and Safety Executive, *How to Deal with SBS: Sick Building Syndrome* (London: HSE Books, 1995).

164. A. F. Marmot et al., "Building Health: An Epidemiological Study of 'Sick Building Syndrome' in the Whitehall II Study," *Occupational and Environmental Medicine* 63, no. 4 (April 2006): 283–289, https://doi.org/10.1136/oem.2005.022889.

165. Nanette Fondas, "Feminization Unveiled: Management Qualities in Contemporary Writings," *Academy of Management Review* 22, no. 1 (1997): 260, https://doi.org/10.2307/259231.

166. Francis Duffy, "A Case for More Collaboration (1986)," in Duffy and Hutton, *Architectural Knowledge*, 113.

167. Forty, *Objects of Desire*, 140.

168. Francis Duffy and Colin Cave, "Bürolandschaft:

An Appraisal," in *Planning Office Space*, ed. Francis Duffy, Colin Cave, and John Worthington (London: Architectural Press, 1976), 72.

169. Joanna Eley and Alexi Marmot, *Understanding Offices: What Every Manager Needs to Know about Office Buildings* (London: Penguin, 1995), 50.

170. Eley and Marmot, *Understanding Offices*, 51.

171. Richter, "Office Furniture."

172. McDowell and Court, "Missing Subjects," 229–238.

173. McDowell and Court, 239.

174. McDowell and Court.

175. McDowell and Court, 238; Bronwen Wood, interview with Katherine Thompson for *City Lives*, British Library National Life Stories Collection, December 8, 1992, British Library Sound Archive; David Kynaston, *The City of London Vol 4, A Club No More, 1945–2000* (London: Chatto & Windus, 2000), 707.

176. Anthony Sampson, *The Changing Anatomy of Britain* (Sevenoaks: Hodder and Stoughton, 1983), 311.

177. Katie Prescott, "Inside the Goldman Sachs Nursery," BBC News, July 20, 2017, https://www.bbc.com/news/business-40658619.

178. Margrit Shildrick, *Leaky Bodies and Boundaries: Feminism, Postmodernism and (Bio)ethics* (London: Routledge, 1997).

179. Linda McDowell, "Capital Culture Revisited: Sex, Testosterone and the City," *International Journal of Urban and Regional Research* 34, no. 3 (2010): 652–658, https://doi.org/10.1111/j.1468-2427.2010.00972.x.

180. Abbi Hobbs, "The Impact of Remote and Flexible Working Arrangements," POST, UK Parliament, April 29, 2021, https://post.parliament.uk /the-impact-of-remote -and-flexible-working -arrangements/.

181. "Women Perceived as Less Productive while WFH: Report," *The Statesman*, March 11, 2021, https://www .thestatesman.com/lifestyle /women-perceived-less -productive-wfh-report -1502956742.html.

Epilogue

1. Jon Coaffee, *Terrorism, Risk and the Global City: Towards Urban Resilience* (London: Ashgate, 2009), 101.

2. "Police Clash with Protesters at Carnival against Capitalism," *The Guardian*, June 18, 1999, http://www .theguardian.com/uk/1999 /jun/18/1.

3. Coaffee, *Terrorism, Risk and the Global City*, 102, 103.

4. According to Coaffee, by the end of 1996 there were over 1,250 private security cameras in the CameraWatch system, eight entry point cameras, thirteen exit cameras, and forty-seven traffic zone control cameras. Coaffee, 128, 131.

5. Coaffee, 106.

6. Mumbai, Riyadh, and Colombo were other prominent centers attacked during this period. Coaffee, 7.

7. Nick Cohen, "Without Prejudice: Last Rotten Borough," *Observer*, June 27, 1999; Maria Kaika, "Architecture and Crisis: Re-Inventing the Icon, Re-imag(in)ing London and Re-branding the City," *Transactions of the Institute of British Geographers* 35, no. 4 (2010): 461.

8. Nigel Lawson et al., *Big Bang 20 Years On: New Challenges Facing the Financial Services Sector* (London: Centre for Policy Studies, October 2006), 27.

9. Richard Roberts and David Kynaston, *City State: How the Markets Came to Rule the World* (London: Profile, 2001), 43. In 2012, Canary Wharf had officially over taken the City as the largest employer of bankers in Europe, with the sixteen biggest banks in the UK employing 44,500 bankers in the area, compared with 43,300 in the City. Patrick Jenkins and Ed Hammond, "Canary Wharf Claims High Ground on City," *Financial Times*, May 13, 2012.

10. Colin Lizieri, Jan Reinert, and Andrew Baum, *Who Owns the City 2011: Change and Global Ownership of City of London Offices* (Cambridge: University of Cambridge, Department of Land Economy, November 2011), 16.

11. Stephen Graham and Simon Marvin, *Splintering Urbanism: Networked Infrastructures, Technological Mobilities and the Urban Condition* (London: Routledge, 2001), 327.

12. Andy Beckett, "Lord of the Ring of Steel," *The Guardian*, November 25, 1999, http://www.theguardian .com/politics/1999/nov/25 /londonmayor.uk.

13. Ali Shalchi, Georgina Hutton, and Matthew Ward, "Financial Services: Contribution to the UK Economy," May 31, 2022, https://com monslibrary.parliament.uk /research-briefings/sn06193/.

14. "Spending Review 2010: Key Points at a Glance," *The Guardian*, October 20, 2010, http://www.theguardian. com/politics/2010/oct/20 /spending-review-2010-key -points.

15. John Summerson, *Georgian London* (New Haven, CT: Published for the Paul Mellon Centre for Studies in British Art by Yale University Press, 2003), 1, http://archive.org /details/georgianlondon 0000summ_06h7.

Index

Brett, Lionel (Lord Esher), 18, 19, 65, 190
Bretton Woods, 46
Bridgland, Aynsley, 167
British Airways, 53
British Empire, xxvi
British Insurance Association, 23
British National Export Council (BNEC), 42
British Pathé, 36
British Telecom (BT), 53, 57, 60, 142, 146, 242
British Telecommunications Act (1981), 60
Broadgate, 52, 53, 56, 66, 67, 131, 133, 133, 147, 196, 197, 197, 233, 233
Broadgate Square, 133
Broad Street railway station, xxvi, 61, 67
Brown, Capability, 92
Brussels Expo (1958), 32, 33
City of London Pavilion 32, 33, 35, 44
Buchanan, Colin, 111, 113
Buchanan, Peter, 206
Bucklersbury, 116
Bucklersbury House, 142, 167
Builder, The (journal), 81
Building Use Studies, 267
Bunning, James Bunstone, 223
Bunshaft, Gordon, 178
Burnet, Sir John, 169
Tait & Partners, 204
Bürolandschaft (office landscaping), 279
Burrow's Guides, 35
Bury Street, London, 197
Butler's Wharf, London, 60
Byrne, Mike, 192
Byron, Robert, 166

CABE, 65
Cain, Peter J., 24
Cambridge, 245
Campbell, Duncan, 139, 140
Canada, 38
Canaletto, 122
Canary Wharf, London, 51, 60, 61, 116, 137, 209, 228, 246
Cannon Street, 116, 247

railway station, xxvi
Canterbury, 178
Capel, James, 229
Capital City (film), 49
Carl Fisher & Associates, 177
Carnival against Capitalism, 299
Carter, Edward J., xxii, 9, 10
Cashmore, Milton, 185
Casson, Hugh, 94, 123, 190
Cave, Colin, 291
Central Criminal Court Extension, 39
Central Moneymarket Operations Office, 121
Centre Point, London, 20
Centre for Policy Studies (CPS), 51
Centre Pompidou, Paris, 256
Chamberlin Powell & Bon, 16, 17, 19
Chandler, Edwin, 116, 117
Change Alley. See Exchange Alley
CHAPS. See Clearing House Automated Payments System
Charles, Prince of Wales, 122, 123, 124, 125, 126, 266
Chase Manhattan bank, 30, 178
Cheapside, London, xxvii, 81, 116, 131, 134, 168, 299
Cheesegrater, the (The Leadenhall Building, 122 Leadinghall Street), 306
C. H. Elsom & Partners, 18
Chicago, 134, 240
Sears Tower, 194
Chicago Board of Trade (CBOT), 237, 240
Chicago Board of Trade II (photograph), 237, 238–239
Chicago Mercantile Exchange (aka the Merc), 240, 242
trading floors, 241, 242
Chicago School, 118, 196
Churn, 200
Citibank, 30
Citicorp Investment Bank, 231
City Churches Commission, 23
City of London

bombings in the, 299
conservation area, 50, 134
demographic of the, 68
historic sites, 50
Information Office, 34, 35
pavilions, mobile or transportable, 43, 44, 45, 46
self-regulation in the, 24, 86, 118, 121, 149, 220, 225, 236, 250, 253, 266
surveillance in the, 147, 148, 149, 273
telecommunications, 143
Various Powers Act, 115
women in the, 267–278, 272, 279, 280, 284, 290, 292, 295, 296, 297, 310
City of London (film), 36, 37
City of London: A Record of Destruction and Survival, The, 12, 85, 90, 91, 92, 105
City of London Club, 176
demolition of the, 184
City of London Corporation (formerly Corporation of London), xx, xxiv, xxvii, 6, 10, 11, 15, 16, 21, 23, 33, 34, 36, 38, 39, 43, 46–50, 59, 61, 62, 64, 69, 109, 113, 144, 164, 181, 182, 184, 192, 210, 301, 306, 310
building program, 40
Common Council, xxv, 36, 48, 49, 110, 111
Court of, 36
Economic Development Unit, 146
Improvements and Town Planning Committee, 6
planning, 50, 110, 113 (see also Draft Local Plan)
Planning and Communications Committee, 48, 63
planning department, 67, 210
"Preliminary Draft Proposals for Post-War Reconstruction" (publication), 3, 4
proactive planning, 63
public relations, 43, 49

This book was set in Haultin Normal by New Best-set Typesetters Ltd. Printed and bound in the United States of America.

Library of Congress Cataloging-in-Publication Data

Names: Thomas, Amy, author.
Title: The City in the city : architecture and change in London's financial district / Amy Thomas.
Description: Cambridge, Massachusetts : The MIT Press, [2023] | Includes bibliographical references and index. | Summary: "This book charts the development of London's financial district, the City of London, in the decades following the Second World War, investigating the relationship between economic and built change"— Provided by publisher.
Identifiers: LCCN 2022054179 (print) | LCCN 2022054180 (ebook) | ISBN 9780262048415 (hardcover) | ISBN 9780262375863 (epub) | ISBN 9780262375856 (pdf)
Subjects: LCSH: Architecture and society—England—London—History—20th century. | City planning—England—London—History—20th century. | City of London (England)—Economic conditions—20th century. | London (England)—Economic conditions—20th century.
Classification: LCC NA2543.S6 T46 2023 (print) | LCC NA2543.S6 (ebook) |DDC 720.9421/2—dc23/eng/20221125
LC record available at https://lccn.loc.gov/2022054179
LC ebook record available at https://lccn.loc.gov/2022054180

10   9   8   7   6   5   4   3   2   1